The Holy Spirit In a Man

Spiritual Warfare,
Intercession, Faith,
Healings and Miracles
in the Modern World

R.B. Watchman

(An Autobiography)

The Holy Spirit in a Man: Spiritual Warfare, Intercession, Faith, Healings and Miracles in the Modern World
by R. B. Watchman

ISBN 978-1-907066-41-2 (paperback)
ISBN 978-1-907066-42-9 (eBook ePub)

British Library Cataloguing In Publication Data
A Record of this Publication is available from the British Library.
First published in March 2015 by ByFaith Media, updated in February 2016 and August 2017.

- Jesus Christ is Lord -

Contents

Contents

'The apostles gathered to Jesus and told Him all things, both what they had done and what they had taught' (Mark 6:30).

'When he had greeted them, he told in detail those things which God had done among the Gentiles through his ministry. And when they heard it, they glorified the Lord' (Acts 21:19-20a).

Preface

My first introduction to spiritual warfare was sudden and traumatic as I lay in my mother's womb. God intended the womb to be a place of complete safety, while He created my inmost being and made me in the secret place (Psalm 139:13-16). However, for me, it was a battlefield, as I faced death before birth and the devil's hatred of God's creation. God's plan was to knit me together in my mother's womb; the devil had another plan to stab me to death with a knitting needle. Who knows, that very same knitting needle may have been used to make a garment of clothing for my sister who was born some years before. Sixty-six years later as I write this, a mother's womb has become one of the most dangerous places to be. I was blessed with life. Millions of others were not, because laws were passed that made it legal to destroy the unborn children before all the days ordained for them, which were written in His Book came to pass. This was only the beginning of spiritual warfare for me. Yes, I escaped with my life but a spirit of rejection had entered me, which would cause me years of heartache and torment.

Many years later, after being born-again by the Spirit of God (John 3:3), and shortly after receiving the baptism of the Holy Spirit (Acts 1:5-8), I was instructed by the Holy Spirit to pray for a woman who had had an abortion and was tormented by a spirit of murder. She had repented and was set free by the grace of God when the spirit was cast out in the name of Jesus Christ.

Back to my birth, I entered this world knowing that I was not wanted. World War II (1939-1945) had not long finished and everything was in short supply. Life for millions was an uphill battle, and in Britain, rationing was still the norm for most people, yet there was another war still raging, as it had for thousands of years against spiritual forces of evil in the heavenly realms (Ephesians 6:12). All other wars are a shadow of this one. This is a spiritual war of good versus evil. God has said that in the last days He will pour out His Spirit on all people (Acts 2:17), and everyone who calls on the name of the Lord will be saved (Acts 2:21). The devil knows he is defeated, but continues to release hordes of demonic forces to blind the eyes of the unbelievers and bring them under demonic bondage (Luke 10:17-20, 2 Corinthians 4:4).

As World War II drew to a close, more than a few bishops, church leaders, government ministers and military leaders, truly believed that Great Britain had been saved for a purpose. They and others believed it was of a spiritual nature. Victory in World War II was won due to spiritual interventions by God.[1] There was another group led by Rees Howells who fully understood that both these wars were not only linked, but one and the same. Led by the Holy Spirit, they knew that just as the devil had entered Judas Iscariot (Luke 22:3), the devil had entered Adolf Hitler to try to stop Jesus' last command, to, "Go and make disciples of all nations" (Matthew 28:19-20 and Mark 16:15). Rees Howells, his son Samuel and over one hundred others, all became channels that the Holy Spirit entered, to fight the devil's schemes, for our struggle is not against flesh and blood, but against the rulers, against the authorities, against the powers of this dark world, and against spiritual forces of evil in heavenly realms (Ephesians 6:12). God's intent was that now through the Church, the manifold wisdom of God should be made known to the rulers and authorities in the heavenly realms (Ephesians 3:10-11). Rees Howells and his team of intercessors, fully understood this and went to war daily, on their knees. Led by the Holy Spirit they fasted, prayed and interceded, to bind the strong man and pull down his strongholds, releasing angelic forces to do battle with the principalities and powers of darkness (Daniel 10).[2]

Before I reached my second birthday, Rees Howells was called home. His life on earth was over and mine had only just begun. Today, prosperity preachers boast that they will not live in lack, but this was not the world that I was born into. I often went to bed hungry and learnt the value of all that God has given me, and knew that nothing should ever be wasted (John 6:12, Luke 16:10).[3]

It is my hope and prayer that by God's grace, as I share some of what I experienced and learnt, it will help others to understand and overcome the difficulties they are experiencing, which may be demonic, or a life that has not been crucified with Christ, so that you too can find victory in Jesus Christ by the power of the Holy Spirit (Galatians 3:20 and Romans 6:6-7).

Chapter One

Glimmers of Hope

It was shortly after World War II and I, unseen in the womb was not desired. Why was I not wanted? Did they not love me? Was I like many others, just another mouth to feed? Did they not know that for every action, there is a consequence? Was lust mistaken for love? My mother was already a single parent having been rejected by the father of her first child; like so many then, and now, they wanted sexual intercourse but not the responsibility that comes with it. My mother's two older brothers decided to teach my father a lesson regarding *another* unwanted pregnancy. My father, a small man, against the odds gave them both such a beating that he finished up in prison (Acts 19:16). This caused a rift that was never bridged, so on his release my parents moved to another town.

After the war, there was a housing shortage in Britain and the government encouraged those with spare rooms to share their homes, so the four of us lived in "rooms" as it was then known. As the years passed by, so the family's name slowly rose up the council housing list. Then with a third child on the way, we moved into a terraced house with neighbours on each side. There was no running hot water and electricity only downstairs. This was to be my home until I married and moved out. My parents did their best I believe, but the thief who comes only to steal, kill and destroy (John 10:10) moved in with us, and Jesus was not welcome; unlike the fortune-tellers and mediums, which my mother ran after, hoping to hear of a better life to come. Over time things went from bad to worse, and were often referred to as "a living hell." Money was always in short supply, but somehow or another, there was always enough for cider, cigars and gambling on the horses. My father became a drunkard and my mother was highly strung. One wrong word and she would lose all self-control, and become hysterical. Her anger was past management and as I later learnt, had opened the door to spirits of anger with other demonic spirits following! Foul-mouthed ructions were on the menu daily, and food was scarce. Our staple diet in the evening was bread and dripping,[1] or an Oxo cube dissolved in water with pieces of bread dipped in it. I was often sent to bed early to sleep off hunger. One dear neighbour always gave me a smile when I helped myself to her dog's biscuits left in a bowl by her back door.

One day, while we were still very young my sister was taken away to live with my mother's relatives. A few years later, my younger brother left home to attend an open-air school for health reasons. Food became more plentiful, as did the beatings, and my parents became more and more abusive, and violent towards each other, and myself. I thought about running away, but fear had such a strong hold over me that I had nightmares and would wet the bed, as I felt blamed for everything. My health suffered as a vulnerable child and I was admitted to hospital on four occasions to be operated on. At the end of it, I was so run down that the doctors wanted to send me away to convalesce. As I was the only child at home, my mother would not agree, so as a compromise, I was sent to stay with one of her sisters who had recently been released from a psychiatric hospital after having a breakdown; she had tried to commit suicide. Within days, my aunt could not cope and I was sent home. I was a long time recovering and did not attend school for many months. Years later, I learnt by the Holy Spirit that my forefathers on my mother's side played with witchcraft and a curse of mental illness came on the family (Exodus 20:1-5, Exodus 34:6-7). Curses are just as real as blessings and both are described in the Bible (Deuteronomy 27-28).

In my early teens, when my mother's father died, I was sent for and as he lay in his coffin, my grandmother *insisted* that I kiss him on the forehead. It was the last thing that I wanted to do, but I was manipulated, intimidated and dominated, against my will to kiss my deceased grandfather's forehead. The Holy Spirit later taught me that any form of manipulation, intimidation or domination is witchcraft, because it seeks control over others, to force them to do something against their will – it is sin. From that moment on, my personality changed for the worst and it would be years before the Holy Spirit was able to reveal to me that there had been a transfer of demonic evil spirits, depression being one of them, from my grandfather's dead body to mine. Evil spirits we learn from the Bible are fallen spirits (fallen angels) who serve Satan. Just as God sends angels to aid us (Hebrews 1:14), so Satan sends evil spirits to oppress and harass people. In Western culture, Satan is often portrayed as an imaginary cartoon character, but Jesus Christ fought against a real evil spiritual being who harms people and who has lesser evil spirits subservient to him. The Lord taught, "The devil and his angels" (Matthew 25:41), will be cast into everlasting fire for all their sins (Revelation 20:10).

In the intervening years, my brother and my sister both attempted suicide but thankfully failed. Some say it was a cry for help, but in hindsight, I know they were driven, tormented by evil spirits, suicide being the name of one of them. To say my family was dysfunctional is an understatement. Where was God in all this darkness you may well ask. He never rejected my family, but we had rejected Him and His Son, Jesus Christ (John 3:16-21). While the demons were busy painting pictures on my imagination and tormenting me to take my own life, God's Holy Spirit was reaching out to me in a way that I could understand. There were three glimmers of hope.

The first one happened when I was eight years of age. One of the local churches sent a minibus onto our poor and dysfunctional part of the estate, inviting the children to a time of fun and games with Jesus at their Gospel Hall. There would be squash and buns (a fruit flavoured drink and a cake). This truly was good news, so I went. I heard that Jesus loved me and I was given a bookmark with a tassel. On it was written the words of Jesus: "It is more blessed to give than to receive" (Acts 20:35). As there were no books in our house at that time, I hung it on the picture rail in my bedroom. I only went once, but twenty-eight years later, the Holy Spirit led me back to this little church to make a fresh start.

The second glimmer of hope came one evening while playing football with friends and the ball went over the fence, once too often. We had been warned by the woman of the house, that because we had been rude to her (when this had happened on previous occasions), that she would no longer throw the ball back. Furthermore, we would have to go round to her garden and apologise for our bad behaviour, before she would give our ball back. I dared not go home without the ball, just the thought of it made me tremble. As the minutes slowly passed by, so fear took a greater hold over me. As I entered the garden gate, I wanted to run, but I had no choice, I would have to take my chances. With my head hung low and my face to the ground, I knocked the door, thinking would she wallop me across the head. This was the accepted practice of the day. She came to the door, smiled at me and in a soft caring voice asked, "Would you and your friends like some lemonade and biscuits?" We did, and as we tucked into them, she explained she lived on her own and enjoyed her garden. However, the ball had damaged some of her plants for which she forgave us, and politely asking us to move the place of our goal, which we did.

God in His goodness and mercy had placed a *truly* Christian woman in my path, who invited my friends and I to go to her church the following Sunday. She would take us on the bus and pay our fares. Over time, all my friends stopped going, but I continued for some years at the Gospel Hall. I never forgot that woman, she lived in the same street, in the same type of house, but she was a lady to me, a light shining in the darkness, a beacon on a hill. Why was she so calm, so forgiving and at peace? With a smile on her face, this was indeed a Divine appointment. God in His sovereign will had orchestrated all the events for His purposes. Thirty years would pass before I saw another smile like hers. This time it was an answer to prayer to which I shall refer to later.

In 1961, I received my third glimmer of hope at the pictures, as we called it then (cinema). I went to see *Whistle Down the Wind*. It's the story of a prisoner on the run from the police who hid himself in a barn on a farm, but was discovered by the farmer's children. They believed he was Jesus and feared that if the adults found out, they might crucify him all over again. They managed to hide him and look after him, but as word got out, more and more children wanted to come and see him. Eventually one of the children let it slip and the police were called. The children sent for help from all the other children in the area, who came in large numbers. However, by the time they arrived, the police had arrested the felon. In a silhouette, the children saw 'Jesus' being frisked with his arms outstretched in the shape of a cross. Later, when all the excitement was over, two small girls turned up asking to see Jesus. The farmer's eldest daughter said she was sorry but they had missed him this time, but assured them of his return a second time at some later date. As I sat there at the pictures, I knew God was speaking to me and I welled up. I was a sinner on the run and could not hide from Him (Psalm 139:6). From that day forth, I have always known that Jesus would return a second time. Forty-three years later, God in His goodness and mercy led me by the Holy Spirit to the farm where the film was set. I stood in that barn with tears in my eyes knowing that one day, Jesus would return.

The day before I left school, I got into a fight with one of my classmates and we were sent to the headmaster's office. In all my years I had never been caned; corporal punishment was encouraged in those days. For gross misconduct, you were given six of the best. I was flogged so much at home with a leather belt by my father, and my mother's copper stick, (this was a piece of wood used to stir the washing while being boiled in the copper)[2] that I had become hardened to it, and was now bold and strong enough to refuse punishment. Many boys had their spirits broken this way, what little life or hope they had was beaten out of them (Proverbs 18:14). The headmaster was full of wisdom that day, when he calmly pointed out to us that we were no longer boys but men, and we would reap what we sowed (Galatians 6:7-8). Yes, we could refuse our punishment and continue down that road of rebellion for the rest of our lives – it was our choice. The next day, every student who was leaving school would shake the headmaster's hand and be given a Bible to help guide them on their way in this life. This all took place in the hall, in full view of all staff and students. However, if we took the easy way out, we would lose not only our invitation, but the gift of a free Bible. I left his office that day smiling. My classmate was in tears, he was in pain, yet I hardly felt it. We both received our Bibles the following day.

Before the spiritual decline and anti-Christian onslaught of the 1960s (inspired by demonic strongholds), the revivalist Rev. Duncan Campbell of the Hebridean Revival (1949-1952), warned the Church, "At this very hour, forces are taking the field that are out to defy every known Christian principle." On another occasion he said, "Unless revival comes, other forces will take the field that will sink us still deeper into the mire of humanism and materialism."[3] How right he was!

This permissive society wanted free love, (which cost millions so much), yet some years later, women would lie on the road to stop cattle trucks (lorries) from boarding the ferries at the port of Dover, which were transporting young calves in cramped conditions to be farmed on the Continent in confined spaces, as compared to the UK farms. However, at the same time, these same women demanded the right to abort their babies, despite the Bible describing how a child is formed in its mother's womb by God.[4] For years, governments have struggled to balance the books between national insurance credits and pension debits, because there are more pensioners receiving their pensions, than young people paying in, because of the deficit left, due to millions of babies having been aborted! And still it continues.

The nation was turning its back on God and the Bible. My parents mockingly enquired, "Are you going to be a vicar?" With no qualifications, not fully knowing the alphabet, I smiled and went my own way, and managed to secure an apprenticeship in the motor trade. With money of my own, I took up smoking and spent any spare money I had at the local boutique (a small shop selling fashionable clothes) and at the record store. Finally, I could choose my own clothes and wear what I liked. I was an extrovert wearing the clothes made popular and trendy by the music stars of the time: Beatle jackets (a jacket without a collar) were all the rage; a white polo necked shirt, as worn by the Dave Clark Five; a pair of trousers with 56 cm (22 inch) circumference flared bottoms, and a pair of winkle-picker shoes with pointed toes. Also, my trousers looked like a chequered flag used at car races, black and white squares like a chessboard. You would see me coming. The reader can be forgiven for smiling, but I assure you it was all the fashion then.

The people at the little Gospel Hall were not impressed or smiling. The youth leader and his wife were very sympathetic, but there was what would become known as a generation gap. These dear people had gone through so much in the war years and paid such a high price. All they wanted was peace and their traditions restored. Who could blame them? Few people like change and most feel secure in their routines. Like it or not, change was relentless and defined in the 1960s. There was a spiritual battle going on for the hearts and minds of a new generation. At this time, protest songs could be heard wherever there was a jukebox or transistor radio. For me, the lyrics of two songs still reside with me: 'The Times, They Are A-Changing' by Bob Dylan, and 'The Eve of Destruction' by Barry McGuire. Both American, both hits here and in the USA. These songs shed light on how millions perceived their society at that time, and were determined to be free, or so they thought. "Make love, not war," they said. "Live for today, there may be no tomorrow." "Ban the bomb, throw off all restraint." "Be a free spirit." This was just the beginning of godlessness in the last days, and as Romans 1-2 explains, God gave them over to the sinful desires of their hearts. He allows sin to run its course as an act of judgement (Psalm 81:11-12, Romans 8:18-31, 1 Timothy 4:1-2, 2 Timothy 3:1-4). The reader would be well advised to open their Bibles, read these verses and meditate on them for a time, for this is the days we are living in. We sowed the wind and have reaped the whirlwind (Hosea 8:7).

Chapter Two

Tides of Anger

Having left school and entered the world of employment, things could only get better, or so I thought. There were no more physical beatings, but on the inside I was troubled. My mind was tormented. There was a battle going on; some days I was so depressed and angry – I had to restrain myself. One day, I was working on my racing bike, trying to set up the gears and I became more and more frustrated, and suddenly I snapped. I lost control and raised the bike over my head and threw it into the air! The headmaster was right, I reaped what I sowed, and it took me several days to repair my bike.

Then there was the time when I was out with my first girlfriend (before I left school); I was very shy back then and she was very quiet. We went for bike rides and walks together. We never kissed or held hands, but enjoyed being together. Until one day, whilst out walking we met another young man, her neighbour, whom I had never met. He started talking to her and was ignoring me. I was overcome with feelings of rejection, and jealousy reared up within me. In anger, I snapped and lost control. I have no idea what I said, but I do recall that he jumped on his bike and peddled away as fast as he could. My girlfriend burst into tears and went home without saying a word to me. The following day, I went to her house and was told by her mother that she never wished to see me again. Later that day, I went looking for her neighbour, whom I believed had come between us. I had a small chain wrapped around my hand; but God is sovereign and on the way I met a friend who talked me out of it.

As I explained before, my sister had to leave home, due to my dad's insane jealously towards her and my mother, because she had another father; in an age when this was culturally unacceptable. Was I, with my jealously, another chip off the old block? Like father like son?

On another occasion, my mates and I were watching a football match, when I noticed a woman looking at us, as if we were not welcome. If looks could kill, I would not be writing this. I turned to one of my mates and inquired, "What's her problem?" To which he replied, "Maybe it's because of your foul language about the referee!" I was not even aware that I had been using bad language. Today, the experts would have diagnosed me with Tourette syndrome; but is that really the problem? Later, I would learn that my problem was something deeper and spiritual, and I was not the only one with these problems. When I was older, one of my friends at work shared with me how he was standing in line in a shop one day when he started, in his words, "Swearing his head off." He was so embarrassed that he ran out of the shop. He also said, "I had no control over this voice that came out of me." What was going on, I wondered.

While at work, on another occasion, I was talking to a colleague, when another person I knew walked up to me and without saying a word, punched me so hard in the arm that I stumbled. I looked at my colleague in disbelief and said, "What was that all about?" To which he replied, "That was probably his way of paying you back." "For what?" I exclaimed. "When you kicked him earlier." I have noticed down the years that some people, especially when they are angry, strike out – one way or another, and when challenged as to why, they will reply, "I don't know," or "I did what?" Today, I would ask the Holy Spirit, "Lord, what are you trying to teach me in this?" But for now, we must move on and will return later to all that the Holy Spirit taught me about the root of these problems and how I could be delivered.

As a young man, I decided never to get married, nor to have children. I feared that whatever it was *in* me, might harm, or damage them, as I had been and still was. As a child, I went to bed for years hearing my parents fight and would awaken, not to a dawn chorus, but a chorus of demonic and fleshly abuse. One thing I was sure of, I could and would work hard to have a better life and be at peace. I was not on my own; there were so many broken families and hurt people. This was not life as God intended, but a miserable existence.

I was now seventeen years old and do not recall ever feeling loved. What did it feel like to be wanted? To be cuddled? To be hugged? I had seen it in the Hollywood films; even the war films of the day were romanticised. But with the coming of the Vietnam War and its true horrors seen daily on our television screens, I better understood why so many who returned home, after World War II (1939-1945), had no wish to talk about it and relive those horrors.

At work, my foreman who was helping to train me was one such man who had lived through war. He was always thoughtful towards me, which for some reason upset one of the skilled men, an amateur boxer, who was five years older than me, and he went out of his way to provoke me. He would deflate the tyres on my bike etc. One day he went too far and put sawdust in my sandwiches. He was a skilled man; I was an apprentice, which placed me in a vulnerable position if I tried to retaliate, but I had to do something and I did. The following day, I filled his lunchbox with sawdust; this stopped him, but he vowed to get revenge outside of work.

One Saturday night, whilst leaving a dance hall he saw me; he was intoxicated and he challenged me to a fight in front of many of our friends. I refused for fear of losing my apprenticeship, which was my passport to a better life. He pushed me to the ground violently and something within me fired up and took over. This was demonic in nature, cruel and relentless. I lost control, so I must ask one simple question – who was in control? I was so shocked by what had happened and so was he, after leaving the Accident and Emergency department at the local hospital! The police had broken up our fight and to my surprise, my opponent stood up for me, explaining that he had started it, which other witnesses confirmed; and we were dismissed, no charges were brought against us.

At work on Monday morning, I was summoned to the manager's office to give an account of myself. Fortunately, the antagonist once again stood up for me, as God was truly watching out for me, but I was yet to know it, or Him.

My foreman, who became a fatherly figure for those few years, later took me to one side at work and calmly told me that he knew my father. He was aware that my father had been banned from most of the drinking houses in the town because of his drunken violent behaviour. This remained our secret and he advised me to stay out of trouble before I ruined my life, as my father had, and others beside. It turned out that my foreman had been in the military police during World War II and had seen too many men go down the wrong path. Something happened at this time – was he a Christian? Was he a praying man? I have no idea. But I was convinced from that time on that God was calling me, doing His very best to get my attention. Yet, at the same time, the devil was not letting go without a fight.

Approximately ten years later, I wrote to my old foreman and thanked him for all his help. The apostle Paul knew the value of becoming a father to others, in Christ Jesus, through the gospel (1 Corinthians 4:15). Jesus taught the apostles and they taught the new disciples of Jesus Christ. Today, there are millions of young people who have not had the benefit of a true father or a mentor. Sadly, for them and for society as a whole, both have been cheated out of God's best for them. Others, like myself, were given a distorted view of what a father should be, which makes it very difficult to view God as a loving and caring Father. Because of the faults of my natural father, my view of God the Father was distorted, and I viewed Him as an angry disciplinarian. It took me years to learn the truth: 'And because you are sons, God has sent forth the Spirit of His Son into your hearts, crying out, "Abba, Father!" Therefore you are no longer a slave but a son and if a son, then an heir of God through Christ' (Galatians 4:6-7).

My mates were growing up and found less interest in having adventures as we had once done, and most of them became more interested in girls. This was the era of 'free love' and yet, we remained ignorant of the long-lasting costs the devil would make people pay, for what he called 'free love.' It wasn't free and it wasn't love – it was lust. Today we can discern that the so-called 'free love' of the 1960s came at a terrible cost to individuals and society as a whole; one night of passion for some, turned into a lifetime of regret. Satan also used this rebellion against God's holy standards to destroy family lives and to crush the spirits of millions of children, brought up in broken homes (1 Thessalonians 4:3-8).

My mates were soon at the age when testosterone was having a great affect upon them, and the girls they came into contact with were longing to be loved and cared for. So one by one, my mates had to get married, as they mistook lust for love and their girlfriends became pregnant. None of us had been taught the difference between sacrificial selfless Christian love and lust. Today, society could not care less; back then, it was accepted by almost all that it was a great sin to have a child outside of marriage (Deuteronomy 23:2, 1 Corinthians 6:18-20, 1 Peter 4:2, 1 John 2:16). As always, it tends to be the children of such arrangements who pay the heaviest price.

Most of the people I grew up with married young and sadly, the majority later got divorced. What was happening was a complete rejection of God's will, as expressed in the Bible – but had anyone told us? According to Scripture and the teaching of the Lord Jesus Christ, marriage is a covenant between one man and one woman for life, witnessed before God. Covenant is sacred and to God, is like a legal binding spiritual agreement and for this reason, and because of the terrible cost of divorce, God hates divorce (Malachi 2:13-16, Mark 10:7-12, Ephesians 5:31-33).

The sad legacy of the 1960s rebellion lives on today, as the overwhelming majority of young men and women do not know the difference between love and lust. This also includes most young Christians, who have not been taught the difference between living according to the will of flesh and the liberty of the life of the Spirit (Galatians 5:16-26). It took me many years to learn that, 'The flesh lusts against the Spirit and the Spirit against the flesh; and these are contrary to one another, so that you do not do the things that you wish' (Galatians 5:17).

I did not follow the same path as my friends. Yes, I did have two other girlfriends, but after three weeks I would always politely end the relationship, for fear of getting emotionally involved. Then, one night I was out with a group of friends and a girl I had never met before decided she wanted to get to know me. My friends encouraged me to meet with her on another occasion, saying, "You have nothing to lose."

I was not a disciple of Jesus Christ at this point in time; I was still living in the dark, and longed to be at peace. I later found out that when the Holy Spirit comes into your life, He comes to guide you into all truth. He is the Spirit of Truth who brings peace (John 16:13); unlike the devil, the father of lies (John 8:44).

Jesus promised that if we will hold to His teaching, then we will become His disciples and we will know the truth, and it will set us free (John 8:31-32). However, it would take years for me to enter into and experience the peace of Christ.

Jesus said, "He who does not love Me does not keep My words; and the word which you hear is not Mine but the Father's who sent Me. These things I have spoken to you while being present with you. But the Helper, the Holy Spirit, whom the Father will send in My name, He will teach you all things, and bring to your remembrance all things that I said to you. Peace I leave with you, My peace I give to you; not as the world gives do I give to you. Let not your heart be troubled, neither let it be afraid" (John 14:24-27).

Chapter Three

Back to the Beginning

My friend who had said, "You have nothing to lose," when this girl wanted to meet me was right, because I had gained much. Sixteen years later, I had a wife, family and a mortgage, and lived in another town. Despite my limited knowledge of God, I was aware that I was by now getting tired of running from the Lord. Something had to happen to get me to bow the knee to God, but when it came, it was a terrible shock.

It was some years later and my son was in very bad health, which required frequent visits to the hospital. In the early hours of the morning, he was rushed into hospital and was admitted, often fighting for his life in an oxygen tent. When the specialist came to see him, which he did on regular occasions because of his deep concern, I pleaded with him to tell me the truth. He said, "There is a possibility that he might not make it to his teenage years."

This battle for my son's health had been going on for months and months, and at the same time, unbeknown to me, the Holy Spirit had instructed an intercessor to pray for my conversion to Christianity. It was a woman who was employed in the same company as myself, but in another department. I had tried and exhausted every human avenue to help my son, and now I had reached the last resort – God. I was so desperate I began to pray daily for my son's life. I promised God in my daily prayers that if He would spare my son's life, He could take mine. I perceived this as a Divine exchange; I would die and my son would live in my place.

I had not attended a church to worship for seventeen years, but now I was so desperate that my wife and I took the child to a Christian healing service at a church, and slowly, but surely, after he received prayer, a quiet confidence grew in me that he would live. Later on, when we were given the all-clear by the doctors and I knew he would not die, I got on my knees thanking God for His mercy. At the same time, offering my life to Him, believing that it was possible that He might end my life, due to my bargaining – my life for my son's.

Within days, God revealed to me that I was already dead in my sins. I did not need to die physically because I was already spiritually dead. God showed me that I needed to repent and be born-again. Jesus said, "Most assuredly, I say to you, unless one is born of water and the Spirit, he cannot enter the Kingdom of God. That which is born of the flesh is flesh, and that which is born of the Spirit is spirit. Do not marvel that I said to you, 'You must be born-again' " (John 3:5-7). This was my need, to be born spiritually and I came under great conviction, as I poured out my heart, pleading for forgiveness and begging for a second chance (John 16:8). As God met with me, His peace flooded into me, and as my heart melted, tears rolled down my face for the first time in perhaps twenty years. This was my born-again experience, as I put my faith in Jesus Christ's death and resurrection. For, 'If you confess with your mouth the Lord Jesus and believe in your heart that God has raised Him from the dead, you will be saved' (Romans 10:9-10).

Upon my conversion I was immediately set free from using foul language, which I later learned from the Holy Spirit was a spirit of unclean speech. Immediately, I became hungry for the truth of God's word, the Bible. As I read the book of Acts, which is the testimony of the early Church, I realised it was the Holy Spirit who had empowered the disciples after they had received the baptism of the Holy Spirit (Acts 1:4-8). I read in Luke's Gospel, how God our heavenly Father is willing to give the Holy Spirit to all those who ask Him (Luke 11:13); so, at home, I got down on my knees and pleaded for this baptism of the Holy Spirit. With my hands raised towards heaven, I asked for the promise of the indwelling of the Spirit of God and He came upon me, and I was not disappointed. He fell upon me in peace and joy, and I swayed with my hands in the air. I had never felt such peace inside.

Fortunately for me, I had not met people who peddle the false teaching that we receive everything at conversion – they do not know what they are missing out on! Paul was converted and sealed by the Spirit for the day of redemption (Ephesians 4:30), but it was not until three days later that he received the baptism of the Holy Spirit (Acts 9:9). After Paul's conversion, whilst he was heading towards Damascus, the Lord Jesus Himself appeared to Ananias and told him to prepare to pray for Paul to receive the Holy Spirit! Ananias said, "Brother Saul, the Lord Jesus, who appeared to you on the road as you came, has sent me that you may receive your sight and be filled with the Holy Spirit" (Acts 9:17).

I too had been converted and had to wait until I was baptised by the Holy Spirit, and when He came upon me, He came in power and I was empowered and began sharing my testimony with all who would listen. Jesus Christ had changed my life and I wanted everyone to know that He can change the lives of all who call upon Him! Some weeks later, I also received the gift of tongues (Acts 19:1-7), and all this took place (as a new Christian) before I had even attended a church meeting. I was converted and baptised in the Holy Spirit in God's way, in His time and outside of the walls and structures of a church building.

Now I knew I needed to learn what being a disciple of Jesus meant, by meeting and worshipping with other Christians. Therefore, I shared all that had happened to me with my wife and explained that I had seen religion when I was young, but what I had experienced was not religion, I had met with God!

As I kept reading the Bible, I realised that Jesus and all His disciples were baptised in water, and it is God's will for all who believe in Him to be baptised. 'Peter said to them, "Repent, and let every one of you be baptised in the name of Jesus Christ for the remission of sins; and you shall receive the gift of the Holy Spirit" ' (Acts 2:38-39).

We began attending a local church on a weekly basis and the pastor was very keen for our baptisms to take place. This church was learning to welcome the Holy Spirit to come and do His work amongst them, and we were all discovering what it meant to invite Him in and allow His gifts to flow amongst us (1 Corinthians 12:4-11). It was all new to the older Christians, but to me as a new convert, this is what it meant to walk with God, to experience the power of the Holy Spirit and to see His gifts at work!

I wanted to obey God in all things, but one of my friends was not keen on the idea, telling me that he had been christened as a baby and that was enough. When I pointed out to him that the apostle Peter had preached repentance and baptism to enter the Kingdom of God, he said, "I have nothing to repent of."

My wife and I were baptised about a month later and testified that we wanted to be, "True disciples of the Lord Jesus Christ." There was a prophecy given about our future lives, also a tongue and its interpretation, most of which have come to pass (1 Corinthians 14:27-34). All of this was new to me, but as I read the Bible, I learned that this was the experience of the believers in the New Testament and it should be our experience too, and it was!

One evening while walking home from work, the Holy Spirit spoke to me and explained that He wanted me to go back to the beginning and start again. What did God mean by this? I was puzzled by this word and yet at the same time excited. I had read in my Bible that the Holy Spirit would speak to Jesus' disciples (Acts 13:1-3), but that was then. Did He still speak today in the same way? The answer was, "Yes!" I was learning that He still speaks today. Jesus taught, "My sheep hear My voice and I know them" (John 10:27). Nevertheless, I never thought to ask God where I was to go. Instead, I pondered all this in my heart, sharing it with my wife when I arrived home.

The next day a letter arrived inviting me to share my testimony of my conversion at a church. Some weeks later, I arrived at the church and discovered that it was the same chapel I had attended when I was just eight years old. Twenty-eight years had passed and I had gone back to the beginning where it all started! I had learnt a great truth. The Holy Spirit can and will guide you, if you will choose to listen to Him and if you are willing to be obedient. This is what happened to the first believers in Jesus Christ. 'As they ministered to the Lord and fasted, the Holy Spirit said, "Now separate to Me Barnabas and Saul for the work to which I have called them" ' (Acts 13:2-3). Who called and sent them? It was the Holy Spirit.

Now, it was the Holy Spirit who had told me to go back to the beginning and He had initiated the journey, which would lead me back to the Christian meeting place, where I first sensed God's call on my life. After giving my testimony at this church, the Holy Spirit suddenly came upon me and I shook from head to toe. My conversion was dramatic, deep and powerful, and not all could understand the experiences with God I had received. Too many had been playing with religion all their lives, but I had met with God, not a religion. As previously stated, my conversion to Christianity and baptism in the Holy Spirit took place outside of the church. God met with me and I was transformed.

Chapter Four

The Deep End

I picked up a leaflet whilst at the church, which explained what a true disciple of Jesus Christ is and the cost (Luke 14:25-33). I learnt that to be a disciple of Jesus Christ you must give up everything. Jesus said, "So likewise, whoever of you does not forsake all that he has cannot be My disciple" (Luke 14:33). I knew this could mean living in a mud hut in Africa as a missionary, but as it turned out, it meant *giving all to God,* and allowing Him to use everything I am, and own, for His glory. It meant being a steward of all He has given me, instead of being the owner.

When we returned home, I invited my wife to join me in a prayer of surrender, giving all we had to the Lord, to use at His disposal, anytime He chose, and to follow Him wherever He might lead us. This was the answer I believe, to the call which I received when I was a teenager. Before we had married, I told my future wife that one day the call would come and my life would change forever. As I was not a Christian, I did not understand the call, nor did I know the Lord at that time, but God allowed me to sense His witness within me.

Today, I still meet many who claim to be disciples of Jesus Christ but who are in truth churchgoers with a nickname 'Christian.' They have not and *will not* lay everything down, and follow Him. Jesus tells us the conditions to be His disciples in the Gospels, and they must be met! Brother, sister, friend, if you are one such a person I implore you, please get down on your knees and repent. Then, read and study Jesus' teaching and definition of discipleship in Matthew 7:13-27. Be very careful what you say and do not be hasty, because words can come cheap, and it is no good later saying, "I meant it at the time." The Bible warns: 'Better not to vow than to vow and not pay' (Ecclesiastes 5:5). Being a fool for Christ is one thing, acting the fool is quite another. We are not permitted as believers to be double-minded, saying one thing and doing another (James 1:5-8, James 4:7-8).

The following Sunday after this wonderful experience, we returned to our home church and a woman came up to me, "I have a letter for you," she said. "From whom?" I inquired. "From the Lord God," she said, as she placed it in my hand. I opened it later and could hardly believe all that I read. One part of it said, "You have submitted your possessions to Me and in this I rejoice. For now I will use them for My glory. But I want all of you; your mind, dreams, desires and yourself. As you give each to Me, I will cleanse your old nature from you and fill you with My Spirit in each one of those areas, and people will see Me in you, and our relationship will deepen and be purified."

We had told no one about our prayer of surrender to the Lord; yet the Lord had heard, acknowledged and accepted our prayer. At our baptism we had been told by the Holy Spirit, "If you will be what I want you to be, together we shall make disciples that are strong, healthy and very active." Why did He say, "If you will be?" Then, it came to me. God is love and will never force us against our wills to do anything; we always have a choice to obey His will and be blessed, or rebel and suffer the consequences. This is one of the great differences between God and the devil. God works through love, the devil through all forms of witchcraft (always seeking to control another). Any type of manipulation, intimidation, fear or domination to force you against your will to do something, is one part of Satan's strategy to get you out of God's perfect pleasing will. Far too often, people in some churches also feel forced to do things they are not called by God to do. This is not the work of the Holy Spirit, but of other spirits working through unsurrendered vessels (1 Timothy 4:1-3).

Now that I had been converted and received the gift of the Holy Spirit, many people at my workplace began to notice the profound difference in my life. Like Saul, I was a changed man and people were talking about it. Therefore, when people spoke to me I was thrilled to share my testimony and many were inspired. At first, there was just one colleague at work who listened intently and wanted to experience the same; so following my lead, he repented of his sins and invited the Lord Jesus into his life. He was born-again and now he wanted more! He wanted to receive the baptism of the Holy Spirit. "Could I help?" he inquired. "Yes," I said, "let's meet up at my house and pray about it."

I thought my friend was coming around to receive the baptism of the Holy Spirit, but God used the occasion to introduce me to another part of spiritual warfare. Before he arrived, I was reading how Jesus Christ had twice cast out an evil spirit from a man in a synagogue (Mark 1:21-28), and it was fresh in my mind when he arrived. We prayed as he invited the Holy Spirit into his life. I laid hands on him, as the disciples of Jesus had done and prayed over him, using my gift of tongues, as they had done in Bible days (1 Corinthians 14:14-15). The Holy Spirit came on him in power and he slipped to the floor. Then he started shaking. At first I thought he was having a fit, but then he started moaning and fear took hold of me, as I backed away from him. I was not sure what to do, and then, the Holy Spirit reminded me of what I had been reading and said, "It is an evil spirit. Command it to go in Jesus' name." So I said, "Come out of him, you evil spirit!" In a gruff voice, the evil spirit replied through the man, "Who are you to tell me to leave?" I was stumped for a few seconds, as I thought to myself, who am I? Then it came to me. "I am a child of God, a servant of Jesus Christ the Lord...come out of him, I command you in Jesus' name, leave!" With that, the demon left him and through this incident the Holy Spirit taught me that it is God's will for believers to exercise all the authority Jesus gave His disciples – including casting out demons.

Demons had fled from people during Jesus' ministry and they had been cast out of people by His disciples. Jesus explained that evangelism, speaking with new tongues, casting out demons, and praying for the sick should be the standard for His disciples (Mark 16:15-17). But I had not learnt this in a church; it was the Holy Spirit who was teaching me.

Still at my house, the man I was praying for struggled to his feet smiling and said, "I have not felt so good in years," and he also received the gift of tongues from the Holy Spirit. This is what happened to Paul. 'And when Paul had laid hands on them, the Holy Spirit came upon them, and they spoke with tongues and prophesied. Now the men were about twelve in all' (Acts 19:6-7).

It was certainly a wonderful time, yet I did feel that I had been thrown into the deep end and wondered, where would all this lead? I had not been attending church for long and I had no theological background; why was so much happening to me in such a short time?

The testimony of this man became very effective. Before his deliverance from this evil spirit, this man was very withdrawn, but the Holy Spirit loosened his tongue and he was now so different. People at our place of employment kept asking him, "What has happened?" Word began to spread that God was moving and though many disbelieved, many others came seeking, and received!

One woman we both worked with came and asked me one day, "Do you think God will help me?" "What do you want?" I asked, and she explained that for thirteen years she and her husband had been trying for a baby. They had been to see many doctors and they found no reason why she had not conceived. She had spoken to her husband and he had agreed to ask me to pray for her. I placed my hand on her shoulder and asked the good Lord to bless her with a baby. Six weeks later she spoke to me again and said, "When you pray for someone and what you pray for happens, do you think it might just be a coincidence?" "Not after thirteen years of trying," I said, pointing out her long battle trying to get pregnant. Then I asked, "Are you pregnant?" "Yes," she replied, "and when the baby is born, we shall attend a church." They had a little girl and to my knowledge, they continued their life just as they had, without the Lord. I saw their daughter when she was eighteen years old, working in a store, and I was reminded of God's answer to this simple prayer.

For the first few months after my conversion I witnessed many powerful healings and at one point, people would simply touch me and get healed. I was concerned for the future after these events. What would happen if this lasted forever? Would I be mobbed in the streets? If you are smiling, remember, I was a young and inexperienced Christian.

Chapter Five

Power and Authority

Jesus gave His disciples power and authority over all demons and over sicknesses (Luke 9:1), and that authority is passed to each generation of Christians. For me, good news was travelling fast, as many people I knew heard that there was a God with power to heal, save and deliver. I was busy for a season, sharing the gospel and praying with those that asked, and God worked in power. Many were converted, many were healed, and many were added to my local church. One of the Christians at my workplace once asked me why no one ever listened to his witness, whilst many were suddenly converted after I was saved. There is no easy answer to this question, but I believe this man was offering people religion and they could see what it had done to him! As for me, God was changing me, pruning me and empowering me; but there was much work to be done!

Over the years, the Holy Spirit taught me that if I was willing to become vulnerable, open and transparent, He would work through me to help others. I was given the gift of the word of knowledge and discerning of spirits, which Paul taught would be given to believers as the Holy Spirit wills (1 Corinthians 12:8-10). Nevertheless, Jesus said, "Only in his home town, among his relatives and in his own house, is a prophet without honour," and the Lord struggled to help His own who were close to Him, because of their lack of faith (Matthew 13:57-58). It was the same with me.

However, I was also struggling myself in different areas of my life and decided it was time that I focused on my own problems, to get fully delivered and set free. Some things are so painful that we bury them deep down and project an image of normality to others; yet at the same time, we are tormented by all that happened.

I was not permitted to hide from my past life of sin and the Holy Spirit had made it plain to me that He wanted to clean up *every* area of my life, but I would have a part to play, as I cooperated with Him. Deep inside, I was still struggling with rebellion, jealousy, depression, fear, pride, self-pity, compulsive eating, lust, anger, rejection and mistrust. Like the Corinthians, I moved in spiritual gifts, but was still very shallow in my faith, with very little of the nature of Christ shining through (1 Corinthians 3:1-4). I had received a measure of freedom at my new birth and a further measure when I was baptised in the Holy Spirit, but there were still strongholds in my life (2 Corinthians 10:3-5).

I was prepared to pay the price to get free, but sadly, most people I knew then in the church, would not even admit that they had problems, and many had no desire, or wish to get involved with casting out evil/unclean spirits. Most were complete strangers to any form of spiritual warfare, despite this being one of the main reasons the Church exists on earth (Ephesians 3:10-11).

Despite being used to help cast a demon out of someone else, I was still struggling, so eventually, I asked for the Lord's help and the answer came when I was later introduced to a man who said he could help me with deliverance. We met over a period of time and he cast the majority of the spirits previously mentioned out of me, one at a time. Some evil spirits would not leave me, until I repented of some specific sin, or forgave someone, because these sins gave them a right to remain. It was a real battle, but I was determined to be free. Like so many men and women, lust was a real problem; but now I had been freed from the demon of lust. I felt clean. I was clean. Praise the lovely name of Jesus Christ. In all of these experiences, I was still learning to give the Holy Spirit every situation as it came to me and to learn what He was trying to teach me from it. The lesson for me was that humility, confession and repentance are the paths to liberty.

'The Lord is near to those who have a broken heart, and saves such as have a contrite spirit' (Psalm 34:18). 'The sacrifices of God are a broken spirit, a broken and contrite heart, these O God, You will not despise' (Psalm 51:17). 'He who covers his sins will not prosper, but whoever confesses and forsakes them will have mercy' (Proverbs 28:13). 'Likewise you younger people, submit yourselves to your elders. Yes, all of you be submissive to one another and be clothed with humility, for God resists the proud, but gives grace to the humble' (1 Peter 5:5).

One of my big problems was that a spirit of depression refused to leave me. In the Bible, many evil spirit have specific names.[1] However, the Holy Spirit taught me that it would only leave when the curse of mental illness, which had come on my forefathers (on my mother's side), had been broken. I had once thought of devils and curses as superstition, but in the Bible, they are all very real. Christ has given us power to be free from all devils/evil spirits,[2] and one of the reasons Jesus Christ died and rose again, was to set us free from all curses (Galatians 3:13, Colossians 1:13). However, I learnt that at each stage of my deliverance, it was imperative that I was led by the Holy Spirit; for He knows the key to all deliverances. Jesus explained that the Holy Spirit is the Teacher and I was learning to listen to and obey Him (John 14:26).

The Holy Spirit also had another lesson for me, and this time, it was that I could *not* blame my sins on evil spirits. Approximately three months after I had been delivered from the spirit of lust, it started to become a problem again. By now, I had read a few books on self-deliverance and had learnt the power Jesus gave to His followers to cast out devils, and I found these books very helpful. I became aware how I had got into this mess and how my sins had given these evil spirits a right to harass me, despite being a child of God.[3]

Convinced that an evil spirit of lust had returned and entered me, I decided I could cast it out on my own. I started to command the spirit of lust to leave in Jesus' mighty name. Eventually, as I was feeling quite worn out, the Holy Spirit said, "You cannot cast self out of self." "What do you mean?" I asked. He replied, "Your problem is not a spirit of lust, but *you*." "Me!" I retorted. "Yes, *you*," He replied. "It is your old sinful nature. Your flesh (1 Peter 4:2), for in your heart, you enjoy lusting. You enjoy fantasying; it gives you pleasure; but it also opens the door for the spirit of lust to enter. You only love the Lord Jesus in measure and only when you truly love Him more than that, will you be free of it." I repented at once and learned another hard lesson. But another much harder lesson would come later.

Today, everywhere you go there are sexual enticements, traps of the devil to lure you into spiritual and emotional bondage. You cannot help the first glance, but if you continue to stare or ogle, you open the door by your lusting and could become more bound than before (Matthew 12:43-45).

My father was bound by a spirit of anger, as was my mother, and when he became one with my mother, a spirit of anger got hold of me whilst I was still in my mother's womb. It was spiritual and hereditary; just as the Old Testament explains (Exodus 34:6-7).[4] I had already been delivered from the spirit of anger, as I have indicated, and it was a real battle, because it was truly a stronghold in me (Mark 3:27). But one evening, I let my guard down and succumbed to uncontrolled anger. This incident began when a person in my church spoke behind my back, and when I heard about it, I was *very* upset. I should have seen the person responsible to discuss the matter, and forgive (Matthew 18:15); but I did not, and the devil began to paint pictures on my imagination.

With an offended person (yourself or the offender) the priority in Christ is forgiveness and reconciliation (Matthew 5:21-26, Matthew 18:15-17, 2 Corinthians 2:10-11), otherwise the devil will take advantage of you and torment you, painting pictures on your mind with imaginary conversations and scenarios. Jesus said, "And whenever you stand praying if you have anything against your brother forgive him, that your Father in heaven may also forgive your trespasses" (Mark 11:25). How I wish I had applied these biblical admonitions!

These taunts from Satan about what he said was going round and round in my mind, and I decided that I had every right to be angry. I lost all restraint and began to verbalise out loud, and within a few seconds, I felt a hard thud in my chest, as a spirit of anger returned.

The spirit had returned, but even after repenting, it would not come out. I humbled myself and two brothers in the Lord from whom I sought help, decided to stand with me and drive it out in Jesus' mighty name. I had to seek help from these Christians because my pastor had publicly banned all who were bound in his church from getting free from devils! He had publicly stated that Christians cannot have demons, despite Jesus' warning of never casting out demons from people who refuse to submit to God and therefore cannot receive the infilling of the Holy Spirit. If non-believers are delivered from the demons and they refuse to submit to God, Jesus warned that the last state of those people will be worst than the beginning! (Matthew 12:43-45). See Appendix A.

Christians and godly people can have, be oppressed, or be under the influence of demons/evil spirits (Job 26:4, Mark 1:23-24, 39, Acts 5:3, 2 Timothy 2:24-26, James 3:14-16). However, a true Christian cannot be completely taken over or 'possessed' (Luke 8:26-31), but Satan did enter Judas, one of the Twelve Disciples chosen by Jesus! (Luke 22:3-6, Matthew 27:5). If you give demons a legal right to 'enter' or harass you, they will! (Matthew 18:34-35, 2 Corinthians 2:10-11).

As these men prayed with me, the demon refused to leave at first, declaring that I had invited him back by my actions. The demon became very angry with one of the men who had commanded him to leave. The demon swore at him (via my voice box) and the man said, "It's a good job your pastor is not here! What would he think?" It was meant as a lighthearted joke, but the demon replied, "You need not concern yourself with him (my pastor), we have him just where we want him." With that, the demon departed and I was free in Jesus' mighty name. I learnt a hard lesson that day, which I have never forgotten. I was born-again, baptised in the Spirit and spoke in tongues – yet the lesson was that Christians who themselves cast out demons cannot afford the luxury of succumbing to the flesh (1 John 1:5-10).

As I thought about all that had taken place, I pondered what the evil spirit had said. I have learnt not to engage with devils when they are being cast out, yet what the demon said stuck in my mind. What did he mean when he declared of my pastor, "We have him just where we want him?" Was the man who denied that Christians could have demons, himself bound? I was soon to find out.

Chapter Six

Led by the Holy Spirit

Life in these last days has become more and more stressful, and will continue to be so. Jesus said, "And because lawlessness will abound, the love of many will grow cold. But he who endures to the end shall be saved" (Matthew 24:12-13). Endurance is key, and yet, as we consider what is happening in the world today, we find that more and more people are struggling with rage and anger, and the secular answer is to seek anger management. The truth is this, when a spirit of anger enters your body, a part of you comes under a new manager. In the area that you have submitted to another, you are no longer in control, you are controlled.

Christians make a big mistake when they think people with demons must be totally possessed. When Jesus helped Mary, He cast seven demons out of her (Mark 16:9). She was not like legion (Mark 5:9), but was simply oppressed in areas and Jesus set her free. It was the same with most of the people who came to Jesus for help. The majority of people who came to Jesus for deliverance from demons were not possessed by them, only oppressed. They were ordinary people who needed help (Matthew 4:24). I was like one of those ordinary people, and so have been most of the people whom God has called me to help. In addition, in Jesus' day, people were in need of healing, but in the case of the woman bent over double, Jesus first cast out a spirit of infirmity, then He laid His hands on her and she was able to stand upright (Luke 13:10-17).

One part of Satan's strategy to keep people bound is to make the Church and Christians afraid of demons and deliverance. When people say, "I don't want to get involved with that," are they following Jesus' command to cast out demons or following what Satan wants them to think and do, by their inaction and sin of omission? (Mark 16:17). I think it is a part of Satan's strategy to keep people bound, by keeping Christians in fear of demons and making them avoid casting them out. The image we are given in the Bible is not of an all-powerful enemy, but of a defeated foe, with demons trembling at the thought of God (James 2:19, Colossians 1:13, 1 John 3:8). Demonic ruling spirits (strong man) only exist where mankind's sin empowers them, and Christ has given us power to bind these strong men in His name (Matthew 12:29-30).

Casting out demons was a central feature of Jesus' ministry and it was absolutely normal for the disciples of Jesus and the apostles to set people free in Jesus' name (Mark 3:15, 6:13, 16:17, Acts 19:12). At least sixty-two times in the Gospels, demons/evil spirits are mentioned, and all true Christians can and must exercise authority over demons in the name of Jesus Christ and command them to go. We can live oppressed by them or master them. It's the same with sin; if you are not the master of it, then you are a slave to it (Romans 6:16). Jesus said, "Most assuredly, I say to you, whoever commits sin is a slave of sin" (John 8:34).

All this is good in theory, but it must also be applied. In my home church I found that my pastor had many human weaknesses just like me. Pastors, vicars and ministers are not perfect and they cannot be superhuman. In truth, they can become more vulnerable to attack because their prominence (as a shepherd of the flock) makes them one of the devil's main targets. My church was thriving and the pastor encouraged the use of spiritual gifts. As I have already stated, I would receive words of knowledge by the Holy Spirit, which I would share. I did this freely in church, but then the pastor asked me, to *always* share with him first, and then I would be allowed to share it with the congregation. As I was young in the faith, perhaps only nine months old, I thought testing my revelations was the reason for his decision; but was it? I knew the church had gone through many splits and thought his caution was to avoid another, or to save me making a grave public mistake.

One morning on the way to our prayer meeting, which the pastor would not be attending, the Holy Spirit told me that there was a spirit of division operating over the church. I was told to share this with the others at the right time, which He would show me, for their prayer. Those present knew that something was wrong in our church and we were concerned that it might have another split. When the time came, I shared my revelation. As they began discussing this warning about the spirit of division, one man became very upset about many things, which had been going on, and a big disagreement ensued. The man concerned stormed out of the meeting and others followed. This was a confirmation to me that this spirit of division was operating over the fellowship and influencing it, for we were unable in unity to tell that spirit to go. Shortly after this, there was another split and I ended up joining the new group, simply because they met near where I lived and money was tight. I was saving money by not using so much petrol/gas, as the church was some distance from my home and held multiple meetings each week.

As we met together, I sensed something was very wrong with our meetings. The Holy Spirit then began to show me that because this fellowship was born out of rebellion, the devil had the right to place a spirit of division over it (Psalm 105:15, Psalm 133:1, 1 Corinthians 16:16, 1 Peter 2:13, 5:5). In our former church we had *not* endeavoured 'to keep the unity of the Spirit in the bond of peace' (Ephesians 4:3), and as such, at some point in the future this church would come to an end. Jesus warned in the book of Revelation that He would close churches that did not obey Him, if they rebelled against His will. In their sin they failed to represent Him and the Lord does not need false witnesses (Revelation 1:20, Revelation 2:5).

Approximately ten months after this split, I was reading from the book of Acts, and the Holy Spirit told me to phone my previous pastor and share some verses of Scripture with him. He probably did not know that I was led to challenge what we (the church I attended) had done, in breaking away from him, yet the Lord told me to give him a warning too. I was told to inform him, that if he repented of all his wrongdoing, he would receive forgiveness; but if he refused to repent of his sins, savage wolves would come into his fellowship again. The Scripture I gave him was: 'Therefore take heed to yourselves and to all the flock, among which the Holy Spirit has made you overseers, to shepherd the Church of God which He purchased with His own blood. For I know this, that after my departure savage wolves will come in among you, not sparing the flock' (Acts 20:28-29).

I was still young in the Lord and was learning to discern the Holy Spirit's voice from all others, including self, the world, and the demonic. Consequently, I was afraid to share this message with my former pastor and told the Holy Spirit that I could not phone him. "Why?" asked the Holy Spirit. "Because he is an ordained minister, a man educated in the Scriptures, a man of God," I replied (Jeremiah 1:6-7). Then the Holy Spirit counteracted my fears by saying, "Yes, but you are My servant." As I pondered this, I thought, 'What if I am wrong?' The more I pondered on this direction, the more I began to hear another voice casting doubts at me. Therefore I said to the Holy Spirit, "If this is You truly speaking to me, then please have him phone me. Then I shall know for sure that it is You speaking to me."

I had not seen or spoken to my former pastor since I had left his church. By now, he had no reason to phone me; I knew I was safe or so I thought! Within minutes, the phone rang and it was him! I shared with him as instructed and he then began to treat me with contempt, pointing out that I was still very young in the faith and had a lot to learn. He warned me that just because I had said it, did not mean it was true. Thirteen months later he was asked to leave his church because he had been having an affair with a member of the fellowship. Years later, I discovered the Lord had sent others with prophetic giftings to warn the pastor (1 Corinthians 14:29, 1 Timothy 5:19). One had spoken in public saying, "There is adultery in this church," but the pastor hardened his heart and did not avail himself of the grace God was offering. 'Or do you despise the riches of His goodness, forbearance and longsuffering, not knowing that the goodness of God leads you to repentance?' (Romans 2:4).

As I later learnt by the direction of the Holy Spirit, my former pastor's sin of adultery had given a spirit of division, the right to enter and five church splits followed! Like King David, my pastor was tasked to protect God's flock (1 Peter 5:2), but his sin and refusal to repent, as in the case of King David's adultery with Bathsheba (1 Chronicles 21:14-17), made a hole in the hedge of protection (Job 1:10). The wall of fire was quenched around the church, their armour was broken and evil spirits came in (Zechariah 2:5, Ephesians 6:11-13). The devil had walked around like a roaring lion seeking to devour (1 Peter 5:8), and he found his way in through the pastor's sin.

The Lord had been very gracious, urging him to repent, without openly revealing his specific sin.

When King David sinned, many innocent people were harmed and it was the same in this church (2 Samuel 24:15-17). This spirit of division had not only caused splits in the church, but also splits in the marriages of many of its members; some of which led to divorce (Hebrews 13:4). Sometime later, the Holy Spirit told me I was partly to blame for what had happened, because I had never prayed for the pastor's protection. This was true and it was sad that I had never been taught by anyone that it is God's will for us to pray for our leaders (1 Timothy 2:1-2).

This was not the first time that I found church leaders living in sin, fearing the gifts of the Spirit. More than a decade after this experience, I was invited by a church leader to share with a small group from his fellowship. As part of my introduction, I mentioned that while praying about the meeting I had received five words of knowledge, which I would share. The leader became agitated and stopped me. But I pointed out to him that the Holy Spirit did not wish to embarrass anyone, because His will is to offer help, deliverance and healing. Later, I learned why this leader was so concerned. Just like my former pastor, he too had something to hide. Is it any wonder that they both wished for me to share the words of knowledge privately first.

Nevertheless, I too was being taught something in all of this by the Holy Spirit, about another stronghold in my life. It was the fear of men in authority. Why? From an early age I learned that those who had authority over me were likely to abuse me and harm me. I also felt inferior to men of learning, but the Holy Spirit taught me that men who had learned from books about the Bible, did not necessarily learn to become sensitive to the Holy Spirit and His will.

Today, my life is not my own, it belongs to Jesus Christ and my body is not my own, it is the temple of the Holy Spirit and belongs to Him (1 Corinthians 6:19), I will share more on this later. All strongholds in our lives, the Lord showed me, must be cast down. The Bible clearly teaches what we should fix our minds on and think about (Philippians 4:8, Colossians 3:2). If we have strongholds in our minds and lives, we are to pull them down and take captive every thought, to make it obedient to Christ (2 Corinthians 10:3-5). We are not to conform to the pattern of this world, but be transformed by the renewing of our minds (Romans 12:1-2). We must live by the Spirit and not gratify the desires of the sinful nature, but crucify that sinful nature with its passions and desires (Galatians 5:16-24). In the lives of these men, lust was a major problem, and lust continues to be a stronghold in the minds of millions, and if not pulled down, can drag us deeper into sin (James 1:14). All these sinful desires are of the flesh, not the Spirit, and must be crucified. If not, the temptation to sin that already has a hold over us, will only become greater. Jesus said, "But I say to you that whoever looks at a woman to lust for her has already committed adultery with her in his heart" (Matthew 5:28-29).

In all these experiences, I was being taught to live the Bible by the Spirit of the Lord and I was learning to know the voice and guidance of the Spirit of God, which is essential if you are to fulfil God's call on your life! If ever there was a generation in the Church that needs to learn to be led by the Holy Spirit it is this generation.[1] Last evening, I was relaxing watching the television when I felt led to go for a walk in my garden. As I did, I heard shouting and screaming coming from a garden shed a few houses away. The woman of the house had shut one of her children in the shed as a punishment, it was just getting dark, and the child was terrified. Fear has now taken hold of this child and in years to come, when he has panic attacks in confined spaces, they will say that he suffers from claustrophobia, which is an abnormal fear of confined spaces. In the future, will Christians try to counsel this child or will he receive the deliverance he needs? Will they follow the teaching of this world, or the pattern of our Lord, who led by the Holy Spirit cast out devils and healed the sick?

Chapter Seven

Heed God, to Your Own Good

In all my experiences with God, the Holy Spirit was teaching me that God is merciful and gracious, and is to be feared in holy respect. He is our Father, but He is not your 'buddy' who can be ignored, mocked and mistreated. Unfortunately, many churches teach from the Bible, verses that are easy, presenting a limited, one-dimensional God, who is merely a 'god' made in their own image. As long as we only take the verses which we like of the Bible and ignore the rest, we will always have a distorted view of Him. The Bible warns: 'Of how much worse punishment, do you suppose, will he be thought worthy who has trampled the Son of God underfoot, counted the blood of the covenant by which he was sanctified a common thing, and insulted the Spirit of grace? For we know Him who said, "Vengeance is Mine, I will repay," says the Lord. And again, "The Lord will judge His people." It is a fearful thing to fall into the hands of the living God' (Hebrews 10:29-31).

In the mid 1980s, the Holy Spirit directed me to return once again to the church in my home town where I had given my testimony years earlier. It was a Sunday evening and there was a visiting speaker. During communion, I noticed a small group of the youth behaving very badly, and making a mockery of remembering the Lord's death and resurrection. The Holy Spirit was grieved, yet not one person attempted to restrain them in the fear of the Lord. Perhaps it was because two of them were children of one of the elders. The Bible warns against taking communion lightly. 'Therefore whoever eats this bread or drinks this cup of the Lord in an unworthy manner will be guilty of the body and blood of the Lord. But let a man examine himself, and so let him eat of the bread and drink of the cup. For he who eats and drinks in an unworthy manner eats and drinks judgment to himself, not discerning the Lord's body. For this reason many are weak and sick among you, and many sleep' (1 Corinthians 11:27-30).

In His love, the Holy Spirit wanted to spare these mistaken young people any difficulties. He instructed me to write on a piece a paper a Scripture, and to give a copy to each of them, to warn them so they could repent. I followed the Holy Spirit's instruction. I have no idea if any of them took the time to find what it said. 'Do not be deceived, God is not mocked; for whatever a man sows, that he will also reap. For he who sows to his flesh will of the flesh reap corruption, but he who sows to the Spirit will of the Spirit reap everlasting life' (Galatians 6:7-8). A few years later, one of the girls present, who had been born-again and spoke with tongues, fell into bad company at secular music festivals and became pregnant. Through events like these, the Holy Spirit taught me that we do reap what we sow, if not now, then later.

In the early Church, two of the new converts believed they could lie to the Holy Spirit and falsify their commitment to God in front of all. They treated God with contempt and through their swift judgment, God set a precedent that all in Christ's Church should serve God with sincerity, in holy fear (Acts 5:3-11). When God is respected as God Almighty, the Church grows rapidly (Acts 5:14-16), but do we realise that we mock Him by committing all to Him in public, yet withdrawing all in private, and God is grieved.

Back to the service – as I sat there troubled by all that was going on, I had a vision in which I saw the floor of the church lifting up and cracks began to appear, just like an earthquake. Then suddenly it stopped. I was trying to understand what had happened, as this was a first for me to see this kind of vision. The Holy Spirit led me to Jeremiah. ' "So it came to pass, through her casual harlotry, that she defiled the land and committed adultery with stones and trees. And yet for all this her treacherous sister Judah has not turned to Me with her whole heart, but in pretence," says the Lord' (Jeremiah 3:9-10).

Some of the leaders of this church had cast off all restraint and were committing spiritual adultery. Many years later, the sins of the leaders were openly revealed. One of the pastor's was having an affair and one of the elders was stealing.

At the time, I kept the vision the Lord showed me to myself. A few weeks later, when driving by the church, I saw a spirit of division, straddling the roof of the building. This was the first time I literally saw into the spiritual realm and witnessed how the Holy Spirit can unveil the boundaries between the natural world and the realm of the invisible, both of which were created by God. In Ephesians, the Holy Spirit presents the structure of this invisible world of demonic powers and how the Church is to defeat them with the authority Jesus Christ gives to His servants. 'For we do not wrestle against flesh and blood, but against principalities, against powers, against the rulers of the darkness of this age, against spiritual hosts of wickedness in the heavenly places. Therefore take up the whole armour of God, that you may be able to withstand in the evil day, and having done all, to stand' (Ephesians 6:12-13).

After seeing this spirit of division, the Holy Spirit instructed me to go immediately to the elder's house and tell him what I had seen. I told him, but was surprised to find that he was not interested. He thought I had been told about their internal divisions by one of the church members! I explained to him that God is sovereign – He is in control of all things, and all things are under His control. He was not impressed by my words and suggested I had been gossiping, which I had not. This leader refused to heed what the Holy Spirit was trying to warn him for the church's own good, and the salt lost its saltiness. Jesus said, "You are the salt of the earth; but if the salt loses its flavour, how shall it be seasoned? It is then good for nothing but to be thrown out and trampled underfoot by men" (Matthew 5:13). Thirteen months elapsed and the Lord removed its lampstand, as the church closed because it was no longer a good testimony of Him (Revelation 1:20, Revelation 2:5). The church remains closed and the building is now used for secular purposes.

Chapter Eight

Death to Self-Reliance

In my place of employment, I was known for being a leader of men, but I made the mistake of thinking that I could apply secular principles of leadership and management to the work of God. Due to my success at work, I was used to achieving my objectives and I had grown confident in my own abilities. What I had yet to learn is that all this self-belief is a great hindrance to the ministry of the Holy Spirit, because when we trust in our own abilities, we get in His way. 'Not many wise according to the flesh, not many mighty, not many noble, are called. But God has chosen the foolish things of the world to put to shame the wise and God has chosen the weak things of the world to put to shame the things which are mighty' (1 Corinthians 1:26-27).

In one of the local villages near where I lived, the young people used to throw stones at one of the churches and the local minister did not know what to do. As I was brimming with self-confidence, I told him that I could deal with the problem and get them all converted, as long as he'd let me use one of his rooms to help disciple them. He was a little sceptical that all these young people could be converted, but gave me his blessing. I led a small group of Christians to reach out to them; we began meeting weekly and shared the gospel with the youth, and over the weeks, many of them made a profession of faith.

As you can imagine, I was proud that we had achieved what this minister was unable to. Each week, these young people came to our Christian meetings, but over time, the numbers began to fall until nobody turned up! This was the opposite of my experiences in my workplace, where many had been converted by the power of God. Why did I experience failure here? I was about to learn another valuable lesson.

One evening, when I was in the village the Holy Spirit asked me, "What are you doing here?" I thought it was obvious. I was sharing the gospel as Jesus commanded; but I had also learned to be very careful what I said to this Holy Person, for He is God. However, I tried to justify to the Holy Spirit what we were doing in this village, then He spoke, "I never sent you here, or asked you to come. Everything you have done to date, counts for nothing!" I was stunned. As Jesus said, "It is the Spirit who gives life; the flesh profits nothing" (John 6:63).

I had been a leader of men and now I thought I could lead God! In the flesh, like so many today, we had shared the gospel to this group of teenagers and encouraged them to pray a 'simple' sinner's prayer for salvation. We were so desperate to see them saved that without realising it, we cheapened the price of entrance. Like many evangelists, we thought that getting someone to quickly pray a short prayer was enough. As I look back, I realise that not one of them came under conviction or truly repented for their sins. They had not experienced the new birth of being 'born-again' (John 3:3-21), and had not passed from 'death to life' (1 John 3:14). Like the Parable of the Sower, "When anyone hears the message of the Kingdom and does not understand it, the evil one comes and snatches away what was sown in his heart" (Matthew 13:18-19).

Through this lesson, the Holy Spirit was trying to teach me the difference between the good works and the ideas of the flesh, as compared to effective spiritual warfare, done His way. Yes, I had received the baptism of the Holy Spirit and I had been empowered by Him, but I was still trusting in myself. I was bold and blessed with a measure of the gifts of the Holy Spirit, but my character still needed to change to be more Christ-like, and my thoughts were still my own. I had not been fully transformed by the renewing of my mind, so I was unable to test and approve what God's good, acceptable and perfect will truly was. 'Be transformed by the renewing of your mind, that you may prove what is that good and acceptable and perfect will of God' (Romans 12:2).

It was true that God had called me to serve Him, but I did not yet know that the call is not the command to commence. Two can only walk together by agreement (Amos 3:3), and I was guilty of the sin of presumption. Through experiences like this, the Holy Spirit began to teach me that the Father only has one plan. It is Plan A and there is no Plan B. This is why Jesus, whilst on earth, would spend time alone with the Father. He only did what the Father showed Him, as He was led by the Holy Spirit (John 5:30, John 10:35-38). Jesus said, "Most assuredly, I say to you, the Son can do nothing of Himself, but what He sees the Father do for whatever He does, the Son also does in like manner" (John 5:19). He did not form a committee and bring in business leaders to get advice – He followed the leading of the Holy Spirit.

As I had previously stepped out into spiritual gifts and witnessed conversions and healings, self-confidence continued to grow in me and it had become a mindset. I could serve the Lord without Him! I thought, 'I can do this!' In my own heart I was trusting in myself and my own abilities, forsaking the grace of God. But now the Holy Spirit was exposing my error and showing me that I had to do things His way, and not my own. He explained it to me like this: If I was to fast and pray, and then go out and share the good news of the gospel, He might choose to bless my efforts. But if I waited for Him to show me where to go and what to do, He would anoint me. The difference is all the world! There is a *big* difference between God blessing a work and God anointing a work. The apostle Paul went on three major missionary journeys. With Timothy, 'they were forbidden by the Holy Spirit to preach the Word in Asia' (a Roman province) and 'after they had come to Mysia they tried to go to Bithynia, but the Spirit did not permit them' (Acts 16:6-10). At Troas, Paul had a vision of a man saying, "Come over to Macedonia and help us." When they arrived, God had prepared the heart of Lydia, and she and her household believed and were baptised (Acts 16:9-15). It was not that God did not want those in Asia to hear the good news, but that the timing was incorrect, for within five or six years, Paul visited the region. After two years of teaching and preaching 'all who dwelt in Asia heard the Word of the Lord' (Acts 19:10), and the verse following informs us that God worked 'unusual miracles by the hand of Paul' because he was anointed for the work, he was in the will of God and the timing was correct.[1]

The world must be reached with the gospel, but we cannot do it without God! The Every Creature Commission of Jesus to His Church is this, "Go into all the world and preach the gospel to every creature. He who believes and is baptised will be saved; but he who does not believe will be condemned. And these signs will follow those who believe: In My name they will cast out demons; they will speak with new tongues; they will take up serpents; and if they drink anything deadly, it will by no means hurt them; they will lay hands on the sick, and they will recover" (Mark 16:15-18).

The Every Creature Commission is Jesus Christ's final and binding command on all Christians and it must be completed, "Not by might, nor by power, but by My Spirit," declares the Lord (Zechariah 4:6). The book of Acts reveals how the disciples of Jesus were led and guided by the Holy Spirit, and how the Spirit through them spread the gospel message all over the Roman Empire. Today, many still rely on all their good ideas, intentions, money and technology, yet we have achieved so little by comparison. The reason we fail is because we are trusting in ourselves, instead of following the pattern of Jesus and the apostles – all of whom followed the Holy Spirit wherever He led. All of the apostles had to learn to be sensitive to the leading of the Spirit and so must we! 'While Peter thought about the vision, the Spirit said to him, "Behold, three men are seeking you. Arise therefore, go down and go with them, doubting nothing; for I have sent them" ' (Acts 10:19-20). For more examples, see Appendix B.

For me, to be led by the Holy Spirit would mean more prayer and some fasting, looking to Him alone, and less thinking and looking to self. I had to learn to become more sensitive to His voice and leading. Trusting in the Holy Spirit and not in myself turned out to be very difficult at first, it was another stronghold in my life. I was used to looking to self, which should be crucified, not followed. Now I had to look to Jesus alone and not to my own abilities. I wanted to be obedient at all times, but I was accustomed to doing things my way.

It seemed strange to me to spend more time quietly with God, instead of being out there 'doing the work.' Yet, as I drew near to God, I saw clearer than ever that I had been doing *my work* and *not His!* One morning, as I was praying at home on my own, as I sought Him more thoroughly God blessed my obedience. As I was praying, I heard someone call my name – audibly. 'Whose that?' I thought, as I was the only person at home. Then it happened a second time! I searched the house trying to find someone, but I found no one. I had read in the

Bible how God called people by name, but was unsure what to do about it. Like Samuel, the Lord began to reveal Himself to me through His Word (1 Samuel 3). I was learning to become sensitive to His inner voice and as a reward, I heard His audible voice!

By now, four years had passed since my conversion to Christianity, and three and a half years since I began attending a local church. Sadly, in that time I had seen too many church splits, and far too many denials of the work and ministry of the Holy Spirit. I was becoming troubled with much of what I witnessed in the Church and I was bored with religious routines devoid of God's power.

If God is welcome in His Church, why is His power often absent? We had witnessed the gifts of the Spirit, but these are manifestations of God's grace, not dependent on spiritual maturity (1 Corinthians 3:1-3). Who knew God the Holy Spirit like the prophets of the Bible? Jesus told His disciples before He left, "It is to your advantage that I go away; for if I do not go away, the Helper will not come to you" (John 16:7). As we can see from the Lord's teaching, the Holy Spirit is just like Jesus, but He does not have a body. That is why He wants ours. He is the Holy Person of God; a Spirit without a body to live in and through. So why is He so unwelcome in so many lives and churches? Instead of finding men and women of the Spirit living in victory in my church, I found people bound. It was like a hospital's Accident and Emergency department, filled with the walking wounded. In our church, we would sing about the power of the blood of Jesus and of our victory over the powers of darkness, but I saw little proof of it in most people's daily lives.

Having been given the gift of discernment by the Holy Spirit, which gave me the ability to discern different spirits, I could see in the spirit that many Christians were secretly struggling. But instead of receiving the deliverance Jesus Christ paid for, many were too afraid to accept God's offer of healing. Was it pride or fear of losing their dignity which kept them silent? I did not know. But when there was a word of knowledge shared to help get people set free, it was not unusual for no one to respond; and then I would see the individual whom the word was given for leave the meeting the same as he or she had arrived – bound. This certainly was not God's will.

Chapter Nine

There Must Be More Than This!

I loved the Lord and dedicated most of my spare time to Him. Yet, I was still a working man, with a young family and a mortgage on an old house that needed repairing. My conversion had been deep and powerful, and I had seen many others converted. By God's grace I had moved in the power of the Spirit, but my local church, outwardly a beacon of the charismatic movement, seemed to be settled into religious routines of singing about God's power and reaching the world, whilst doing little or nothing, and being satisfied with shallow experiences with our almighty God! Even when I was working, I was pondering in my heart, "There has to be more than this!" However, the Holy Spirit was silent, but like the persistent widow, I refused to give up (Luke 18:1-8). Night after night I cried out, "There has to be more!"

The answer to my persistent prayers, seeking God came through a book called *Rees Howells Intercessor* by Norman Grubb (1952). Upon finishing the book, I prayed, "My Lord and My God, this is it. My search is over. There *is* more!" This book contained the testimony of a man who had what I was looking for. The reality of living the Bible life today and witnessing God's power at work.

The book describes the work achieved when the Holy Spirit began working in and through an individual, later a small company of believers and then a whole fellowship of disciples. I could not put Rees Howells' biography down and read it from cover to cover, repeatedly. Rees Howells, who went to be with God in 1950, was used by God to transform a village, minister healings, carry revival and in world-changing powerful intercession. As I read about his life, I knew that the offer God gave to Rees Howells, of complete surrender and to truly be filled with the Holy Spirit, was an offer God gives to all people. The Holy Spirit lived through Rees Howells because he gave God permission to live His Divine life through his surrendered vessel, and the Lord wants this kind of life for all believers! Sadly, my close friend was not impressed with this and inquired when I was going to settle down like the other Christians in church, and be content with singing hymns and hearing a sermon every week. I smiled thinking to myself, 'What a horrible thought!'

Jesus did not suffer, die and be resurrected so we could play at religion. The Bible states: 'Jesus Christ is the same yesterday, today and forever' (Hebrews 13:8). There were two things I really wanted. First, to truly know the Holy Spirit like Rees Howells had. The second was to meet someone who was truly filled with the Holy Spirit. As you might be aware, many claim to be filled with the Holy Spirit, but few are truly filled. The Holy Spirit had taken full possession of Rees Howells and lived His life in and through him. Rees Howells' body truly became a temple of the Holy Spirit and I would not settle for anything less.

At last I knew there was something far deeper to experience than simply going to church, or even moving in the gifts; I decided to set aside one week for prayer and fasting to this end, so I could meet the Holy Spirit in such a way. But, as ever, the Holy Spirit led me another way. I planned to pray and fast in the hills whilst living in a tent; it was all very spiritual from a human point of view and then the Holy Spirit said, "Go to Scotland!" As I pondered, "Why Scotland?" He used the Scripture, Numbers 13:1-25, to indicate that I had to explore the land, just like the Hebrew spies who went throughout Canaan and brought back some of the fruit of the land.

In the late 1980s, I booked time off from work and set off to Scotland with a Christian brother. As we did not know where we were going, I had to trust the Holy Spirit to lead us daily and we were not disappointed. I was learning on this journey that the Holy Spirit could, and would, guide us daily, if only we would learn to trust Him and be obedient to all He said.

On the first day of our mission north into Britain, we stopped at a campsite in the Lake District of England. We met a couple and started talking to them whilst in the hills. They shared that they had come away for a few days, to get away from their neighbours. They had once all been good friends and one-by-one, all their friends and neighbours had become born-again Christians, and their lifestyles changed so much that this couple felt really bad about their own. However, they had no wish to change themselves. Things had come to a head, they left home for a break, so they could think things through, but felt guilty.

My friend and I were smiling when one of them said, "Oh, no, you can't be, can you?" They had travelled almost the entire length of the nation to get away from the Holy Spirit's conviction and now we told them, "Yes, we are born-again Christians!" Then I asked them, "Is it possible that God loves you so much that He has arranged this meeting?" They stood there speechless. I suggested they go back home, and share what had happened to their friends and neighbours. We left it at that because the Holy Spirit had orchestrated this encounter and He could be trusted to finish His work in them.

The following day we crossed the border from England to Scotland and because it was Sunday, we asked the Holy Spirit to lead us to a church. We were guided to a church and while in the service the Holy Spirit said, "At the end of the meeting, ask the pastor if you can have a private word with him." After the service, I met with him in private and he inquired, "How can I help you?" I replied, "You cannot help me. I've been sent to help you!" I shared with him the things which the Holy Spirit had showed me about his future in this church and to my surprise, he fell to the ground weeping. He later shared he had decided to leave the ministry. In desperation, he had told the Lord that if he was truly called here, the only way he would stay was if the Holy Spirit sent a complete stranger to him that day. I was that stranger and had travelled some distance to get there!

A few days later, in the Highlands of Scotland, we were once again staying on a cheap campsite. We met two local people and shared the gospel with them. They told us that there was a Salvation Army captain in the town and he was desperate for any help or encouragement. They asked if we would go and see him to encourage him. When we arrived, I could see him through the window sat at his desk, with his head in his hands. We knocked the door and entered. "Can I help you?" he asked. "No," I politely said, and explained how we came to be there. As we talked, he shared that he no longer had anything to give in the ministry, he was tired and worn out. I asked him, "Have you received the baptism of the Holy Spirit?" He told me that he did not believe in such an experience, as he had been taught it was not for today. He also explained that he had opposed those who taught from the Bible that it is for today. No wonder that he was exhausted, we all would be without God's power!

After a long chat based on the Bible, he still did not fully agree that the baptism in the Holy Spirit existed or was possible, so I said, "Let me pray for you and you will see it *is* for today!" He was humble enough to agree for us to pray for him, and as we stood for prayer, he told us, on no account were we to touch him. Most of his resistance to receiving the baptism of the Spirit was because of the negative stories he had heard, but now he was at his end. He finally came to a place of accepting that if the baptism of the Holy Spirit is for now, he wanted it.

As we prayed for him, he slipped gently to the ground, whilst pointing to his throat. God was touching him, but the enemy also had a hold on him. We commanded whatever evil spirit it was to leave him and suddenly he was free, and burst into tongues! He now had received the power he needed for the work! It is amazing how one experience with God can flush away years of bad teaching.

When we left, a different man was sat in his office and through this experience I learnt that God the Holy Spirit, can, and will, lead us, not only through His inner voice in our spirit, but also through using other people to lead us into Divine appointments.

A few days later we headed south and stopped at Kinross in Scotland. As we got out of the car, we saw a notice advertising a meeting of Christians from different denominations. Believing this to be a sign from God for another Divine appointment, we went to the meeting. The meeting was in progress and as we entered, the man at the front quipped that we were late. We respectfully responded, "No, we are on the Lord's time," and explained we were in the region serving the Lord. The leader had to leave early, but invited us to the front to share what the Lord was doing.

Speaking to the congregation, I shared the burden the Holy Spirit had placed upon me, which was our great need for a Christian revival, and my confidence that one would come. Suddenly, the Holy Spirit drew to my attention a woman and I told her that the Holy Spirit had a special blessing for her, if she was willing to receive. She came forward and as we prayed for her, the Holy Spirit came upon her, and she slipped gently to the ground. Many of the group, unfamiliar with the working of the Holy Spirit thought she had fainted, and some went to get water!

Once again, we were meeting very good religious people who did not know that the Holy Spirit is a Person who can change their lives. I explained what the baptism of the Holy Spirit is and as a living testimony to God's power, this woman stood up with a radiant smile, and was continually thankful to the Lord. I later learnt she had lived through a time of great devastation in the past few months of her life and when she went home, other people in the street mentioned that she was shining like Moses when he met with God (Exodus 34:35). God was comforting His people, setting them free and giving them His joy (Isaiah 61:3).

As we were about to leave this meeting, three other women invited us to join them for refreshments. The Holy Spirit was once again leading us through the simple invitation of these people. These dear sisters in Christ were interested in learning how the Holy Spirit was leading us, when one of them asked, "Where are you going when you leave?" We told her we were heading south towards England. "Oh, good," she replied. "Then you will be passing Inverkeithing. There is a house meeting there tonight, would you please come and you will be made very welcome." Another of the group said, "Before you leave, you must visit our Loch. Just follow the signs."

We said our farewells to these sisters in Christ and drove the short distance to Loch Leven in Scotland. As we parked the car, we noticed a man and a woman, lying on the grass in a very passionate embrace. The Holy Spirit said in my spirit, "Adultery." I knew immediately I had to speak to them. I was thinking, 'What is the best way to approach them?' feeling concerned that this could quickly erupt. Then my friend said to me, "You had the word of knowledge," and once again, I was in the deep end, because it was me who had to deal with it. At that very moment, I received a word of wisdom that I should give them a copy of a Christian booklet called *Living Together God's Way.*[1] 'It seemed good to the Holy Spirit and to us' (Acts 15:28), to approach the subject this way.

We walked over to them and tried to get their attention, but they were too focused on each other in their passionate embrace. I began to whistle and they looked up at me. I shared with them that the Holy Spirit has told me to speak to them and that He wanted me to give them this booklet. I did not know if they were Christians or how they would respond. They took one look at the cover and their faces went pale. The message had been delivered and we left them because we could see the job was done. God did not want to embarrass them and we were simply messengers sent by Him for their good. As we looked back over our shoulders, they stood up and both ran to different cars. I marvelled at God's goodness and mercy. Perhaps at least one, or maybe two marriages were saved that day.

When evening came, we went to the house meeting in Inverkeithing. One of the words that I shared was, "If there are any intercessors here tonight, this is a word for you, the battle for our nation (UK) is only just beginning." We made no mention of our experiences that day, but did share that we had visited the Loch and the cemetery, which stands on its edge. On one of the headstones was inscribed: 'This was a man filled with faith and the Holy Spirit, Acts 6:5.' I used this text as my message that evening. While I spoke, I kept thinking of Rees Howells and how he truly was a man filled with the Holy Spirit. Yes, it was true that I had a measure of faith, but I could not claim in all honesty to be *full* of the Holy Spirit and I knew no one else who could too. Our experiences with God were all very shallow when we compared them to the prophets and apostles of the Bible.

After the meeting, one of the brothers in Christ invited us to stay at his house for the night. The following morning, I awoke early to seek the Lord as the sun was rising, and so was my level of faith. Something was different about this day, but I was unsure what. Something was about to happen which would change my outlook on the Holy Spirit of God, and the future of Britain. Within minutes, my life would never be the same. Before this moment, I saw little hope for the United Kingdom, and then, suddenly, the Holy Spirit spoke to me in a clear voice within my spirit and I saw a vision of revival for the UK and beyond.

Twenty-five years have passed since that day, but the reader must understand that God is outside of our conception of time, because He is the Beginning and the End (Revelation 1:8, 11, 17, Revelation 22:13). As Peter stated: 'But, beloved, do not forget this one thing, that with the Lord one day is as a thousand years and a thousand years as one day. The Lord is not slack concerning His promise' (2 Peter 3:8-9). Likewise, "God is not a man, that He should lie, nor a son of man, that He should repent. Has He said, and will He not do? Or has He spoken, and will He not make it good?" (Numbers 23:19). Also, "He who is the glory of Israel does not lie or change His mind, for He is not a man that He should change His mind" (1 Samuel 15:29).

Like many other people who have seen visions of revival or received a clear word from God about a coming spiritual awakening, I truly believe the problem and the answer lies with us, Christ's Church – obeying God and meeting the conditions. "If My people who are called by My name will humble themselves, and pray and seek My face, and turn from their wicked ways, then I will hear from heaven, and will forgive their sin and heal their land" (2 Chronicles 7:14). I have noticed we often quote this Scripture in our churches and large gatherings, but rarely do we actually meet the conditions![2] God did not say, "If you read out this verse," but instructed His people to humble themselves before Him, pray, seek His face and turn from their wicked ways. We don't have revival because we don't want to pay the price. God never has a discount sale; the price is always everything.

Chapter Ten

Meeting God Almighty

After breakfast, we continued south on our journey from Scotland and arrived in Gateshead in England. Whilst driving, we saw a large sign on a hill which read: 'Have Faith in God,' in very large letters. We knew God was leading us again and decided to take a closer look, and found a Christian fellowship. When I entered the building as my friend parked the car, the pastor greeted me, "Are there two of you?" he asked. "Yes," I replied. "Are you evangelists?" he asked. "Yes," I replied, "but we're part-time." He responded, "That's good," and continued, "at our prayer meeting this morning the Holy Spirit told us you were coming and you are to speak tonight at the community centre." We were experiencing being led by God just as Peter had been (Acts 10:19-43).

That evening, I shared the gospel with the people at the community centre. Afterwards we returned to the main church centre, which had living accommodation for visiting evangelists. A man asked us to pray for him and was delivered from evil spirits, and we went to bed tired. In the early hours of the morning, I left my bed to go and pray in the church sanctuary. As I sat there, I poured out my heart to the Lord. "Lord, I cannot go back to play at church and religious tradition, after all you have done," I prayed, "I want to know you, as Rees Howells did." There was a short silence and He said, "Can you not get any lower?" I was sitting at the time and I bowed my head saying, "Sorry." The Lord replied, "Can you not get any lower?" So I knelt down repeating my apology, "Sorry, I am out of my depth, I don't know what to do!" He replied a third time, "Can you not get any lower?" I bent forward and my head touched the floor as I repeated that I was sorry. Once again, in a gentle loving voice, He said, "Can you not get any lower?" After all these wonderful experiences I was being humbled before the Lord, as I lay face down with my arms and legs spread out before Him.

As I lay there, I was unsure what would happen next, when suddenly I felt a hand gently cover the back of my head, and very slowly turn my head from one side to the other, which brushed my nose on the carpet. I knew I was still on my own in the sanctuary and I felt a sense of holy awe. I was in a spiritual state, but I was quickly brought back to reality. From behind, I heard the sound of door hinges moving as my friend came in to see if I was all right. "Are you ok?" he enquired. "Yes," I replied. However, deep inside I was now far from happy with him, because he had disturbed me at the moment I thought God was going to meet with me. After I had felt God's touch on my head, my friend entered, and the moment felt lost.

My friend was concerned for me and encouraged me to have a cup of tea with him, and so we headed towards the kitchen. The sun was now rising and as the door to the kitchen opened, the rays of the rising sun shone through the window and struck me, and I fell to the ground![1] At that very moment, the Holy Spirit entered my body as a Person to dwell and abide.

I had been converted and baptised in the Holy Spirit, and at the time I thought that was all there was. But now He had come to enter me in His fullness; He had come in as an indwelling Person to take control of my life. He was no longer the visiting guest in my life; it was now His life! This was not the blessing of His presence; this was God possessing my body and now my will would have to be submitted to His in every area of my life. The apostle Paul had explained that this experience was possible and he wished all believers, 'May be filled with all the fullness of God' (Ephesians 3:19).

Within a few moments, I went through a physical experience which to an onlooker would have looked like crucifixion. With my feet placed together and my arms held out at the side, the experience was so real that I looked at my hands expecting to see holes. This physical experience was given to me to teach me that the crucifixion of my flesh life would need to be undertaken for the rest of my life (Galatians 2:20, Galatians 5:24). Jesus said, "If anyone desires to come after Me, let him deny himself and take up his cross daily, and follow Me. For whoever desires to save his life will lose it, but whoever loses his life for My sake will save it" (Luke 9:23-25).

After this, I lay on the floor motionless for approximately thirty-five minutes. In a trance-like state, as had Peter (Acts 10:10), the Lord showed me I was called to a life of crucifixion. My old self was to be nailed on the cross, so that He could work in and through me to do His will. This was just the beginning, and these dealings of sanctification would go on year-after-year, as He changed my human self-centered nature to His selfless giving nature.

When we read the stories of the lives of the prophets, apostles and great servants of God of previous ages, we find these common themes – complete surrender and a desire for the fullness and leading of the Holy Spirit. Today, it has become acceptable for many in their churches to declare with ease that they are, "Full of the Holy Spirit," but their characters (and often their lifestyles) give them away. Jesus said, "By their fruits you will know them" (Matthew 7:20). Being baptised in the Holy Spirit is what it says. You are baptised, washed over, as He comes upon you. When I was baptised in water, it washed all over me, but I did not drink the pool dry! I was not full of water. I was washed over. If we say we are full of the Holy Spirit and have surrendered *all* to Him, why is it that sin still has a hold over us, and our thoughts and actions are still focused on self? I am not speaking about the false doctrine of sinless perfection; but I am referring to the deluded belief that we can be, "Full of the Holy Spirit," whilst none can tell the difference between our lives and non-believers!

The extreme view of sinless perfection is that sin is eradicated from one's life and therefore it is impossible to sin, and one will never sin again. The sin of pride or *false humility, (*which is pride) is often attached to those professing sinless perfection! James wrote that 'we all stumble in many things' (James 3:2), but thank God for the cleansing blood of Jesus Christ, and God's grace to forgive us for our failings, whether sins of commission or omission. We must always try our best to live holy lives before a Holy God, but like Abraham, Moses, King David, Peter or "doubting" Thomas, we will make mistakes, and should learn from them. When Jesus Christ said, "You shall be perfect..." (Matthew 5:48), the word perfect means "to be complete," "in moral character," and the more we love Christ and fear God, the less we will want to sin, and the more we will be stronger to stand firm and resist temptation. The more God has of us, the less the devil has use of us!

Many Christians claim to have met with an all-powerful God, but their characters and lifestyles are unchanged! We claim that our bodies have received His touch and are His temples. We claim so much! But if we had *truly* met with Him, would we continue to live for self? When the Holy Spirit comes in to abide, you have to pack all your bags of the old lies, self-deceit and deception, and anything else that grieves Him and leave! (John 15:5-8).

Some have asked, "Why did the Christians of a former age see so many revivals and experience so much of the power of God?" The answer is found in their surrender and willingness to obey. If you study the lives of the saints which have gone before us, (whom the Holy Spirit entered as a Person to live His life), you will notice many turned the world upside down (Acts 17:6). First, He turned their personal world upside down, and through them, He turned the world outside of them upside down! Now, ask yourself this: Did they have Someone in them that we lack?

Evan Roberts, the revivalist of the Welsh Revival (1904-1905), pondered the question, why if God is all-powerful and lived in His people, how come no one seemed to notice? It's the same today. Bold claims about the power of God are made by many Christians, but if God was truly in the house, as many have declared, the demons would flee and people would fall on their faces before Him! Have you not read what happened to the prophets and the testimonies in the Gospels? 'At evening, when the sun had set, they brought to Him [Jesus] all who were sick and those who were demon-possessed. And the whole city was gathered together at the door. Then He healed many who were sick with various diseases, and cast out many demons; and He did not allow the demons to speak, because they knew Him' (Mark 1:32-34). When God the Holy Spirit truly turns up, so will thousands and potentially, millions of others, to see what He is doing!

Even in the life of our Lord, we learn there is a difference between receiving the fullness of the Holy Spirit at His baptism and walking in the power of the Spirit. 'Jesus, being filled with the Holy Spirit, returned from the Jordan and was led by the Spirit into the wilderness' (Luke 4:1-2); and later, 'Jesus returned in the power of the Spirit to Galilee' (Luke 4:14). The evangelist Steve Hill, now in glory, often said, "If your shadow is not healing the sick, then God has more for you."

After receiving this powerful encounter with God the Holy Spirit, when He entered me in His fullness, according to my prayer, we prepared to leave. The next day, as this journey was nearing its completion, we walked in the hills near Haworth. As we enjoyed the view I was thinking about my experience with God the previous day. Suddenly, the Holy Spirit said, "You are standing on holy ground. Take off your boots" (Acts 7:33). As I removed them, I was overpowered by Him again and fell to the ground. As I lay in His presence for thirty minutes He spoke to me about things to come.

Now, I am very reluctant to testify to this, but my editors have urged me not to avoid this part of my story. Something happened as I lay on the flecked grass which cannot be explained by any human reasoning. My body lay on the ground, but I know the Lord took me somewhere and we talked in another realm. Many Christians have noted what happened to Enoch, the prophets and the apostle Paul, who crossed the invisible barrier from this world into the next, and of Moses and Elijah who crossed back (Genesis 5:24, Mark 9:4, Acts 7:56, 2 Corinthians 12:2). I cannot tell you where I went because I was not told. Nevertheless, when I read accounts in the Bible concerning people being moved to other realms of God's creation, I feel confident that these things have happened, and still do happen. 'In the visions of God He took me...' (Ezekiel 40:2). I have heard it said by others, that it is possible for the Lord to take people up into the heaven and walk amongst the clouds of heaven to talk (Mark 14:62).[2] Did not such a thing happen to the apostle John, whose testimony is recorded in the book of Revelation? As such things must still be possible, then perhaps the Lord will not allow such people to remember what they heard and saw, to guard them from their foolish pride (2 Corinthians 12:7).

Once again, I do not know where I went and am unwilling to try to name the place, if it were possible. What I am sure of is, I went somewhere and the Lord, or one of His servants, spoke with me and we talked of the future; and when I awoke in those hills, I had no memory of what was said. Nevertheless, in the past few decades I can testify that I have been to places and found myself in situations, wherein I knew exactly what I should say or do. In those moments it felt like I had already discussed these events and would just 'know' what to do or say (Luke 9:30-31).

On our final day of this trip around Britain, as we looked back, we had fulfilled our commission to explore the land, and we brought back some of its fruit (a tin of haggis), and what I have shared is only a portion of what we experienced.

As a final testimony of this journey, I must tell you something wonderful which we were told. During this trip we met one pastor in one town and a church leader in another, both of whom asked, "Are you aware that you have two angels traveling with you?" These two men did not know each other, yet both saw things in the spiritual realm, which we did not see. Nevertheless, their testimonies did help explain many strange events that happened to us which had no natural explanation.

During the trip we were traveling on the A74 in Scotland, where it meets the A7, and as we drove around the roundabout seeking the exit to Gretna Green, I was unable to turn the steering wheel in that direction. As I missed our chosen exit, we had to go around the roundabout a second time and once again, I was unable to steer the car in that direction. It was as if an unseen hand was moving us in a direction we had not planned, and the car turned off onto the A7 to Hawick instead, where we experienced a wonderful Divine appointment. For a few moments, someone else was driving the car in a direction we had not planned to go! These Divine interventions, I had once believed, did not happen today, but they do!

Chapter Eleven

The Hidden Life

Four and a half years had passed since I accepted my initial offer of full surrender to the Lord. It had taken all this time for God to clean me up and teach me His ways, to prepare me for Him to enter me as a Person. In the letter I had received all those years previously (see chapter four), He had informed me that He would remove all that was dear to me, as I choose to give it to Him.

Over these years, I continually sought the Lord and was learning to become sensitive to the voice and leading of the Holy Spirit. Written down, it may seem like I was receiving direction from the Lord all the time, but as you may know twenty-four hours can be a long time, and so can a week, a month or a year. These events, compacted onto the page must be put into the context of daily life continuing as normal. In my experiences, I have learnt that on rare occasions the Holy Spirit will have a conversation with me, but they are often very short. When it has happened, it seems most natural at the time, but the moment I realise in my mind what is happening, it comes to an end. He never speaks in sentences when a few words will suffice, and more often than not; He is silent, entrusting us to the words of Jesus Christ.

Jesus said, "When He, the Spirit of Truth has come, He will guide you into all truth; for He will not speak on His own authority, but whatever He hears He will speak; and He will tell you things to come. He will glorify Me, for He will take of what is Mine and declare it to you. All things that the Father has are Mine. Therefore I said that He will take of Mine and declare it to you" (John 16:13-15).

When the Holy Spirit enters you as a Person, (a distinct experience from being washed over in baptism by Him), any thought of independence is unreal, as you become more and more dependent upon Him for everything. When Paul testified, 'I have been crucified with Christ; it is no longer I who live, but

Christ lives in me' (Galatians 2:20), it was no theoretical thing! The old man, Saul, was dead, and now lived a man called Paul, who had no claim on his life. He lived for Jesus Christ and the Holy Spirit through Paul lived to glorify Jesus – God wants the same for all believers, but there is a price to pay.

After all the signs and wonders I had seen traveling the nation as I was led by the Holy Spirit, trying to settle back down to a normal working day was not easy; but this too was coming to an end. The Lord began to cash-in the claim He had on my life. I had told Him, everything I was, and owned, belonged to Him, now He came and asked for it! You never know how unreal your claims of surrender are, until He comes seeking the payment for the things you have promised!

The Holy Spirit told me that I must lay down my right to work for an earthly master and not be beholden to them for my living. From now on, I was to trust in Him alone. I was very nervous and unsure what to do. I did not understand just how dear a regular wage was; but soon I found out. I worked as an engineer in a factory, I still had a mortgage, a wife and a family to support, so I told my wife the little I knew. This was and still remains a daily abiding in Him, looking to Him in every situation. It was not easy for me and my family, but this was only the beginning. Like Abraham, I was being called out, but I did not know to where (Genesis 12:1-5).

I had shared with a few close friends that the Lord had told me I would be leaving my secular employment and they were very unsure about it. The Holy Spirit had spoken to me, not to them. I expected I would leave in a blaze of glory, but like Moses who knew He was called by God, I left under a cloud of disappointment (Exodus 2:15, Acts 7:35).

Thirteen weeks later I was in hospital, lying on my back and in great pain. Some hours earlier, I had been given a tablet which did not help and I was given an injection to ease the pain. I was in a very bad state of health. 'How could all this be happening?' I thought. 'What has gone wrong?' I called out to My God, the One who had done all those signs and wonders in Scotland – "Where are you now?" Due to the heavy drugs to ease the pain, I was drowsy, but still aware of my surroundings. Why was the Holy Spirit silent?

In all my life I had never felt pain like this before. My urine turned blood red and I felt my life was over. I sensed death was not far away. As my eyes opened, I could see a dark angel in the spiritual realm, standing in the ward and looking at me. It was an angel of death. He never said a word, but his menacing stare said it all! He was waiting for me to die and then, suddenly, the Holy Spirit said, "It has taken a long time to get you in this position." I knew exactly what He meant. For the first time in my adult life, I was truly vulnerable and was unable to defend myself. The swaggering leader of men and effective evangelist was now broken and vulnerable, and an evil spirit was waiting to kill me. The Holy Spirit said, "Tell him to depart in Jesus' name." As I did, he fled with speed, as he submitted to the name of Jesus, One far stronger than he (Mark 3:27, 1 John 4:4). Jesus tells us that all authority has been given to Him, in heaven and on earth, and now I exercised that authority over an evil stronghold in His name and the Lord saved me from him (Matthew 28:18).

I was discharged from the hospital and informed by my doctor that my kidneys were diseased, and that I would not be able to work again. We still had a small mortgage that would take another ten years to pay off, and I was not overly concerned or surprised when the company I worked for terminated my contract. The Holy Spirit reminded me that I was to look to Him in every situation and I did. My source of income had suddenly been cut off, but it turned out that the company had acted illegally, by not following industrial employment procedures and my trade union intervened on my behalf. As I was unfairly dismissed, I was reinstated, with all the benefits of an employee backdated.

The company, trying to avoid going to an industrial tribunal, due to my unfair dismissal agreed that I should have a medical with the company's chief medical officer in London, with a view that I should receive ill-health early retirement pension. This doctor was very reluctant to award me the ill-health early retirement, as I was only forty-two years old, and he told me that if I was no better in eighteen months he would reconsider his decision.

Through these hard experiences the Holy Spirit was teaching me faith; not only in finances but also in His way of doing things, which are always different with each person, yet still follow similar principles of sacrifice, obedience, death to self and resurrection. Speaking through Isaiah the Lord said,

"For My thoughts are not your thoughts, nor are your ways My ways" (Isaiah 55:8).

In my employment I had worked with a degreasing agent for over a decade and a renal specialist, who treated me, believed the chemicals in the degreasing agent caused my illness. This agent, I learned, had already been banned from use in parts of the USA, and when my employers were informed, they stopped using it. At the same time, a solicitor, (which is a lawyer in Britain, attorney in America), was appointed by my union to represent me in a claim for compensation which would take years. In the meantime, an agreement was reached and I left the company because of my ill health.

Through the blessing and foresight of the Lord, I received a sum of money, not related to my company, which enabled us to pay off our mortgage, and I used some of the funds to open a ministry account for the work of the Lord. A few years later, I also received my ill health early retirement pension, by which time the benefits had improved. As this has been my main source of income for decades, I have never claimed to live by faith, but I was given a faith ministry by the Lord for His work. When the Lord's work needed money, I was to fast and pray, and look to the Holy Spirit to provide my needs – and the Lord has always answered those prayers.

The following six months was a time of intense pruning. From my initial prayer of surrender till the day the Holy Spirit entered me in Gateshead, I was led by the Holy Spirit to give up many hobbies and pleasures. But now He was dealing with people, my friends etc. I was a founder member with others, of a small but active ministry, which the Lord told me I could no longer be a part off. This ministry had replaced all the time I spent on my old hobbies, friends and interests, and consumed a large part of my life. I was also busy from time-to-time visiting various people. They too had to go to the cross, but I was unable to give most of them an explanation why my visits had to end. Some were relatives on both sides of the family, who were no longer to be visited. Some we had met up with for years, but rarely did they come to us. Sometimes, I struggled, but I was told by the Holy Spirit that if I was not obedient, He would arrange to bring a relationship to an end His way. With the exception of one family, the Holy Spirit never gave a reason for the severance of these friendships, and I never asked. But in the future, it would all become clear.

Dying to self is one thing, but the fear of man is quite another. Dying to what others think or say takes time. Then there was my home church. I was told, "Leave and never return." As always, no explanation was necessary. I had been busy in the work of evangelism and praying with others, and all this ended, as I was led into the hidden life.

My health was still poorly and I was still very unwell, and for six months I spent a lot of time sat in an armchair reading and praying. Moses had to set-up his tent outside of the camp to truly meet with God (Exodus 33:7), and John the Baptist, amongst many others, was called into the hidden life to meet with the Lord (Luke 1:80). The world and even churches can be very noisy places, and often the Holy Spirit, the Gentle Dove flies away and is to be found in the quiet places. Some of the greatest men and women of faith, the Bible declares, are those who 'wandered in deserts and mountains, in dens and caves of the earth' (Hebrews 11:38). Whilst you are under the influence of the world it can be hard to tell how much it still influences the Church, and this is one reason God called me to Himself.

Chapter Twelve

The Cost of the Call

The Holy Spirit encouraged me to read the Lord's teaching in John 15. Jesus said, "Greater love has no one than this, than to lay down one's life for his friends. You are My friends if you do whatever I command you. No longer do I call you servants, for a servant does not know what his master is doing; but I have called you friends, for all things that I heard from My Father I have made known to you" (John 15:13-15). Through this, the Lord showed me that I was no longer a servant of His, but a friend, and with every friendship there is a cost, a giving and a taking.

To go further with God, I also learnt that my life would be a challenge for others (to do the same). As I went deeper with God, I found that many Christians were challenged by my commitment to Him. I learnt that some friends are closer than others, and you need wisdom to know what to share with one, but not with another. I assumed my Christian friends would be an encouragement in all of this, but sadly, I was mistaken.

I was now called to walk in the Spirit, but a few who were close to me were still working in the flesh, and did not know this, just as I had not many weeks before. Nevertheless, they were still friends and I shared with them that the Lord was now calling me into a hidden life of service and intercession. This would mean a life of prayer, broken up with occasional trips, which the Lord sent me on. Nevertheless, instead of being pleased for me, I began to understand a little of how Job felt with his friends. "You can't do that," one said. "Why not?" I retorted. "You have to go to Bible College," said another. "Who said so?" I responded. This may have been a prophetic word that I was to be taught by the Spirit, and not by men, but I did not know that at the time. One person said to me, "No! This is not for now; this is for some time in the future." Another contradicted my call saying, "God does not do it this way!" I discovered that many Christians are *very* quick to share their opinions about other people's call, but very reluctant to pay the full price for their call!

One of the sources of conflict I had with believers was that I had been called out of wage earning, in a way even I had not expected. My poor health led to me receiving an ill health early retirement pension and additional aid from the government. Many believed that if I was to be called out from secular work, the only way God does this is to provide by numerous financial miracles. This did take place, but it was not to meet my needs, but others. Like Elijah who was led to a widow's house, the miracles of provision I witnessed for the Lord's work were veiled by humility of God's source of supply (1 Kings 17:8-10, Luke 4:25-26).

I was very surprised by all this opposition, where was it coming from? As Job asked, "To whom have you uttered words? And whose spirit came from you?" (Job 26:4). It certainly was not coming from the Holy Spirit. In fairness to those who opposed what God was doing in my life, I had not told them that the Holy Spirit had met with me as He did, as I felt this experience was far too precious to share. In addition, even I struggled with some of the ways I was being led by God, so I could not be too critical of others who doubted me. "For My thoughts are not your thoughts, nor are your ways My ways," says the Lord (Isaiah 55:8)

As I have found all my life, there are many Christians who want to serve the Lord in full-time ministry, as long as they can do what *they* want, on *their* own terms, giving them the ability to remain in absolute control of their lives. To my very great surprise, my friend who had travelled with me on the trip, and seen all the signs and wonders, was also far from happy at God's work in my life. In the past, he had made it very plain that if God would arrange for him to have redundancy, with all the financial security it would bring; he too would serve the Lord in full-time ministry. I thought to myself, 'That would be nice, but it's not faith.'

The Lord has said, "No servant can serve two masters; for either he will hate the one and love the other, or else he will be loyal to the one and despise the other. You cannot serve God and mammon" (Luke 16:13). Therefore, we must put God first and accept the means of supply He provides, in the way He chooses. Jesus said, "Therefore do not worry, saying, 'What shall we eat?' or 'What shall we drink?' or 'What shall we wear?' For after all these things the Gentiles seek. For your heavenly Father knows that you need all these things. But seek first the Kingdom of God and His righteousness, and all these things shall be added to you" (Matthew 6:31-33).

My supply came from a different method than I expected and there was little glory in being sacked from work due to ill health, than the miraculous route. Nevertheless, the pathway of humility must be walked to break our hearts in preparation for future success.

'The sacrifices of God are a broken spirit, a broken and contrite heart, these O God, you will not despise' (Psalm 51:17). Please notice the spiritual principle of brokenness and humility before fruit bearing. 'Those who sow in tears shall reap in joy. He who continually goes forth weeping, bearing seed for sowing, shall doubtless come again with rejoicing, bringing his sheaves with him' (Psalm 126:5-6).

I was hoping to find people who would encourage me in my call, but instead, all this opposition became a daily dying to self, and a separation from others close to me, who had refused to surrender all to the Lord. "This is a time of transition," the Holy Spirit explained. He said, "It is the way others have gone before you and others will follow; if their relationship with Me means more than anything else to them." As always, the emphasis is on the 'if.' As I looked back, many years before the Holy Spirit had spoken to my wife and me at our baptisms, saying, "If you will be what I want you to be." The detail and conditions for fruitfulness are always in what He wants, and when He wants it. His good, pleasing and perfect will must come first. There is one plan only, Plan A, as I have already mentioned, there is no Plan B. If we reject His Plan A, He can and will, find another who will pay the price.

Through this time of separation and physical pain, God the Father began to prune my life, according to the teaching of Jesus in John 15, and there was a daily dying to self and the separation of many Christian friends. This was not easy for me or for those close to me. I had no one to turn to, only the Holy Spirit. Sadly, as you go further with the Holy Spirit you do find yourself walking a path that few Christians in local churches have walked. Many have done so, but usually you need to turn to the Scriptures or biographies of servants of God to find such examples. For me, Rees Howells[1] was a great help and on occasions, I met others walking this path.

Like the prophets of the Bible, I was being separated so I could draw close to God. In addition, because of my difficult childhood, I was not close to any of my relatives; nevertheless, they all had their very strong opinions about my life and Christian walk, which they insisted on sharing!

If you have set your heart on serving God in complete obedience, do not be discouraged if you have opposition – think of Jeremiah the prophet and the Lord's lament on Jerusalem's disobedience (Luke 13:34-35). As for me, regardless of what was said, I had made my choice to follow the Lord Jesus Christ and obey Him unconditionally, and due to this, there was a further parting of the waves (ways) with those who were set to oppose what God was doing in my life (Matthew 10:34-42).

Knowing that some of these people had chosen to do all they could to reject the will of God for their lives, and resist His work in mine, the Holy Spirit forbade me to visit some of them, and when some of them died, I was not permitted by the Holy Spirit to attend their funerals. Once I would have thought this impossible, but then the Lord confirmed that the Jesus I thought I knew from the Bible was very different from the One who really existed! Jesus never limited the cost of discipleship. Jesus said to one person, "Let the dead bury their own dead, but you go and preach the Kingdom of God." Another said, "Lord, I will follow You, but let me first go and bid them farewell who are at my house." But Jesus said to him, "No one, having put his hand to the plough and looking back, is fit for the Kingdom of God" (Luke 9:60-62). On another occasion, Jesus said, "Do not think that I came to bring peace on earth. I did not come to bring peace but a sword. For I have come to 'set a man against his father, a daughter against her mother and a daughter-in-law against her mother-in-law,' and 'a man's enemies will be those of his own household.' He who loves father or mother more than Me is not worthy of Me. And he who loves son or daughter more than Me is not worthy of Me. And he who does not take his cross and follow after Me is not worthy of Me" (Matthew 10:34-38).

As you can imagine, all sorts of rumours abounded, but I never gave one explanation for my actions (Ezekiel 24:17-19).

It was very hard for my mother, when my grandmother and my sibling died. For me, this became the final test regarding the fear of man, and whether Satan could use what others thought to control me, and thus to get me to disobey the Lord. For my mother, not attending these funerals was the last straw, which broke the camel's back. It was the same with other family and my oldest friend, and this caused conflict. But as the Lord taught His disciples, there are many distractions which will keep us so busy that we will never fulfil His will, and these must go to the cross (Luke 14:18-24). Jesus warned all His disciples that they could be "weighed down" with the "cares of this life" and the "desires for things" (Mark 4:19, Luke 21:34).

There is a price to pay for serving the Lord, as He removes you from the influence of the world, the flesh and the devil. Nevertheless, if we are not willing to do what He asks, His way and in His time, then He will wait for someone else, even in another generation (Deuteronomy 2:14). God said, "Therefore I was angry with that generation and said, 'They always go astray in their heart and they have not known My ways.' So I swore in My wrath, 'They shall not enter My rest' " (Hebrews 3:10-11). The Lord is in no rush, as we understand and perceive it, for He is the Alpha and the Omega, the beginning and the end (Revelation 1:8). The Bible clearly reveals that it is not unusual for God to start a new work with the birth of a child; for example, Moses, Samson, Samuel, John the Baptist and Jesus Christ.

Why did God want to draw me aside? Because in this busy world, people often do not have the time to learn how to become sensitive to His voice, leading and guidance of the Holy Spirit. If Satan cannot use sin to keep us from God, he will try to use distractions – hobbies, meetings, friendships, extended family and so forth, they must all go to the cross and Jesus Christ must come first. Now I had hours to sit in my chair with the Lord and to become closer to Him. Some might say, "Why do we need the Spirit, we have Jesus!" We need the Holy Spirit because Jesus said we need Him! (John 14:16-17, John 15:26, John 16:7-14, Acts 1:8).

Our wonderful Lord and Saviour lived on earth approximately thirty-three years, whilst His ministry lasted around three years in and around Israel. Meanwhile, the work of the Holy Spirit, since Pentecost, has been ongoing for two millennia! However, most churches choose to focus exclusively on Jesus' work and ministry, to the exclusion of the One He sent to continue His work. Just as the Jews rejected God in Christ, the Messiah, when He came in Jesus, so the Church often rejects God, when He comes to lead us as the Holy Spirit. We choose to remain strangers to the Holy Spirit, whilst we pronounce we love the Lord, who sent the Spirit to continue His ministry on earth!

While Jesus was on the earth, He could only be in one place at one time, but the Holy Spirit is everywhere (Psalm 139:7), looking to do His work, if only we will let Him. How would you feel, if you returned home to your house and knocked on the door, but was told by your family that you are not welcome. You would be grieved and so is the Holy Spirit. Yet this is what happens to God the Holy Spirit, who is 'the Spirit of Christ' (1 Peter 1:11).

In Jesus' final revelation to His Church, He told us to listen to and obey the will of the Holy Spirit. Jesus said, "Whoever has ears, let them hear what the Spirit says to the churches" (Revelation 2:7). The exact same phrase is then repeated another five times! (Revelation 2:17, 2:29, 3:6, 3:13, 3:22). This six-fold exhortation represents Christ's last exhortation in Scripture to the Church – "Hear what the Spirit says!" The Holy Spirit is often outside of the Church. Is it any wonder the Lord Jesus said, "As many as I love, I rebuke and chasten. Therefore, be zealous and repent. Behold, I stand at the door and knock. If anyone hears My voice and opens the door, I will come in to him and dine with him, and he with Me. To him who overcomes I will grant to sit with Me on My throne, as I also overcame and sat down with My Father on His throne" (Revelation 3:19-21). Brother, sister, friend, ask yourself, is your body *truly* a temple of the Holy Spirit or is He knocking on your door? If He is, do not reject Him. Please note this – the book of Revelation was given to Christians, not to unbelievers. God is knocking on the doors of His Church wanting to come in, and saying, "Whoever has ears, let them hear what the Spirit says to the churches."[2]

In every generation, there are those who truly believe Jesus is about to return and yet we are still waiting (2 Peter 3:1-9); are we 'hastening the coming of the day of God'? (2 Peter 3:12). The reason we wait is because only the Holy Spirit can complete God's work on earth, and we must submit to Him, to allow Him to have the supremacy in our lives and churches. The Lord will not return until His Every Creature Commission is completed. This commission is to take the gospel to every creature (Mark 16:15-18). This is the work of the Holy Spirit, working in and through the Body of Christ; this truly is the crux of the matter. When Jesus came to earth, He was rejected by the religious people who were looking for the Messiah's coming, just as the Holy Spirit is rejected today. Furthermore, the Lord made it plain to those who did believe, that it was for their good that He was going away, so the Spirit could come (John 16:5-11).

As the Bible explains, Jesus will remain in heaven until the time comes for God the Father to restore all things, as He promised long ago, through His holy prophets (Acts 3:21). In the meantime, Jesus is sat at the right hand of God and is interceding for us (Romans 8:34). Why is Jesus still interceding for the believers? One reason is because many who claim to know Him, reject the Holy Spirit, just as He was rejected by those who claimed to love God and were looking for their Messiah. Now, we are all without excuse.

Jesus made it very plain that many will *claim* to know Him and serve Him, but are not His, because they did not follow the plan God the Father has for them. Jesus said, "Not everyone who says to Me, 'Lord, Lord,' shall enter the Kingdom of heaven, but he who does the will of My Father in heaven. Many will say to Me in that day, 'Lord, Lord, have we not prophesied in Your name, cast out demons in Your name, and done many wonders in Your name?' And then I will declare to them, 'I never knew you; depart from Me, you who practice lawlessness!' " (Matthew 7:21-23).

Chapter Thirteen

Limiting the Lord

Many in my generation have a deep rooted fear of poverty, going back to the struggles of childhood and my call-out from wage earning concerned friends and family. In His Word, the Lord has promised to provide all our needs (Matthew 6:25-34, Philippians 4:19), and He was, but like so many, it is in the 'wants' that we are caught out. He will provide our needs but not necessarily all our wants. Our security and worth must be found in Him, not in the type of car we drive, the accommodation we live in or the 'brands and logos' that prop-up low self-worth. Nevertheless, the love of money, or the fear of not having enough, keeps many awake at night. But Jesus has promised, "And everyone who has left houses or brothers or sisters or father or mother or wife or children or lands, for My name's sake, shall receive a hundredfold, and inherit eternal life" (Matthew 19:29).

I had made progress on this path, but I was unaware that I too still had strongholds in my own life, relating to finances. I had prayed for a second-hand car, of a particular make and model, which was in good mechanical order, with an official certificate of twelve month's road worthiness (MOT), for £250 ($400). In Britain in the late 1980s, this was a fair price for an old second-hand family vehicle, at the lower end of the market. God did answer my prayer, but when it came, it turned out to be the biggest heap of rubbish/trash I had ever purchased! I was not happy.

As I had given up my right to earn a wage, money was tight, so I felt very cross with God that I had spent the little money I had on a bad car. Underneath it was full of rust and at the end of the twelve months it would need to be scrapped, at a financial loss. When I challenged God on this issue, the Holy Spirit pointed out to me that this car was everything I had asked for! I had been very specific, but in doing so I had limited Him. Through this, the Lord taught me that I must never limit Him in my prayers. I realised my mistake and was willing to learn. When I needed a new car in the future, I agreed not to go looking for a new one, but instead, I was to wait for the Lord to bring my next car to my attention, and He did!

A neighbour of mine who worked in the motor trade knew I needed a new car and found one for £1,050 ($1,680), but I could have it for £950 ($1,520), with three months warranty; as an extra blessing from God. My neighbour would give it a free service because, even as a non-believer, he said, "You will be using it on the Lord's work." This was the first of many cars the Lord provided for me, which were excellent for the ministry He gave me. None on the outside looked special, (most were more than ten years old, and one minister repeatedly asked me not to drop him off outside his house), but mechanically they did the job, and the money saved by not owning expensive popular models (especially the initial outlay and its annual or mileage service by the 'branded' garage to keep the warranty valid) could be poured back into Kingdom work.

I was making progress, but I still had financial strongholds in my life, one was that I tried to hang onto money for as long as I could. The Lord began challenging my hold on money when I would meet homeless people, and the Holy Spirit would tell me to empty my wallet to help them (Matthew 25:34-40). This happened so many times that I began to go out without money just in case! Yes, the flesh is strong. Then, as the Holy Spirit continued to place a deep concern in my heart for homeless people, I was led to bring some back to my house, to let them wash, and try to help them into a better life. I still wonder today if one of them was an angel (Hebrews 13:2).

All this was good, but the Spirit was soon going to challenge me to give far larger amounts to help others. One evening whilst out walking, I passed a house where one of the men I had worked with lived and the Holy Spirit said, "You were never able to reach this man with the gospel," and I thought this was very true, but it was not for the lack of trying. Then the Holy Spirit said, "This man is having mortgage difficulties and I wish to show him a practical demonstration of My love through you." I was told to knock on his door and offer to give him £1,000 ($1,600). "One thousand pounds!" I protested, as I had a limited income and he was a working man. "Yes," said the Holy Spirit, "it's My money, not yours. Have you not declared you have a Lord's Account," which was the ministry account I set up for the Lord's work. "Yes," I replied and the Holy Spirit said, "Then do as I ask."

I was not sure how my wife was going to take this news, so I went to the man's house and as I opened his garden gate, the Holy Spirit said, "That's fine. You can leave now. I was only testing you." As I went up the road, I was happy. I rejoiced on my way home and then the Holy Spirit asked me, "Why are you so happy?" I replied, "Because I have the victory!" The Holy Spirit was searching for my true motives when He said, "But you have done nothing! The reason you are so happy is because you still have the money." He was right and then He said, "If you are willing to give a non-believer £1,000, how much more would you give to a believer, double?" I thought about it and replied, "Yes," without knowing I was digging a hole that I would fall into.

The following evening, a brother in Christ phoned me, one who had aggressively challenged my call, asking me to come around to his house and pray with him immediately. On the way, the Holy Spirit reminded me of our conversation the night before and the promise I had made. Arriving at his house he told me that his business had a cash-flow problem and he needed £2,000 ($3,200) within the next few days! After what the Lord had said to me, I thought, 'What is there to pray about?' I looked up into the air in prayer and looking down said, "It will be here tomorrow morning, how do you want it cash or cheque?" He was thrilled but I knew I still had to go home and tell my wife. 'Therefore, as we have opportunity, let us do good to all, especially to those who are of the household of faith' (Galatians 6:10).

I had supported my wife as the main provider for more than two decades, had paid the mortgage, but now my income had been greatly reduced, we had to trust further in the Lord's provision, and she was keen to return to work. I suggested that she return for six months and I would intercede during those months for finances, and then we would see if the Holy Spirit was able to provide more than an earthly master could!

By this time, the Holy Spirit had already spoken to me about my next step of faith. I had been sat in my garden enjoying the sun, as I was still slowly recovering from my time in hospital. I was still weak and lacked energy, when the Holy Spirit revealed to me that I was to return to Scotland on a trip, but this time I was to go further north and visit Barvas in the Outer Hebrides. This is where a Christian awakening/revival had taken place during 1949-1952, with Duncan Campbell taking a prominent leadership role.[1]

On my first visit to Scotland, I had explored the land in keeping with Numbers 13. This time, I was told to go through the length and breadth of the United Kingdom. The Lord said, "Go through its length and its width" (Genesis 13:17), and wherever I went, I was to claim the ground I stood on (Joshua 1:1-9). Little did I know, that this second trip would be followed by many others, and I would be sent to so many cities, towns, islands and villages of Britain, that one day I would have a map of Britain filled to the brim with red dots where the Lord had sent me. Yes, it would take seventeen years to complete this commission to claim the ground in Britain, as I was led every step of the way, year-by-year. As well as this, there would be further trips to other nations.

One of the lessons the Holy Spirit taught me was the difference between following His leading by His supply, and storming ahead presumptuously by building up debts and expecting Him to clear them. Friends had done this and when they were delivered, they went and did the same again! Therefore, I believed that the only way I could be sure that I was hearing the Holy Spirit was to work out how much each journey would cost, and pray the money in. I felt this was a failsafe system and the principle, which guided me, was, "No dough, no go." Dough is a slang word for money. The Holy Spirit had made it very plain to me that my financial needs were only ever to be known by Him. I was never to send out newsletters, seek partners or drop hints to get people to give. If the work was the Lord's, He would pay for it – there would be NO solicitations.

My wife had now been working for six months and my period of daily intercession for finances came to completion. When I tallied the results of our test, I had received all I needed for the trip to Scotland, which amounted to more money than my wife had earned in secular employment. I thought this spoke volumes and was reminded of what the Holy Spirit had said from the beginning, "If you will be what I want you to be."

When I was baptised I had publicly testified that I wanted to be a true disciple of the Lord Jesus Christ. The words had been said, the promises had been made and I was acting on them. Actions must speak louder than words.

It was the same with Jesus' disciples, who had followed Him for some time, but had to make their minds up, when He taught them who He truly was and what was expected of them. Many of His disciples exclaimed that the Lord's teaching was hard, and, 'From that time many of His disciples went back and walked with Him no more' (John 6:66).

Words and promises may seem very cheap in our culture and age, but God has always taken them very seriously. "If a man makes a vow to the Lord, or swears an oath to bind himself by some agreement, he shall not break his word; he shall do according to all that proceeds out of his mouth" (Numbers 30:2). "When you make a vow to the Lord your God, you shall not delay to pay it; for the Lord your God will surely require it of you, and it would be sin to you. But if you abstain from vowing, it shall not be sin to you. That which has gone from your lips you shall keep and perform, for you voluntarily vowed to the Lord your God what you have promised with your mouth" (Deuteronomy 23:21-23). The Lord Jesus Himself warned of the dangers of vowing (Matthew 5:33-37).

Chapter Fourteen

The Staff and Shofar

Over the months since I was discharged from hospital, I had chronic back pain and whenever I raised this issue with the Holy Spirit, He said, "Go see your doctor." This was not what I wanted to hear. I was in such pain that at times, I needed to use a walking stick, as I tended to lean forward to ease the pain. I knew Jesus Christ still healed the sick (Exodus 15:26, Isaiah 53:5, Matthew 8:17, 1 Peter 2:24), and now I thought it was my turn, but every time I raised this question, I received the same answer. One night things came to a head. "Why will You not heal me?" I asked the Lord and He led me to this Scripture: 'For to you it has been granted on behalf of Christ, not only to believe in Him, but also to suffer for His sake' (Philippians 1:29).

The Lord reminded me that crucifixion is slow and painful, and I withdrew my complaint at once. I had seen many people healed, but by sending me to the doctors God was dealing with my pride. Since my conversion, I had always believed that faith in Jesus' name could, and does heal the sick, and now the doctor prescribed me some painkillers. This medicine eased the pain, but I still stooped when I walked. To my surprise, the Lord suddenly told me that I was to have a staff, made of hazel wood and I went searching in the local woods for something suitable. After looking through four different woods and coppices, I was unable to find one. Whilst I was wasting my time, the Holy Spirit was waiting patiently for me to ask for His help. Eventually, I asked Him to guide me to the right woods, and He said, "Return to the last woods you visited and I will show you the one I have chosen for you."

I obeyed and returned to the woods I last visited, and followed the path through the forested area. Once again, I walked from one end to the other finding nothing; 'What was I doing wrong?' I wondered. Then halfway through the woods as I was exiting, I slipped on the wet earth and as I lost my balance, I reached out by instinct to grab hold of the nearest thing. My heart was beating faster than normal and as I regained my composure, I noticed what I had grabbed hold of. I was hanging onto a hazel branch which was made to measure for me. This was my staff! I cut it out from the base and took it home to be dried and oiled. This staff was to accompany me on most of my trips around Britain for all the years I travelled.

Many years after I received this staff from the Lord, I was told by the Holy Spirit that I would require a shofar. At that time, they were not popular in Britain, and as far as I was aware, they were only available to purchase in Israel and America (this was before the popular advent of the internet). The Holy Spirit showed me the type He wished me to have – a large multi-spiral polished shofar. I had learnt from previous experience to ask Him to provide me with what He wanted me to have, rather than go looking, but where would it come from?

I told only one person what the Lord had said to me and when she spoke with a Christian friend on the phone, their conversation unexpectedly led to shofars. This Christian on the phone had been to Israel several times and said to my friend, "Do you want one?" "I do not need one," she replied, "but I know someone who is praying about getting one." With that, the woman on the phone explained that the night before in a prayer meeting, someone had prophesied, "The Holy Spirit says, 'Someone present has two shofars[1] and he is to give one away, as the Lord has need of it!' "

The staff that the Lord provided was helpful to aid me with walking, but that was not its true function, and often whenever the Lord had something very serious to say or do, I was told to take the staff with me and prophesy. On one such occasion, I was told to drive to a church building with my son, stretch forth my staff, declaring its closure, if it continued with its present leadership, who were in open rebellion to the Lord and His will! They had become so deluded that they were teaching a small vulnerable flock that Jesus Christ was to return in the year 1997, without regard to the Lord's warning that no one knows when He will return (Mark 13:32-37). Some of these people were the most vulnerable in society and could have easily responded unwisely. However, God in His goodness and mercy was watching over them. This church with its unrepentant leaders did close, as they were no longer a light to the Lord, but became a mire of false teaching and hypocrisy (Revelation 1:20, Revelation 2:1).

The shofar's function was similar to the staff – it was only to be used as instructed by the Holy Spirit. That is not to say that I did not have some fun learning how to make the correct sound! In the future, sometimes when I was involved with spiritual warfare, the Holy Spirit would direct me to blow the shofar as a sign to the principalities and powers of the Lord's victory in the intercession. The staff and the shofar have no power in themselves, and were useless if I did not use them as directed by the Holy Spirit. The shofar was blown on several occasions, but not that many in regards to all the work the Lord led me into.

Today, this staff and shofar stand side-by-side in a small wooden structure, which the Lord told me to erect. Over the years, I have learnt that if God shows me something or somewhere in a dream, I was not to go in search of it, but to view it as a Divine appointment to be brought about by Him. I had searched for the staff in vain, but the Lord brought it and the shofar to me in His good, pleasing and perfect timing.

Chapter Fifteen

The Wiper Blade

The Lord told me that I must head north for the second time, to Scotland. I was to go further than I had gone before and the time to depart soon came. A year had passed since my last trip and much had taken place. This time my son came with me and he did much of the driving, which was helpful.

It was a Sunday morning in August when we departed. We were only ten miles away from home, on the next town's bypass, when I kept thinking that we should go into the town and attend a church service. As I thought about all the miles we had to travel to get to Scotland, we passed three junctions leading into town, and with only one left, I had to make a decision and prayed, "If this is of you Holy Spirit, please make it plain to me." Suddenly there was a cloudburst and heavy rain fell from the heavens, and we were forced to slow down significantly. The windscreen wiper blades were turned on to full and working hard, when suddenly, one flew off onto the bonnet. We had to stop and refit it. The weather quickly cleared and as I fixed the wiper blade, right in front of us was the last junction, which led back into town.

We drove into town and entered the first church we came to. The meeting had already started and within minutes the Holy Spirit said, "When I tell you, stand up and repeat the words I give to you." Approximately fifteen minutes later, I stood up and spoke out as instructed. I was moved by the Holy Spirit and said, "My children what do I have to do to get your attention? What will it take to get you to stop and listen to Me, and to get you to do what I want you to do?" I was a complete stranger and when I sat back down there was silence. No one was sure how to respond and the congregation looked around at each other. Eventually the pastor went to the front and said, "So the Lord can speak to us in other ways!" Immediately the Holy Spirit told me to leave and I did.

Some months later, I heard that what I shared with the Church that morning became a catalyst to them accepting the ministry of the Holy Spirit in their church. They had a routine planned for each meeting, with every minute accounted for, and the Holy Spirit was outside of the church, knocking and asking to come in. When they responded in the positive to this word from the Lord, the Holy Spirit entered to glorify Jesus Christ. Jesus said when the Holy Spirit comes, "He will glorify Me, for He will take of what is Mine and declare it to you" (John 16:14). That Church soon outgrew their meeting place and also began to hold conferences. This is what happens when God is invited into His Church!

I was only ten miles from home and the Holy Spirit was already beginning to lay the foundational teaching for me, for this mission. I learnt that those who welcome the Holy Spirit and obey Him will be blessed, and will bear good fruit. But those who resist, rebel and reject the ministry of the Holy Spirit will live in a spiritual wilderness of their own choosing (Hebrews 3:8). Jesus is the Head of the Body of Christ and He said, "Every branch in Me that does not bear fruit He takes away; and every branch that bears fruit He prunes, that it may bear more fruit" (John 15:2).

After this encounter at the church, we continued our journey to Malliag in Scotland, where we were going to catch the ferry to the Isle of Skye. I had heard it was possible to purchase an island hopping ticket, which was the cheapest way to visit these Scottish islands. Early one evening I entered the ferry office at Malliag and told the ticket salesperson of my plan to visit eight islands. He was polite, yet told me that it was the height of the summer season and I should have booked months ahead. He stated it would be impossible for me to travel to all those islands and said they were shutting the office in thirty minutes!

I was shocked for a second. God had instructed me where to go and now we were told it was impossible! I stepped outside to pray and asked the Holy Spirit to help me. I heard the ticket salesperson joking with his assistant about inexperienced people thinking they can just come up to the islands and get the tickets they wanted, but felt compelled to go straight back in. I told the ticket salesperson that I had been talking to my Heavenly Father about the situation, and asked the salesperson when I could book up to go to the Isle of Skye, which was the first island on my journey. "That's no problem," he said, indicating that I could travel over on the morning ferry. Having made progress, I asked him when it would be possible to leave the Isle of Skye for the next island, and he said I could arrive on Tabert the following morning, on the Isle of Lewis and Harris.[1]

I was pleased we had made much progress, but he explained that these first two islands were simple to book. The problem would be with the next islands. However, as we continued trying to book a ticket for each of the eight islands, each time there was an opening and with a couple last minute cancellations, we had all the tickets we needed! As an experienced ticket salesperson, he knew how impossible it is to get these tickets in the summer and I was thrilled. "That's not possible," he said, as he checked and re-checked the tickets in disbelief, "you've been very lucky," but luck did not come into it.

On the short journey over to the Isle of Skye, the Holy Spirit spoke to me saying, "I want you to get used to these ferries, they will be a part of your life for a time." We spent the night in a tent and the following morning, we got the ferry to Lewis and Harris. On our arrival, we drove to Barvas. I was very excited to be there. Many months previously, the Lord had spoken to me, saying, "Barabbas." I tried to write it down, but was not familiar with the word and did not know what it meant. Later, as I was reading a book about revival, I came across the name (which is in the Gaelic language) and its English rendering. When I arrived in Barvas, I saw the sign and asked a local person to pronounce it, and when he spoke it aloud, I said to myself, 'That's it. That's exactly what the Lord said to me.'

In Barvas, I noticed some caravans parked in the gardens and asked a local man if there was one I could hire/rent. "Yes," he replied, "but you will have to drive back across the island," from where we had already been. "All the bookings are made at the tourist office," he said. As I pondered this and my reluctance to drive the length of the island, a car pulled up and the driver asked, "Can I help you?" I explained the situation and she said, "No, no, you can stay in mine," pointing across the road. When we began talking about the cost, she discovered we were here on the Lord's work and said, "Oh no, let's not talk about money if your serving the Lord," and we were given its use for a nominal fee.

It was a Saturday evening when we arrived and on Sunday morning, I went for a walk to find what time the church service would start. A spiritual awakening had broken out in this church in revival power only four decades previously, and as I walked towards the building, the Holy Spirit told me to walk in an attitude of prayer. I interpreted this as meaning with my head bowed in reverence of the Lord. I had only taken a few steps when I became aware that the Holy Spirit was still hovering over the area. I felt His presence brooding over the place and I was too afraid to look up. He was still there and I knew it.

If I had to testify what His presence felt like in the spirit, then I would say, imagine a large electricity power grid, which has so much power in it that it continues to emit a low base humming sound, as it hummed in peaks, high and low. Only a fool would go near without respect to that immense power. However, if you wanted to experience it, you would still need to find a way to reconnect to that source of power.

I have been told that once the Holy Spirit comes in revival power and awakens an area, He never truly leaves and I believe this is true. I was reminded of what Evan Roberts, the Welsh revivalist said on his brief return to South Wales some years after the revival. He explained that the same Holy Spirit who visited their land in the 1904-1905 revival was still there waiting for someone to meet His conditions and pray Him down! As Isaiah prayed, "Oh, that You would rend the heavens! That You would come down! That the mountains might shake at Your presence!" (Isaiah 64:1).

During the church service, I was saddened to see how the numbers had reduced greatly. This is often the case when revival ends, and the traditions and empty religious rules and rituals still seemed to dominate life. Nevertheless, one of the members from the church invited me to his house that evening to share about the 1949-1952 revival. There was a small group present. We spoke of revival and when I began to share about the work of the Holy Spirit today, barriers in people's hearts were raised and the atmosphere changed. They had no wish to hear and this was made plain to me, so I left early. The Holy Spirit had been welcomed here in the past, but He was no longer welcome by some, at the time of my visit. New wine must be put into new wineskins, otherwise it will burst and both will be ruined. Some people still prefer the old and cannot immediately embrace the new, for they say, "The old is better" (Luke 5:38-39).

The following day, we went out to pray as the Holy Spirit directed me and soon we were on the ferry to another island. Here we met an elder of the local church, who invited me to share. Many of the people of the Highlands and Islands of Scotland have a truly wonderful gift of hospitality, but as I once again shared about the work of the Holy Spirit, the atmosphere changed. This island had seen revival in the past, so what had happened? The elder was keen for me to leave, but he was kind and directed me to someone who might be interested in the testimony, which God told me to share.

When I met this interested individual, she invited us into her home where a retired minister was staying on holiday. Around the meal table, the minister asked why I had come to the islands, and I told him how the Holy Spirit had spoken to me and led me there. Immediately, he got up and left. I did not think anything about it, until he came back and apologised. The minister told me that he had been in Christian ministry for more than thirty-five years and God had never spoken to Him! He was visibly upset and the evening was soon over! It was very sad to hear, and alarming. Here was a minister, someone who had been to Bible College or who had received training in theological studies; he had been ordained, yet was spiritually deaf, or dead! Jesus said, "My sheep hear My voice..." (John 10:27).

The Spirit had sent me north and yet all the people I seemed to meet at first did not want to know Him! I was shocked that many people were resistant to the Person and work of the Holy Spirit, but I did discover one of the reasons people were hesitant. Another person we shared with stated that they had been baptised in the Holy Spirit and spoken in tongues in the past. However, when the others found out, they were so concerned that they took this person to the doctors for evaluation! Many of these people claimed to follow Jesus and it was He who said of believers, "They will speak with new tongues" (Mark 16:17). They declared they loved Jesus but rejected His teaching and His Spirit! They had rejected God

Himself! See Acts 5:3-5, to lie to the Holy Spirit is to lie to God, therefore to reject the Holy Spirit is to reject God!

As I was preparing to leave, a woman said, "Wait, I have some friends on the next island who would love to meet you." She gave us the directions to them and we drove over the causeway and spent a few days with believers there. The small meeting in a home was full and I was given several words of knowledge by the Holy Spirit to share. The Lord showed me that one woman was desperate to be baptised in the Holy Spirit and receive the gifts of tongues, and after permission, I prayed with her and she exploded with joy as the Holy Spirit gave her the gift of tongues. Afterwards, I shared the words of knowledge but no one responded. I looked at the leader and he said, "Could you have gotten it wrong?" I acknowledged that it is possible, but said, "Not this time." There was silence for a while when one of the women suddenly stood up and said, "I can't sit here any longer. The Holy Spirit has spoken to me and told me that if I do not get up now, I will never be free and neither will anyone else here."

Then she said something which shocked me. She explained she was the wife of a bishop, (they were on holiday in the region). Immediately I pictured her telling me off and trying to find reasons to denounce this ministry! Instead, she confessed that she had spent years projecting an image that everything was perfect in her life, whilst she suffered greatly inside and was never given the opportunity to be free. As soon as she confessed, this mature woman stood up, and the Holy Spirit told me how she was to be freed. I spoke to the evil spirit in her, saying, "You spirit of rejection, in the name of Jesus..." when suddenly, this woman fell softly back onto the ground, and with strength beyond human ability, jumped straight back up, and starting dancing and shouting, "I'm free, I'm free. It's left me, I'm free!"

The next person in the line confessed her problem, which the Spirit had already pinpointed with His word of knowledge. I spoke out saying, "In the name of Jesus I speak to you spirit of depression," and once again, this person fell down and was immediately free! In the past this kind of deliverance often took a long time, but now the Holy Spirit was taking over and freeing people in power (Isaiah 61:1-3, Matthew 8:16).

All who had previously been silent when the words of knowledge were given had now responded and were free, and as this unusual power had been released, all the people in the meeting sought prayer. One by one, the Holy Spirit came upon the believers and they fell down to the ground and rested in the peace of the Holy Spirit. When the first room was filled with people laying/resting in the Holy Spirit, those who still wanted prayer moved to the next room and soon the floor was covered! Then we had go to upstairs. Finally, every person was laying in the Spirit, as He had come in power. The Kingdom of God truly is righteousness, joy and peace in the Holy Spirit (Romans 14:17). 'For the Kingdom of God is not in word but in power' (1 Corinthians 4:20).

Something very special had happened, and I was shocked and felt the fear of the Lord (Haggai 1:12). Everyone was resting in the Spirit on the floor and I had no one to preach to or pray for, therefore I went to the kitchen and began washing up (cleaning the dishes). Finally, the leader, stumbling into the kitchen came to me and said, "What are you doing?" I did not know what to do or say. Nothing like this had ever happened before and I felt I had to get out of the way of God, and humble myself before Him.

Chapter Sixteen

The Suit

Two weeks before my second trip to Scotland, I walked past a clothes shop and the Holy Spirit said, "Go in there, you will find a suit which will fit you. Purchase it and take it with you." Suits were very expensive then (this was before the rise of supermarket's clothes range), and I only had £50 ($80) in my wallet. The only suit I could find was twice the amount I had – what was I to do? As I was thinking about this, the sales assistant came over to me saying, "Everything is half price," and I gave God praise in my heart.

I purchased the suit and took it with me to Scotland, but why did I need it? It was only when I was on the islands of Scotland that I realised *why* this suit was so important. In many of these islands, which are separated from mainland Britain, the religious culture is still very traditional. Back then, in some places people locked-up the children's swings on the Sabbath, not understanding that the Lord loves joy and He 'gives us all things richly to enjoy' (1 Timothy 6:17).

If I had not worn the sombre black suit, I would not have been accepted in some of the church meetings, as I would not have been deemed suitably dressed. Even the revivalist Duncan Campbell in the 1950s was shunned by some because he wore brown shoes to a meeting once, which was considered worldly!

The following day as I was packing in readiness to leave, I was led to leave the suit with the leader of the fellowship. I explained to him that someone who had need of a suit would make it known to him. As I was about to leave, his wife came in and shared how one of their neighbours had sold his clothes to buy alcohol and was in desperate need of help. Was it not to such people the Lord called us to help? (Matthew 25:36).

The next part of our trip took us to South Uist, to take the ferry to Oban. We had not been long at the port when I saw the name of the ferry, *The Lord of the Isles*. I knew the One who is the true Lord of the Isles and as the ferry sailed, I fell asleep and was awakened hours later by the clatter of pots and pans smashing about in the galley. The ferry found its way into a storm with high seas and was being tossed about. It crashed up and down in the boisterous sea and people were now being sick everywhere, including my son, and children were also crying in distress. Suddenly the Holy Spirit told me, "Command the waves to be calm in Jesus' name." I followed the instruction and within ten to fifteen minutes, the conditions completely changed and it was calm again.

We were all shaken by the events, but I was very shaken by the direction the Holy Spirit had given me and the results. I could understand the storm, but to command the waves had disturbed me. I was very challenged by all these events and felt unable to share with anyone at the time. God had done so much and a lot of it I was unable to truly understand. We had been blessed by Scottish Highland hospitality and along the journey, the Lord had provided for us. In the times of ministry, the Holy Spirit had delivered people from demonic bondages, others were empowered, and others now spoke in tongues. Finally, when we reached Oban, we had to drive to the Isle of Arran and claim the ground in Jesus' name, as we had been directed by the Holy Spirit.

When I later pondered these events and recalled all that had taken place, the Holy Spirit brought to my attention the fact that He was no longer moving in power in the places where He had moved before. He was not present in the church in Barvas and He was not welcome in the house in Barvas, nor in the house on another island, but the Lord had found a houseful of believers who were willing to meet with God again, on His terms and He moved in a powerful way.

On my first trip to Scotland the previous year, I found the same was true – God always expected me to meet Him on His terms. He had not met with me in the sanctuary in Gateshead, but in the kitchen, and the following day, He met with me unexpectedly in the hills. I believe it is true that the Holy Spirit never gives up an area to the devil where He has moved in revival power, even after it has come to an end. Instead, He patiently waits, hovering over the area, for a time to come when He can again work through others who are willing to do things His way.

In each generation, God is ever doing new things, which cannot be the same as in previous generations, and His new work is always controversial to those who love religion and tradition more than the Lord. Jesus said, "No one puts a piece of unshrunk cloth on an old garment; for the patch pulls away from the garment, and the tear is made worse. Nor do people put new wine into old wineskins, or else the wineskins break, the wine is spilled, and the wineskins are ruined. But they put new wine into new wineskins, and both are preserved" (Matthew 9:16-17). There is a danger that some of those who witnessed the last move of God may oppose a new move of God. This is because it looks different than the previous one, but Jesus stated that new wine must have new wine skins, and those who have tasted the old do not immediately desire the new because they believe the old is better (Luke 5:38-39).[1] The Jews rejected Jesus because they were ever looking to the past and hoping to find God moving in similar patterns. They said to Jesus, "We know that God spoke to Moses; as for this fellow, we do not know where He is from" (John 9:29). Today it is the same, many rejoice at past moves of God and resist His moving today, because it is controversial or because people are offended at supernatural manifestations (John 10:20). They rejected the Lord Jesus because He was also controversial (Luke 7:33-35).

Yes, the Holy Spirit is still ready to do a new work in this generation but if He is not welcome in our church buildings, He will be grieved and leave; yet I believe He still broods over many of these areas waiting. From this trip, I found that He is most willing to meet with individuals or groups anywhere, if they will pay the price. Yet our traditions can be a great offence to the Lord. One church I attended once saw a great miracle of healing in the 1930s and hung the leg brace of the man up as a testimony for all. However, six decades later the leadership rejected the ministry of the Holy Spirit and I was given this word for them, "The blessing God has for you will be given to another on your very doorstep!" They had rejected God, but He still wanted to give His blessing to anyone nearby who would welcome it! There are people who will seize this moment in obedience, but also, I have discovered that the moment the Holy Spirit is taken for granted, or sin gets a hold, especially in the church leadership, the spirit of division will move in and fill the vacuum left by the Holy Spirit's departure. Even in a revival, the Holy Spirit might leave, but it can be months before those involved, now running on adrenalin, momentum and past blessings, notice His departure.

In my experience, I have found that a person with a powerful anointing may minister for a time in a dead church and because of his (or her) walk with God, the Holy Spirit may move again. Nevertheless, unless the people themselves welcome Him, the Spirit may well leave with the person with the anointing, who may or may not be the minister. If the people of God do not wake up, they will slip and slide back into a deep spiritual sleep. Paul warned the Romans that 'now it is high time to awake out of sleep' (Romans 13:11). The reader would be well advised to read, study and meditate on the warnings of Jesus in Matthew 7:13-27.

In the past, I have ministered in places under the anointing of the Holy Spirit and God has moved powerfully, but on my return to the same places, very little has happened because the people did not fully obey the direction of the Holy Spirit. In such circumstances, the Holy Spirit showed me there was nothing I could do about it because of the sins and backslidings of the people. Furthermore, I have attended fellowships where the gifts of the Spirit, tongues and their interpretations, prophecy, and words of knowledge etc., were a regular feature, but it had little to do with the Holy Spirit. I will deal with this in later chapters concerning tares and weeds.

Chapter Seventeen

Not Again

When I arrived home to England, after this most unexpected journey, I shared with a small group of Christians the things I felt free to share at the church which met at my house.

We had been meeting with other Christians in my home for some time, but the Lord told me that this season was now to close, as we had to join another fellowship of believers in another town. I had just lived through the most powerful encounter I had ever witnessed as a Christian and the thought of returning to a church bound by religious routines and ceremonies was troubling. "Oh not again," I said!

The Lord showed me where to take my family and at the very first service, I discerned that some of the people needed deliverance, and there was demonic activity going on in the building. I was new to the fellowship, so I kept this to myself, but as I soon found out, there had been prolonged infighting between the members for many months. I had been trying to avoid this kind of entanglement and now the Lord led me back into it! Trouble had been brewing and after the meetings, instead of Christian fellowship, the people turned to gossiping and subtle infighting. As I became aware of this, instead of joining in after the service to gossip I withdrew into the kitchen to help with cleaning up (Psalm 1:1, 1 Timothy 5:13).

I learnt that this infighting had been going on for years and caused many problems for the pastor. As this was the case, very severe demonic strongholds had been enveloping the church. When I felt it was the right time, I told the pastor and shared that we could command these spirits to go. He had little experience of spiritual warfare and was anxious not to get involved himself. Nevertheless, he was very keen that I should command these spirits to go in Jesus' name and take-back the spiritual landscape that division had given to the enemy. As the pastor did not want to get involved, he invited an African brother to join me.

One evening, we went to the church when it was quiet, and one by one, we commanded the demonic beings to leave. The Holy Spirit would give us words of knowledge and we would speak out the name of each demon, and command it to go in Jesus' mighty name. After much victory, there was still one demon, who seemed to reside over the loft/attic, who refused to depart. His name, was the spirit of division. We had cast many spirits out of the church, with the full blessing of the pastor, but this one spirit refused to depart and we could not force him out. As we prayed about this, the Holy Spirit showed me that we had no authority over him, because those in leadership had given him a legal right to enter in, and only those in leadership could cast him out. This was new teaching for me, concerning the importance of authority in spiritual warfare over buildings and the great strongholds, which can be established over churches by sin. The devil is a legalist who has 'legal rights,' but only if we relinquish them by our sin, or the sin of others, especially those in leadership. On an individual level, when we plead the blood of Jesus Christ over our lives and we are not living in wilful unrepentant sin (1 John 1:5-10), then the devil, and his demons have to let us go as they have no legal right or hold over us (1 John 5:18-19). The Advocate, the Lord Jesus Christ, pleads our case and is Himself the propitiation for our sins (1 John 2:1-3).[1]

I shared with the pastor what the Holy Spirit had told me and he went away to pray about it. Several days later, the pastor joined me and we returned to the church building, and he commanded the spirit of division out of the building in the powerful name of Jesus Christ. The following Sunday, people began to comment that there was a completely different atmosphere in the service.

Chapter Eighteen

Praying in Money

When I was not travelling on the Lord's work, I would attend a local fellowship and support its pastor. The exception to this rule was when we would host a church in my home, with local Christians joining us. Now, I was meeting with a new set of believers and at the same time, the Holy Spirit would begin leading me to intercede through me for their circumstances.

Before the Lord sent me on His work, more often than not, the Holy Spirit would show me well in advance the next place I should go. After receiving my first direction, I would pray about it over a period of months, most of the time in private, in tongues (1 Corinthians 14:4). There is always a limitation to what can be prayed in the vernacular and the Holy Spirit is the only Person who knows *exactly* what must be prayed and when. 'Likewise the Spirit also helps in our weaknesses. For we do not know what we should pray for as we ought, but the Spirit Himself makes intercession for us with groanings which cannot be uttered. Now He who searches the hearts knows what the mind of the Spirit is, because He makes intercession for the saints according to the will of God. And we know that all things work together for good to those who love God, to those who are the called according to His purpose' (Romans 8:26-28).

Whenever I sought to discern the Lord's will for my next trip, I had to be cautious. I learnt from experience that the flesh is *very* eager to step ahead of the Lord, and it rushes forward hoping the Lord is following! I had done this in my outreach to the local villages when the Lord told me, "Everything you have done to date, counts for nothing!" Therefore, from then on, I took the rule that if it is God's will for me to travel on His work, then He would send the money.

As long as we have money, we can be like Jonah and pay for a ticket to go in the opposite direction from God's will (Jonah 1:3), and finances is often a great problem in Christian endeavours. Everyday you will find Christian ministries on television claiming that if you send them money as a seed offering, the Lord will meet your every need, because they will pray for you in the 'special season.' They use special techniques which includes 'countdowns' to put you under pressure, to give *now,* they provide manipulative 'prophetic' words and exploit the poor, the sick and vulnerable as the viewers are urged to give *now,* if their problems are to be solved.

Many of these people use cunning half-truths and Scriptures taken out of context to push their point, make their objective and claim their goals, yet what they promise does not appear to work for them, because their needs and debts persist every year! If they practiced what they preached and sowed a seed 'at this time of year' and it worked, (even the miracle 'debt cancellation' or the '24hr blessing'), they would not need to keep on and on, manipulating their viewers! Many of these ministries are in serious debt and they themselves testify to this when they come to the end of their financial year. They bring shame to the name of Jesus Christ by using His name, and as their ministries struggle, they always appear to have enough money to furnish themselves with expensive mansions, second homes, luxury cars, high-end designer clothes and even private jets! Their examples are in complete contrast to the Lord's life and His apostles (1 Corinthians 4:6-13). What the viewers of these programmes forget is that their luxurious lifestyles have been paid for by the sacrificial giving of others, who themselves are often struggling to make ends meet. Peter and the apostles lived sacrificial lives for God, so that nothing of the Lord's provision was wasted, and they warned us of others who would claim to serve Christ, who would live by other principles: 'By covetousness they will exploit you with deceptive words' (2 Peter 2:3).

It is right to support genuine works of God and all should not be blamed for what the minority do, but these charlatans who persistently abuse the generosity of Christians for their own financial gain have no shame, and claim there is not enough to meet their needs. However, when we look at Christian history we find that many of the most effective servants of God lived sacrificially and because of this, were able to pray-in great sums of money for the Lord's true work. George Müller (of

Bristol, England with his orphanages), J. Hudson Taylor (founder of the China Inland Mission), Rees Howells (founder of the Bible College of Wales), his son Samuel Rees Howells, and many others in our day, have allowed the Holy Spirit to gain a position of intercession for finances through His intercession in and through them.

Yes, the flesh is very powerful and we can always find an excuse to do what we want to, when we have the money, or if we take a loan out. Nevertheless, the Holy Spirit showed me that to take out a loan for His work was never His will for me. To take a loan to do 'God's work,' when not called to, and then believe Him for the payments to be made, is not faith but foolishness. I have been called a few times to pray in thousands for those who have got themselves into debt whilst serving the Lord and every time God delivers them, they go and do the same thing. As long as we trust in our own incomes, or in what we can borrow, we are never truly the Holy Spirit's. I say again, "Where the Lord guides, the Lord provides," and as I say in slang, "No dough, no go!" Remember, God pays His own invoices, that which He commissions.

The apostles lived in simplicity enabling God's power and money to flow through them to others, and the prophets did the same (Mark 1:6, Luke 9:58). I was also led to live in simplicity and yet, the Lord also showed me that my sacrificial lifestyle was sometimes too austere and I had limited Him by my lack of faith.

Chapter Nineteen

Strongholds Broken

In May 1991, as directed by the Holy Spirit and after months of prayer, I was accompanied by my son to Cornwall, a county in England. As we were packing the car, I placed our tent in the boot (trunk) and the Holy Spirit said, "You will not need that." I replied in my heart, "I will take it just in case, you never know when you might need it." Of course, the Holy Spirit knew I would not need it. He was telling me to trust Him because He knows the future. My plan was to hire/rent a caravan from a farmer whom I had rented from in the past. When we arrived at the farm the man recognised us. I asked him if the caravan was available. "Sorry," he said, "we no longer use it." I thought to myself it was a good job I brought the tent, when the farmer continued, "What is available is my new Scandinavian style pine lodge and its brand new, never been used." It was a short-let holiday home and I thought it would be too expensive, but the Holy Spirit was reminding me not to limit Him. Suddenly the farmer said, "How long are you down here?" "Five days," I replied. "Give me £50 ($80)," he said, "is that ok?" The Lord provided for us wonderfully and it was still cheap!

The farmer and his wife invited us to their church celebration on the Saturday evening. At the meeting, I met a man who invited me to his home to share what I had learnt about prayer and intercession. We had a wonderful time of fellowship and on Sunday, I joined him at his local church. As they were taking up their tithes and offerings, I wondered to myself, how much I should put in. I thought about what others might say if I gave nothing or even a lot, and I realised that I was not going to give for the glory of God, but because of the pressure I felt from others. My true motive in giving was to be seen to be giving! Suddenly, the Holy Spirit said to me, "If I wish for you to give an offering here, I will provide it." I watched the offering plate come towards me and as I had nothing in my hand, I thought it will be interesting to see what happens next. Will the Spirit provide for me to give, or not? Suddenly, the man who invited me, without any expectation passed me some money and told me to put it on the offering plate! He knew nothing of what God had said to me and the lesson I learnt was simple. When we give, we must give to God alone and never to impress others, or be compelled by others to give, and this enables us to receive what we need to serve the Lord. 'So let each one give as he purposes in his heart, not grudgingly or of necessity; for God loves a cheerful giver. And God is able to make all grace abound toward you, that you, always having all sufficiency in all things, may have an abundance for every good work' (2 Corinthians 9:7-9).

A little later in the service I was moved by the Holy Spirit to speak out in tongues, and one of the leaders gave the interpretation. My new friend immediately looked at me and asked, "Why is it that the interpretation to your tongue came as a prophecy, instead of praise and adoration to God?" I replied, "You must ask the Holy Spirit" (1 Corinthians 14:6). This was the first time they had ever received a prophetic word, which began with tongues and it helped them take spiritual gifts more seriously (Acts 19:6).

The prophecy caused quite a stir in this church and at the end of the service, many leaders who were unhappy about the word surrounded me. The prophecy given concerned the importance of the leaders putting their house in order (1 Peter 4:17). As they portrayed their displeasure at the prophecy, I pointed out to them that it was one of their leaders who gave the interpretation and not me. Regardless of who gave the interpretation, they pressed me asking, "Do you believe the prophecy was correct?" I knew the answer immediately and then the Holy Spirit gave me something extra. "Oh, yes, and you will be in serious trouble if you do not remove the freemasons from the fellowship."

As Christians, we are only permitted to have supernatural fellowship with God, and our pledges and promises must be made to Him alone. We are to have no other gods before Him. Many Freemasons may be unaware that they are serving another spirit, when they make secret vows and partake of rituals before the 'Great Architect of the Universe.' Paul warns, we must not embrace another spirit (2 Corinthians 11:4), and all other spirits, which people serve are really demons (1 Corinthians 10:20-22), sent by Satan to keep people cursed and devoid of blessing from the true God. As Paul states, we cannot take the Lord's cup and the cup of demons; we must choose, repent and renounce the other!

In this church, I knew nothing of their problems with freemasons, but I was aware at this point that Christians who become freemasons are being led down a dark road, into confessions and rituals, which ultimately ends in glorifying demons (Revelation 9:20). The leaders in this church must have known of this sin because some boasted in confidence, "That's all been dealt with." Everyone began to listen and I replied by the Holy Spirit, "No, that's not been dealt with." Unhappy at this, they made it plain that I was no longer welcome and I left with one of the leaders who shared their surprise at what I said. As he tried to belittle the word, the Holy Spirit came upon me in power and I cried out from the car park (parking lot), back to the church giving a prophecy which was similar to all that had been said in the church. As the leaders were unwilling to receive the word the first time, the Holy Spirit chose to give it again with more power and gusto, so all could hear! What I always find strange concerning the Church's unwillingness to repent, is that our disobedience hinders the blessing and goodness of God reaching us! Why do we resist the God who wills our good and wants the very best for us?

The next day my son and I were sent to Boscastle, (a small village, very close to the sea), in Cornwall, where we were called to spend most of the day praying. Within the spiritual realm, I sensed that the enemy had a stronghold here and they even had a museum of witchcraft. The Holy Spirit led us to pray all over the area, and as He directed us we found secret areas of pagan worship, witchcraft and ancient demonic strongholds. The Holy Spirit would tell us to walk up a road, look over a fence or climb into an area, which was not permitted by the ordinance of a sign. This area had such a stronghold of witchcraft that was blocking out God's blessing and grace from reaching the people.

I believe God wanted the people of Boscastle to repent of seeking and honouring demonic powers, so He could bless them. Repentance is a choice we must make and if we do not, we shall reap what we sow. If people honour Satan, those same people do so at their own cost and lay a trap for their own feet. Thirteen years after we prayed around Boscastle, an unusual, localised and persistent flood swept through the centre of Boscastle, and caused much damage and destruction, which made national headlines. Some residents were winched to safety by rescue helicopters as it was the only means of escape. The museum itself was also damaged and many of its irreplaceable artefacts were washed out to sea! There are fourteen references in the Bible to the land being defiled and we are warned, that if we serve other gods to beware: 'Lest the land vomit you out also when you defile it...' (Leviticus 18:28a).

Through all of these experiences, the Holy Spirit was teaching me that there are only two sources of supernatural power being manifest on earth. God is the source of all good power, noticeable through the manifestation of the Holy Spirit, and Satan is the centre of all the other sources, because through them, people are kept from Christ's salvation. Satan will even use signs and wonders to keep people from Christ (Deuteronomy 13:13), and John saw evil spirits performing signs to keep people in darkness (Revelation 16:14). All witchcraft, tarot cards, horoscopes, mediums and the like, are all part of Satan's snare; but we have forgotten all this, as the laws banning witchcraft in England were repealed by parliament in 1953.

On the final day of our trip in Cornwall, we were told to go to Collinford Lake and the Holy Spirit made it very plain to me that we must do exactly what He said, as He led us up a narrow pathway with a bank of earth on one side, and Collinford Lake on the other. The bank of earth was high and there was a 'keep-off' sign, warning all to stay away. But the Holy Spirit said, "Climb up the bank." As we reached the top, we could clearly see a large stone circle, and the Holy Spirit told us to sing one of the Christian victory songs again and again. This was another stronghold of Satan in the area and Christ wanted to set the people free. As we continued to sing, we looked up at the sky and saw directly above us, the dense cloud cover started swirling! This is unusual in England and it appeared as if the battles of the spiritual realm spilt over into the natural realm, as the struggle threw the clouds into confusion. Then, in an instant, the cloud was torn apart and a shaft of sunlight blazed down upon the lake, as if it were a laser beam with a large circumference. This light was so bright that the water reflected the rays all over the lake and we were in no doubt that the spiritual battle was on, but we were on the winning side. Nonetheless, these were early days and we were still learning.

As a Christian, I was aware that Christians dedicate buildings and areas of land over to the Lord, often anointing them with oil, but only through my experiences was I beginning to be taught by the Holy Spirit the difference between holy consecrated land and demonic strongholds over buildings, villages, towns and cities (Ephesians 6:12). I learnt that defiled structures and buildings could be cleansed and territorial spirits over areas can be commanded to leave. All of this is clear in the Bible, but until the Holy Spirit makes it real, you just don't see it. Babylon was 'a habitation of demons' (Revelation 18:2), and Daniel saw two demonic strongholds called the 'prince of Persia and Greece' (Daniel 10:13, 20). Before Israel entered the Promised Land they were told that there were high places where demons were worshipped and they had to be completely removed (Deuteronomy 12:2-4), or there will be a curse on the land and people (Jeremiah 3:1-9). But as a word of caution, unless the Holy Spirit directs *you* to confront a stronghold over a geographical area, do not get involved, as you may bite off more than you can chew, and get yourself into trouble![1]

I was not aware of this at the time, but my trips around Britain over the subsequent two decades would concentrate on claiming and cleansing the land from demonic bondage, in preparation for a future move of the Holy Spirit. In past revivals and awakenings, it has become clear that moves of God have been restricted by unseen geographical boundaries in the spiritual realm, and these must be removed, *but* only as the Holy Spirit leads.

On my way home after all I experienced, I pondered all that had happened. We had witnessed a new level of spiritual warfare. Where was all this leading? I soon discovered it was to a home of intercession and spiritual warfare, the Bible College of Wales, in Britain, where many intercessors had reached the highest levels of spiritual warfare to bind the enemy and set the captives free!

Chapter Twenty

The College of Intercession

After the mission to Cornwall, life returned to the normal routines, when one day the Holy Spirit said, "Go to the Bible College of Wales." I wasted many weeks trying to work out what this meant and became frustrated, all because I was not listening, and tried to read more into this command than I should have. I was flustered by the thought of becoming a student again, sitting behind a desk at lectures for two-three years. As a practical man, academia is not where I flourish and the enemy used this struggle to rob me of my peace.

One thing I have learned the hard way, if you are not walking with your feet fitted with the readiness, which comes from the sandals of the gospel of peace, you will not hear the Holy Spirit's voice. He abides and speaks in peace. If you do not choose the path of peace, your mind will be in turmoil and you will no longer be standing firm with the belt of truth around your waist. In addition, your shield of faith, which can extinguish all the flaming arrows of the evil one, also drops. In such circumstances, you become a target for all the devil's lies, deceit and deceptive arrows that poison your mind. In this state of mind you become very vulnerable, just like a non-believer who has no helmet of salvation to protect his or her mind. Even the sword of the Spirit, which is the Word of God becomes a little hazy and with poisonous arrows in your breast, your righteous walk will also come under attack (Ephesians 6:11-20).

As I found, when you come under very severe attacks from the enemy, you may even lose the desire to pick up the sword of the Spirit, the Word of God, the Bible, and have no desire to pray in the Spirit. However, thank God for Jesus, who is sat at the right hand of God, interceding for us. With this in mind, the Holy Spirit knows the ones who are alert and will call them to pray for you (Ephesians 6:10-18). If deemed necessary, God may even dispatch angels, ministering spirits to help you (Daniel 10:2-13, Hebrews 1:14).

The Holy Spirit had told me to go to the Bible College of Wales (BCW), and it was that plain, that simple. I was told to visit, but the enemy, somehow or another convinced me I was to enrol as a student! Like the prodigal son, when I came to my senses, the first thing I did was to repent and ask the Lord's forgiveness. Shortly afterwards, I had an invitation from a friend who was a student at the College, to visit him and this was the confirmation I needed.

The Holy Spirit revealed to me that I was to invite this student to join me on my next trip which the Lord was sending me on. I went to pick him up at BCW and was thrilled to visit the Derwen Fawr Estate in Swansea, where Rees Howells used to live, and where his son, Samuel Rees Howells was continuing the ministry of worldwide intercession. In the early hours of the morning, I walked around these grounds where the Holy Spirit came to visit after Rees Howells presented the vision that all should surrender their lives to the Holy Spirit, so that every creature could hear the gospel.

Rees Howells had received the Every Creature Vision in the front room of Derwen Fawr House on Boxing Day (26 December) 1934. He explained that if they responded to the Holy Spirit's call, all who accepted would be bondservants for the rest of their lives to this one task – to intercede for every creature to hear the gospel, to serve those who went as missionaries, and to forever carry this living burden.

Intercession, for Rees Howells and the team he led was not ritualised prayer with little meaning, but it was targeted and specific as they abided in the Vine (John 15:1-11). They were led by the Holy Spirit to intercede on national and international levels concerning any situation which affected world evangelisation. As every creature had to hear the gospel, the doors had to be opened and kept open. In world events, their prayers became strategic and defined. Wherever the enemy used rogue governments or dictators to oppose the freedom to share the gospel with the unsaved, they had to intercede and become an army fighting on their knees in spiritual battles. They were to wrestle, not against flesh or blood, but against spiritual powers of darkness, principalities, powers, rulers of evil darkness and the host of demonic powers in the heavenlies. Paul used the word 'wrestle' because spiritual warfare can be a long drawn out battle of strengths between the Holy Spirit in His intercessors and the demonic strongholds who resist (Ephesians 6:12-13). Victory belongs to Christ, but the battle continues.

On my first day at BCW, I met Peggy Coulthard, who I believe was in her seventies. She walked across the Prayer Room in Derwen Fawr House smiling at me and clasped my hands, looked me straight in the eye and said, "Here stands a man that God can use." I was speechless. After all these years, my prayers had been answered. Stood before me was a woman full of the Holy Spirit. When she smiled, I could have been forgiven for thinking that she was a teenager. Eventually I said with emotion in my voice, "You are an answer to my prayers." I explained to her that I had pleaded with the Lord to meet someone truly filled with the Holy Spirit. She smiled gracefully and said, "It's not me, it's the Lord you see." As the apostle Paul wrote: 'But we all, with unveiled face, beholding as in a mirror the glory of the Lord, are being transformed into the same image from glory to glory, just as by the Spirit of the Lord' (2 Corinthians 3:18).

In my calling, I received a lot of opposition and have been called to give words to pastors and Christian leaders who refused to repent, or receive the word. The Lord would later honour me and some have been sent to me by the Holy Spirit to confess their sin, or to hear the word of the Lord, but it was terrible at the time. God said to Ezekiel, "So they come to you as people do, they sit before you as My people, and they hear your words, but they do not do them; for with their mouth they show much love, but their hearts pursue their own gain. Indeed you are to them as a very lovely song of one who has a pleasant voice and can play well on an instrument; for they hear your words, but they do not do them. And when this comes to pass – surely it will come – then they will know that a prophet has been among them" (Ezekiel 33:31-33).

During times of opposition, when I was a lone voice against the crowd, it could be very discouraging. In one situation I even prayed, "Lord they can't all be wrong, can they?" When the Lord showed me the life of Jeremiah, I knew I was not alone. A few times after a word or a prophecy I received was rejected by a pastor or an elder, the Holy Spirit would say,

"Don't worry, it's not you they are rejecting but Me." However it was hard for me not to be disappointed or even grieve (1 Samuel 16:1), because those who rejected God's will put themselves outside of His blessing, and for most, tragic events unfolded due to their disobedience and rebellion. Like Israel and Judah, many did not listen and were taken into captivity by the enemy, (read and study the books of Isaiah, Jeremiah and Ezekiel). Prophets can and still do bear heaven's burdens, I was told. Thankfully, some pastors and elders received these words, embraced them, made amends or whatever else they were called to do and bore much fruit for the glory of God.

Now I was visiting the Bible College founded by Rees Howells in 1924, the man who had inspired me to give my body to the Holy Spirit for His possession. Rees Howells had trained a team of intercessors, who had prayed through with him to victory during international crisis's leading up to the war, from 1936 and all the major battles of World War II (1939-1945) and beyond! These were men and women who knew what it meant to intercede and see the world bending to the prayers given by the Holy Spirit! After all the rejection and opposition I had received, I found myself welcomed by others who had walked a similar path.

Peggy Coulthard took me by the hand and led me to meet the other ladies, all who had been intercessors with Rees Howells and with his son Samuel. We had sweet fellowship. I have never met anyone like Peggy, who gave herself wholeheartedly to the Lord and was filled with His presence. Over the following years, I would visit the College from time to time and was able to sit at their feet, to listen and learn about the cost of spiritual warfare, and see what it meant to live as a temple of the Holy Spirit. For me, these times were priceless.

These dear ladies at the Bible College were not just Christians or even disciples, as I understand disciples to be. They were overcomers. Jesus said, "He who overcomes and keeps My will until the end, to him I will give authority over the nations" (Revelation 2:26). They surely had authority over the nations during the twentieth century.

All Christians are in different stages in their walk with God and in my estimation, there are basic church goers, committed believers, disciples and overcomers. The last are those who have surrendered *all* to the Lord, for Him to use their bodies and to live His life through them, and they have the victory in Christ. In the letters written to the seven churches in the book of Revelation, it is the overcomers who receive: The right to eat from the tree of life in paradise (Revelation 2:7), and they will not be hurt by the second death (Revelation 2:11). They will receive some of the hidden manna and a white stone with a new name on it (Revelation 2:17). They will be given authority over the nations (Revelation 2:26), and they will be dressed in white, their names will be in the Book of Life, as they are acknowledged by God the Father and His angels (Revelation 3:5-6). They will be pillars in the temple of God (Revelation 3:12), and will be given the right to sit with Jesus, just as He overcame and sat down with His Father (Revelation 3:21). Finally, when the Holy Spirit enters you as a Person, He will lead you to become an overcomer, to walk as Jesus did, and I believe just as Rees Howells and his intercessors did.

During my first visit, I was present when Dr. Priddy, a close friend of Rees Howells, led the College to pray during the Gulf War of 1990-1991. Saddam Hussein's army had invaded Kuwait and the College was given specific prayers to plead before the throne of God. This conflict, like all conflicts, has deep spiritual roots. Dr. Priddy, whilst leading the meeting quoted from Rees Howells' journals from World War II, telling his audience, including all the elderly ladies I had been speaking with, that they should pray as they had back then, for the allied forces to have a minimum of casualties. Their prayers were answered and are told in the book *Samuel Rees Howells: A Life of Intercession* by Richard Maton (2012).

My friend at the College also introduced me to one of the gardeners who shared with me how he had received a baptism of love some years before (Romans 5:5). "Do you mean the baptism of the Holy Spirit?" I inquired. "No," he replied, "this is something quite different." This was something new, which I had never heard of before. I thought about it and believed it to be real. Later I found that it was Scriptural and prayed to receive it myself. Paul testified: 'The love of God has been poured out in our hearts by the Holy Spirit who was given to us' (Romans 5:5). Some may ask, "Why did you need a baptism of love, because you already have the Holy Spirit living in you?" I would testify that He had come to live in me, but there were still times, when some people chose to be so difficult to deal with that I struggled to love them as Jesus did! This bothered me. I had a lack of compassion and because of this, compassion did not always flow as naturally as it should. As a young person, I had been a man's man and this made me strong, but it also made me appear harsh to some, and I wanted to surrender this area to the Lord and allow Him to fill it with His mercy instead.

My time at BCW was sweet and the last night before we set out on our trip, we attended an induction service for an Indian student to become a local pastor in Wales. Peggy informed me that the Holy Spirit told her that I was to accompany her and two of the other ladies, to sit with them during the service. They explained that this church could not afford to pay the pastor a wage, so he would have to live by faith, just as Rees Howells and his staff had and still were.

Early the next morning, the Holy Spirit told me to place £100 ($160) in an envelope and give it to this new pastor. I was a little concerned because I had already worked out how much this journey would cost and had prayed in all the money over many months. Yet, the Holy Spirit reminded me it was His money and my brother in Christ had a need of it *now*. As I walked across the grounds at BCW I saw him and he walked over, saying, "The Holy Spirit told me to give you a blessing towards your work. I'm sorry it's not a lot, but it is all I have." Wrapped in a piece of brown paper was £1 ($1.60). This was his first day as an unpaid pastor and he was called to give all the money he had to me! His gift reminded me of the widow's mite (Luke 21:1-4), but in return he received a hundredfold, just as Jesus said he would (Matthew 19:29).

I shall always cherish those times at BCW, especially with the elderly ladies, but Peggy's smile took me back all those years before to another lady, who smiled at me when I was a child and said, "Would you and your friends like some lemonade and biscuits?" and later we went to church with her.

Chapter Twenty-One

Onwards and Forwards

I left the Bible College of Wales with my friend, and the Holy Spirit led us to Bethlehem and Nazareth, villages in Wales, UK. We were asked to hold a Sunday service in one of the chapel's in Nazareth, but only five people turned up. The church was a traditional place, where faith had been projected onto rituals and because of this, attendance had dried up. My young student friend, following the teaching he had received, preached the gospel, following through with many quotes from Scripture and asked for a response. There was none. I pondered what should be done. These were religious people, but not born-again believers.

There was silence in the church and I stood up and spoke as God led me, "I know that I am going to heaven and I would be very sad if I do not see all of you in heaven too," I said. "Are you all born-again, as Jesus said you must be?" Then, instead of following a pattern or routine, which had been taught by men, I gave the testimony of my father-in-law, who had lived without Christ. Nevertheless, on his deathbed, I once again shared the gospel with him and prompted him to respond. He was unable to speak at the time, but I told him if he wanted to receive Jesus as his Lord and Saviour that he should squeeze my hand, and he did. Suddenly, a new light dawned on his face, as he accepted Christ and his eyes became wide open, as I believe he saw eternity. He was certainly converted and yet, I warned these people that they may not get the last minute chance as he did, and asked who would like to receive Jesus Christ as their Saviour and Lord. That evening, four out of the five people accepted Jesus' offer of new life, but the fifth person resisted, insisting that she had her own faith, and that faith was solely in her *Prayer Book*. We laid hands on the other four who had responded to receive the Holy Spirit. Later the Holy Spirit told me that He lit a fire there, which would never go out.

The Lord was guiding us and showed us that He could provide us with cheap accommodation, as another lesson of faith. One of the local shopkeeper's rented us a Welsh hillside cottage for just £5 ($8) a night! The following morning we continued on our journey towards Oban in Scotland, where we boarded a ferry to the Western Isles. We were unable to pre-book a place on the ferry, because we were on the Lord's time and did not know when we would arrive. Entering the ticket office, we were told there were no vacancies for three days, and all the standby places were taken!

I had been in such a situation before and my friend said, "What are we going to do?" There was only one thing to do, pray and trust God. The Holy Spirit then told me to ask the man on the quayside, 'What time can the cars begin queuing?' and to proceed in faith. We returned a few hours later and parked in a one of the standby lanes, which meant we could only board if called. When the ferry arrived we were the second car to drive on! We bought the ticket onboard and learnt that two articulated lorries had failed to turn up, freeing up space.

We travelled to one of the islands and went immediately to a Christian meeting. Everyday we held open house meetings, from morning through to late evening; where people dropped in, as and when they could. We shared the gospel and prayed for all who were bound by the devil.

After our meetings on the islands, we returned to the mainland and en route, we met a pastor who asked us to join him in door-to-door evangelism, and invited us to stay at his house as his guests. To conclude a fruitful period of evangelism we were asked to meet with his elders to pray. However, the elders were reluctant to meet us. My student friend decided the best way to deal with the situation was to pray aloud in tongues! This seemed to make the situation worse. With many cold shoulders, I was already looking forward to leaving when the Holy Spirit instructed me to pray that the church would be purged of witchcraft and freemasonry. The meeting was struck with silence and remained in this state for the next forty minutes or so. At the end of the meeting, one of the elders, who appeared to be in charge said to the pastor, "Perhaps you should pray to close the meeting."

On the way out, all the elders were unwilling to shake our hands and we returned to the car, by which time the pastor shared how angry he was. He shouted and asked what we thought we were doing, and demanded an explanation. I told him the truth concerning the church being bound with witchcraft and being run by freemasons, who without always knowing it, were serving evil spirits. He said, "But I have to face these men tomorrow!" The Holy Spirit came upon me and I prophesied, "Don't worry, in six weeks you won't have a church." In shock, he said, "Oh, just because you said so!" "No," I replied, "because the Holy Spirit told me and when it comes to pass, phone me and I'll help you." When we returned to his house the phone was ringing off the hook, and the pastor told one of the men on the other end of the line, "You're the third person to ring me tonight in great anger. Now let me ask you this simple question. If none of you are freemasons why has this situation caused so many problems?" The man went silent.

Once again, God was trying to purge His Church of all sin, witchcraft and demonic bondages, and as expected, the enemy did not want to leave without a fight! Up until this point, the pastor was a very kind and quiet man, who decided to turn a blind eye and get on with his ministry, but the Spirit would not allow this situation to continue. Six weeks after this event, I received a phone call from this pastor, "You were right," he said, he no longer had a church, and I replied, "No, the Holy Spirit was right."

Our trip continued as we made our way towards Scrabster, when I had a vision of a bridge with three arches. The Holy Spirit said nothing to me concerning what it meant. I shared the vision with my friend and suggested we keep our eyes open, to look out for it. There was only one road into Scrabster, which had a very sharp bend in it. As we travelled on this part of the road, we saw the three arches of a bridge that I had seen in the vision. Approaching the bridge, we slowed down to a crawl, as I wondered what was so important about this structure. Suddenly, I noticed a large dark demonic angel standing astride the bridge. I said to God in prayer in my heart, "What is that?" The Holy Spirit replied, "His name is unbelief. Rebuke him in Jesus' name and command Him to leave," and as I did so, he quickly disappeared.

This was again something new to me, and the best way I can explain is that for a time, I was given eyes to see, and when I commanded the demonic stronghold to leave, it did. My friend knew something had happened, but was unable to see what the Lord had shown me. Having shared with my friend, I asked the Holy Spirit to confirm to us both in a way we could understand, that what I just saw had really taken place. We drove over the bridge to the quay and waited for the ferry to come, and were approached by a man and two women. One of the women said, "Excuse me, are you two born-again Christians?" We told them that we were, and she said, "Would you please share with us how to become born-again!" This was as good a confirmation and explanation as any could ask for! Unbelief was gone and complete strangers asked us how to get saved! From this incident, I understood that the spirit of unbelief had gained a stronghold and influence over this community, but his authority came to an end when One stronger than he, the Holy Spirit, said his time was up.

In some Christian circles it has become fashionable to try to bind demonic strong men (plural of strong man) without the leading of the Holy Spirit and after all the noise has come to an end, nothing has changed. However, when the Lord leads you, and He does the work, God is able to move in and do something wonderful. The lesson is this: If you have a teachable spirit, the Holy Spirit will teach you, if you are willing to take the time and be obedient to all His leadings (John 14:26).

We took the ferry to the Orkney Isles and were kept busy travelling between the different islands. One night in a vision, I saw a road, with water on one side and a church on another. The following day, we came upon it and stopped. We went for a walk to discern why we had been led there, and saw a church building that had been converted into a home. Right next to the church was an ancient graveyard and the gate was locked. As we walked away the Holy Spirit said, "Go back and look over the wall." When we did so, we found that someone had mowed the grass around the headstones in a ceremonial circle. They had placed a circle of large standing stones in the graveyard and it was a coven, a gathering place for witches. I am not at liberty to share any further, but the Holy Spirit did lead us to deal with the situation.

Being a Christian can never be limited to going to church on Sundays. While much of the Church in Britain has been sleeping in the last few generations, playing at our weekly rituals, the devil has been very busy. Furthermore, witches and warlocks once excluded from our nation when it was committed to Christianity, have been very active, and have exercised power in Satan's name against the Church. Our refusal to learn how to be led by the Holy Spirit in spiritual warfare to defeat them has only empowered them and weakened believers who have not taken a stand.

These people only serve weak defeated demons, but they are empowered by an army who refuse to fight! Christians who live holy lives and are led by the Holy Spirit can see tremendous power released by the authority of Jesus Christ. The name of Jesus, the King of kings and Lord of lords, and the power of His blood is spiritual dynamite. There is nothing that can stop it. Previous generations knew and understood the power and efficacious of the blood of Jesus Christ (see the end of the chapter), but we have been asleep so long that much of the Church seems powerless. Did you know that some covens of witches send their women to churches to seduce the pastor or his elders? In addition, there is a spirit of Islam bringing strongholds from the east into the west. This is a spirit, not a religion, which is a power and a principality that seeks to break the power of Christianity (Daniel 10:13, 20). When did you last fast and pray about such powers?

After several days of prayer, as we were led by the Holy Spirit to claim the ground, we left the Orkney Isles and arrived on the Shetland Isles in the extreme north of Scotland. The Holy Spirit led us to hire/rent a caravan to use as our base camp. Months previously, I was told by the Lord to go to the Isle of Yell, which can be reached by a small passenger ferry, and walk to a small hamlet called Setter. As with many of the small islands, they do not have many named signs. I saw a man in the field turning the hay with a large wooden rake, we called out to him, "Are we in Setter?" and he replied, "Yes." He was pleased to see us because not many visitors came his way and he asked us what we were doing here. "Jesus has sent us," we exclaimed. Suddenly, this dear man poured out his heart to us. "Is there any hope for a poor sinner like me?" he asked. We shared the good news with him and invited him to kneel before God, in the hay with us. Right there, he repented for all his sins and pleaded with Jesus for forgiveness as he gave himself to the Lord. We were amazed at the length and breadth God would go to, to get us to reach one soul for Him. The Holy Spirit now had another temple to clean up and live in. As the Scriptures declare, "Whoever calls on the name of the Lord shall be saved" (Acts 2:21).

Never forget, all spiritual warfare exists for the purpose of making Jesus Christ known. We are led to cleanse the land and bind strong men, in order that people can hear and respond to the gospel message. This is the heart of the Every Creature Vision given to Rees Howells in 1934. Therefore, I am very troubled when I hear Christians say, "I am not called to be an evangelist," nor was pastor Timothy, but he still had to do the work of an evangelist! (2 Timothy 4:5). Peter stated, we must always be ready to share our testimony, to give a defence as to what we believe (1 Peter 3:15). All Christians are called to be disciples of the Lord Jesus Christ, and all disciples of Jesus have been commanded to, "Go into all the world and preach the gospel to every creature" (Matthew 28:19-20, Mark 16:15). You may not be called to go to the ends of the earth, but you must go and share with someone! You are Christ's light in your community!

As I pondered the conversion of the man in Setter, I realised that God so loved this one person that months before we departed, He spoke to me about Setter, on the island of Yell. He sent us from South Wales, all that way to meet a man working in his field who wanted to be saved, yet no one was willing, or able to tell him before! There was other work on the island, which included further claiming the ground and praying over places, which the Holy Spirit led us to, then we returned to the mainland and arrived in Aberdeen, Scotland. We had now been away for more than a month and my student friend would soon have to return to his studies for another year.

Nine Blood-Bought Privileges

1. We have been purchased by Jesus' blood (Acts 20:28). 'According to the law almost all things are purged with blood, and without the shedding of blood there is no remission [forgiveness]' (Hebrews 9:22).

2. We are at peace with God having been reconciled. 'By Him to reconcile all things to Himself, by Him, whether things on earth or things in heaven, having made peace through the blood of the cross' (Colossians 1:20).
3. We are brought near to God. 'In Christ Jesus you who were once far off have been made near by the blood of Christ' (Ephesians 2:13).
4. We can receive forgiveness of our sins. 'In Him we have redemption through His blood, the forgiveness of sins, according to the riches of His grace' (Ephesians 1:7).
5. We are justified (declared not guilty). '...Having now been justified by His blood, we shall be saved from wrath through Him' (Romans 5:9).
6. We are righteous. 'For if by the one man's [Adam's] offence death reigned through the one, much more those who receive abundance of grace and of the gift of righteousness will reign in life through the One, Jesus Christ' (Romans 5:17).
7. We are sanctified (made holy). 'Jesus also, that He might sanctify the people with His own blood, suffered outside the gate' (Hebrews 13:12). '...The blood of Jesus Christ His Son cleanses us from all sin' (1 John 1:7b).
8. We have access to the Holy Place, the throne room of God and access to the Father through Jesus the Mediator (in prayer). 'Brethren, having boldness to enter the Holiest by the blood of Jesus' (Hebrews 10:19).
9. Healing (for body, mind and soul). 'He was wounded for our transgression...by His stripes we are healed...It pleased the Lord to bruise Him...He bore the sins of many...' (Isaiah 53:5, 10, 12). 'He Himself took our infirmities and bore our sicknesses' (Matthew 8:17). 'Who Himself bore our sins in His own body on the tree...by whose stripes you were healed' (1 Peter 2:24).[1]

Chapter Twenty-Two

Prayers for Peace

Ireland is an island nation sat next to mainland Britain. Due to its closeness to Britain, there have been numerous wars and battles in history for English kings to control Ireland, and the entire island was ruled from London for years, often to its detriment. In the twentieth century, unrest grew and a desire for home rule reached its height. In 1921, independence was gained when 26 of 32 counties comprising the island voted for home rule, whilst eight counties voted to remain part of Britain. This division of the emerald isle led to The Troubles, as they are known, which began in the 1960s and resulted in more than 3,600 deaths. The key issue was the constitutional status of Northern Ireland and the relationship between the divided communities; the Unionists wanted to remain part of Britain and the Loyalists wanted a united Ireland. The subsequent decades of violence on the streets of Northern Ireland hardened the divide, and it spilt over onto the streets of England and even onto mainland Europe.

Like others, I had followed the troubles on the news, but had not thought about it as a spiritual conflict, as well as the practical one, but the Lord was to change this view. The years 1992-1993 turned out to be a very busy time for me, which was a time of prayer and fasting that ultimately led to me visiting Ireland, both north and south. I was told by the Holy Spirit that I must go on my own, starting at Belfast, where I was to hire/rent a car. I had to drive around the coast roads and circumnavigate all of Ireland. I had learnt a few lessons about spiritual warfare and claiming the ground in previous trips, but in Ireland, I received no special revelation. I had to allow the Holy Spirit to pray through me and follow His every leading.

I was also directed to Inishmore, part of the Aran Islands. As I drove, only the Holy Spirit knew what must be prayed, so I was told to pray in tongues, which I did for hours each day.

Whenever I felt led by the Lord, I had to stop and read out portions of Scripture, as a declaration of the Lord's power and sovereignty to the principalities and powers.

It took me seven days to complete the journey around Ireland and I returned home to England; however two months later, the Holy Spirit gave me two days notice that I must return to Ireland, and go to Belfast, the capital of Northern Ireland to continue the work. I had already been fasting and praying about my next trip, so I was already prepared. In almost every trip I had ever been on, I took another person with me, but when the Lord sent me to Ireland to intercede I had to go alone, and the same was true for Northern Ireland. The Holy Spirit told me that this trip, and the outcome, would have very little to do with me because it would be a work of the Holy Spirit.

The troubles in Ireland had been and were very severe and many had been called to pray and intercede about it. I learned by the Spirit that I would in a spiritual sense, be surfing into Ireland on the back of the prayers of others. Yes, I would be protected and guided because of the prayers and intercession of thousands of believers, around the clock, around the world. Because of the importance of this journey, I would be led every step of the way.

At the airport, when I checked-in to leave England for Northern Ireland, I had to go into a special room where police-security tried to find out what I would be doing visiting such a troubled spot. At one point, I was a little light hearted and the guard said, "Now don't get smart with me, this is very serious stuff." After this intense conversation, they put everything they could about me into their computer and I was allowed to fly to Belfast.

On my first day, the Holy Spirit spoke to me and forbade me from using the black taxis in Belfast. I did not know why, but later, a local man told me that they were forced to pay a tithe to an illegal organisation, who were very much involved in the Northern Ireland troubles. I was told to walk the streets and pray in tongues, and the Lord led me past all the buildings and organisations of significance. In front of all these buildings, including government ones, transport hubs, police, council, town hall and hospital etc., I would quietly stop and intercede. I spent five long days walking the streets of Belfast and the Holy

Spirit would pray through me. There was much groaning as I walked the streets of this divided city, in deep prayer and intercession (Romans 8:26-27). There is very little I can share about this time, apart from the fact that the Holy Spirit would lead me where to pray and He would do the praying.

My time in the Shankill and Falls area was very intense. This area was the fault-line of the tensions between the Catholics and Protestants and I found myself in the centre of the sectarian divide. As I walked through the streets praying in tongues, people would look out of their front doors and windows, wondering who this person was. On every corner, there was a soldier holding his gun, and bags were checked and overcoats had to be opened before you were permitted to enter into some shops. It was one of those situations where you never really knew who the people were and if they were being friendly, or searching for information. The Lord told me clearly that I must always return to my hotel before it got dark. A few people asked why I was there, and one said, "I know that accent, you're a Canadian!" I smiled and continued my ministry, despite the fact that I was very afraid, and the Lord used my weaknesses for Him to be strong in me (1 Corinthians 1:27-30).

These five very long and costly days of intercession culminated on the last day when I went to Stormont, the parliament building of Northern Ireland to pray and prophesy for peace. I boarded a bus in Belfast city centre for Stormont, but I was told that because of the terrorism threat, only those with an official pass could enter the Stormont grounds, which led up to the parliament. The bus driver asked to see my official pass and I told him I did not have one. He stated I would have to leave the bus when we arrived at the gates of Stormont. As I did not have all the paperwork I needed, he asked me to sit on the seat closest to him. As we pulled up to the gates at Stormont, the bus stopped and the driver told his passengers to get off.

I knew the Lord wanted me to go up to Stormont Parliament to lay hands on the building and pray for peace, so I continued to sit on the bus without paying any attention to what the driver said. In deadlock, the armed security guard came onto the bus to search for bombs. By now, everybody else had left the bus, so I was the only person who needed his pass checked. "Can I see your pass please?" asked the armed security guard. "I'm sorry, I don't have one," I replied. He had a look of shock on his face and went to the driver and said, "How did he get a ticket on this bus, without a pass?" They talked it through and he came back to search the bus again. Then the security guard said to me, "I know where you're from, you're from Northfolk." I certainly wasn't from anywhere near that region, but I wasn't going to argue and just smiled at him. Then the guard said to the driver, "Drive on," and the driver's jaw dropped in shock. I said with a smile and a joke, as if I was in charge, "Ok driver!"

As we drove into the Stormont grounds the Holy Spirit said to me, "I want you to pray all around that building in tongues." What I did not know until later, was that the British prime minister was flying into Stormont that day and because of this, security was tightened. The bus drove closer to the building and the driver said to me, "Whatever happens now, you must get off at the next checkpoint, because you are not allowed to go around the back of the building. Only I'm allowed to go round the back. The guards must be able to see you at all times and when I return, I will pick you up by the side."

As we drove closer, we came to another checkpoint and the guard asked to see my official pass. Having learned that I had no official documentation to give me permission to enter the grounds, the guard interrogated the driver, asking what was going on. "What's he doing down here?" he exclaimed. "You know he has no right to be here! He's got no pass. What were you thinking man? You know he can't come down here. You know it!" The driver, under pressure said, "The first guard said, 'drive on,' and I have to obey his official instructions, and so I did." The second guard said, "You know its not official procedure; it's not right. But, well, if he's let you through it must be ok. Ok, go on." The driver looked at me in disbelief again, because I had already been told that I must get off at this point, and so I said jokingly, "Ok driver. I'm with you!"

The driver took the bus all around the building and I prayed in tongues as the Lord told me. The driver told me that I only had one hour and a half and he would return. He said, "At all times you must stay where the guard can see you. On no account are you to ever go up those steps towards the building or go near to it." Yet, I already knew that the Holy Spirit told me I had to lay hands on the building to pray.

The bus left and as I walked around, I noticed the guard kept walking out to see where I was, and then he returned to his hut and disappeared for a while. So quickly, I walked up the steps where I had been forbidden and laid hands on the main entrance to the building. I stood leaning on the pillars of the front door praying in tongues, which must have been an unusual sight to anyone looking for suspicious activity. After completing my commission, I walked back down the steps to the 'safe area' and just at that moment, the guard walked out.

That evening I returned by bus to Belfast and packed my bags to return home. As I explained before, this journey was one of the rare occasions when I was sent out on my own. The reason for this, I believe, was that my mind had to be truly focused on the Holy Spirit and tuned into His will. I needed this extra sensitivity because had there been two of us, much time would have been wasted talking about nothing. The Holy Spirit can be very strict about such things. To protect me from pride, I was allowed by Him to be nervous, as I walked into the red-hot areas of conflict and with armed soldiers around, which I was not used to. In addition, someone who I later learned was a tare was doing all they could to discourage me. The Holy Spirit allowed all this for my protection.

As the Holy Spirit sent me out to pray and guided me in such a miraculous manner, I knew something had happened; but what, I knew not. Though there were many political and practical reasons for the troubles, there are also higher spiritual battles that influence conflicts. As I was soon to learn, one of the battles the Holy Spirit can wage is to cast down arguments and strongholds in people's minds, which are contrary to the peace and will of God (2 Corinthians 10:5). Therefore, millions around the world were thrilled to see the prayers of many answered, when the 10 April 1998 Good Friday Agreement brought peace to Northern Ireland. Certainly, there was a reason the Lord allowed the talks to be concluded on Good Friday, the day we remember the crucifixion of our Lord.

Life as I knew it with the Holy Spirit would continue in similar patterns for well over the subsequent two decades as I would be sent on numerous trips, with at least one each year, to claim the ground and serve the Lord from Land's End in the most south-eastern part of Britain, to John' O Groats in Scotland. I was sent to cities, towns and numerous villages all over Britain. In fact, there are very few places in Britain where I have not travelled to, or at least been very close to. I was also sent to the islands of Britain, from the Scilly Isles, and Channel Islands near France, to the Inner and Outer Hebrides in Scotland, and Lundi Island in the Bristol Channel. Some Islands like Barra or the Isle of Man, I spent a week on, others would only take one day, but all as led by the Holy Spirit.

This long season of travel in the Lord's service, claiming the ground and working with the Holy Spirit on the road culminated in 2004 when I was told to go to the heart of the British nation, to pray and prophesy as the Holy Spirit led me. After seeking the Lord, I received a prophetic word, which made reference to the heart being at the centre of man. I searched and discovered that the centre of mainland Britain, taking into account the islands, is in Lancashire, England. It is also very near the farm where the film *Whistle Down the Wind* was made. This film, concerning a group of children who are convinced that a man in hiding is Jesus Christ, made a huge impact on my life as a child, as you may remember from earlier chapters.

One day I was reading a booklet and found an advertisement for a farm in Lancashire, which claimed that their village, called Dunsop Bridge was the exact centre of Britain! This was the heart of the nation! The Holy Spirit told me to make a booking and when we arrived, we discovered the farm we were staying on is part of the Duchy of Lancashire. This is the land, which belongs to Queen Elizabeth II, who has the official title as Supreme Governor of the Church of England and the Defender of the Faith. In 1953, with sincere personal conviction, Queen Elizabeth II vowed in her Coronation Oath, "To uphold to the utmost of my power, the laws of God within this realm and the true profession of the Christian faith." We were now in the centre of the nation, but the Lord wanted us to go to the exact centre! In this village, I could not receive any signal on my mobile/cell phone, so we walked down to the heart of the village to search for a public phone box. There was nothing unusual in this, or so I thought!

It was Sunday, 6 June 2004, Trinity Sunday and the sixtieth anniversary of D-Day. As I write this today, it is the same day, but it is now the seventieth anniversary of D-Day! Surely, this is not just another coincidence. We walked to the phone box and engraved upon it is this: 'This phone box marks the exact centre of Great Britain and the 401 associated islands. As supplied by The Ordinance Survey.' Here we were, at the heart of the nation! After two decades of prayer, intercession and claiming the ground, the Lord led me to pray and prophesy, with full assurance, that the ground had been claimed for the time to come when God's people will meet the conditions for revival to flow from heaven (2 Chronicles 7:14).

We spent some considerable time there in prayer and prophesied as the Lord led us. We left with the assurance that a Christian revival/awakening would come and that God's D-Day for the nations would come. The Holy Spirit, in His timing, will find the men and women who will meet His conditions for an awakening to take place again, as they cry out, "Oh, that You would rend the heavens! That You would come down! That the mountains might shake at Your presence, as fire burns brushwood, as fire causes water to boil, to make Your name known to Your adversaries, that the nations may tremble at Your presence!" (Isaiah 64:1-2).

This was not to be the last trip that the Lord sent me on, but now as I look back, I see that it completed the job of claiming the ground, which the Lord called me to on my first trip in 1989, a fifteen year task. I also know that many others have done similar things and are also expecting a Christian revival to come. Jesus said, "If you abide in Me, and My words abide in you, you will ask what you desire, and it shall be done for you" (John 15:7-8). I don't think we are waiting on God to move anymore, He is waiting upon His Church to pray Him down, as they meet all the conditions for Him to come again. 'After two days He will revive us; on the third day He will raise us up, that we may live in His sight. Let us know, let us pursue the knowledge of the Lord. His going forth is established as the morning; He will come to us like the rain, like the latter and former rain to the earth' (Hosea 6:2-3).[1]

Chapter Twenty-Three

The Second D-Day

In the late 1980s, the Holy Spirit had told me that revival, (which I saw in a vision), would begin in Scotland and flow south, cross the Channel and flow into mainland Europe; so it came as no surprise when I was sent to France to help prepare the way for the Spirit's outpouring on the other side of the Channel. Of course, the last days outpouring of the Holy Spirit will probably breakout in many areas of the world simultaneously, but I can only share with you, what the Holy Spirit showed me in His vision.

When I asked the Lord why I should go to France, He told me by the Holy Spirit to go to Normandy, in northwestern France, to pray over the D-Day landing beaches, where tens of thousands of men from Britain, America, Canada and other Allied nations died to liberate Europe from the Nazi regime. These Allied soldiers were heroes who had died in the cause of liberty whilst there were many other soldiers, deceived by demonic spirits operating through Hitler, who had also died because of the sins of their nation, with its antichrist leadership.

For me, this journey turned out to be a very emotional time, as the Holy Spirit in me grieved for the pain, sorrow and loss of life that the devil had orchestrated, with the express intent to delay the fulfilment of the Every Creature Commission and the Lord's second coming. Satan knew that in war, the doors to world evangelism are often closed and money would be tight, making it harder to support missionary endeavour. He could also take many lives before they responded to the good news of the gospel.

As I walked slowly across the D-Day beaches in intercession, there were times that the burden was so great that I would fall to my knees, as if heartbroken. The pain of pouring out my heart in repentance for the loss of life, and the sins of the war on all sides was overwhelming. Day-by-day, I walked all the beaches, repenting, claiming the ground and praying in the Holy Spirit. On the last day, I visited the American war graves in Normandy, which numbered almost ten thousand. These men and millions of others during this conflict, laid down their lives, so we could live in freedom. Forever etched in my memory is the seemly endless row upon row of white crosses.

In all my prayers, the Holy Spirit interceded as He chose, and in many ways, I was not always aware in my understanding what the Lord was doing; but I do believe my repentance had much to do with cleansing the land from the loss of lives. There was so much innocent blood shed in the war, especially on these D-Day beaches and it had defiled the land. 'You shall not pollute the land where you are; for blood defiles the land' (Numbers 35:33). This principle is repeated in Scripture (Deuteronomy 21:1-9, 1 Kings 2:32, 1 Chronicles 22:8, Revelation 6:10).

As I write this, we have just remembered the seventieth anniversary of the D-Day landings and the sacrifice of these men. This is a very important thing to do, and yet I wondered how could we, in this generation, still forget what it cost our Lord and Saviour, when He was nailed to a cross for our liberation from sin and Satan? (1 John 3:8). Jesus laid down His life for all of mankind and one day, we will all stand before the Lord God to give an account for our lives, and He may ask, "What did *you* lay down for Me?" (Revelation 20:12). The Lord's good, pleasing and perfect will is for you to be transformed into the image of Jesus Christ, and walk in the light as He is in the light. Without the Holy Spirit in us, we will all fail to achieve this (Romans 8:29, 1 John 1:5-10).

I spent five days praying on the D-Day beaches and I was led to visit every beach, where I prayed as the Holy Spirit guided me. It is not easy to understand the way the loss of innocent life has a profound negative influence on our land, and only in the spiritual realm are we able to understand how this loss pollutes the nations; but this is a principle of God and repentance must be made, as the Holy Spirit leads (Genesis 4:10, Deuteronomy 21:1-9, Jeremiah 22:13-19, Ezekiel 9:9). When my commission was complete and I had returned home, I wondered what had been achieved. The Holy Spirit explained, "The D-Day landings was the beginning of the physical deliverance of Europe, but the next one will be spiritual."

I was not fully aware of all the Holy Spirit had been doing through me in prayer and was surprised when He sent me back to France again to intercede. This time, I was sent to the region of the Somme, where so many laid down their lives during World War One (1914-1918). I was sent to many of the great battle sites, memorials and to the war cemeteries. In addition, the Lord specifically told me to go to Crucifix Corner. I was led to pray in tongues and repent for the sins and the crime of war itself. So much innocent blood was shed because of the sins of the few in power. Twenty-four times in the Bible, shedding innocent blood is mentioned and fourteen times the Scriptures mention the defilement of the land (Leviticus 18:24-29, Jeremiah 22:7, Ezekiel 36:17-18).

My visit was in the summertime and there were fields of glorious sunflowers. The Holy Spirit showed me that my intercessions, along with many others, were preparing the way for Holy Spirit revival to flood from Scotland, into the rest of Britain and over onto the Continent.

On one of the trips, the Lord God sent me on the ferry in the south west of England to France, yet the next time, He forbade me to go any other route other than via the Channel Tunnel in the south east. Through this, the Lord showed me that His move of the Spirit leading to a spiritual awakening would flood into Europe, like a pincer movement, one from the East and one from the West of England over into Europe. This would be the second D-Day landings, but this time it would be the Holy Spirit flooding over, a Divine Armada.

Through these visits to France, the Holy Spirit was showing me the true cost of the two World Wars, in lives lost and in shattered hopes of those who lived on, then He showed me the eternal cost of those who lives were cut-short without accepting Jesus Christ as their Saviour and Lord. This is the unseen eternal cost. The Lord's great desire is for *all* to hear and be saved (1 Timothy 2:4). The Holy Spirit showed me that there was a price to be paid, a heavy cost, in intercession and spiritual warfare to see demonic strongholds bound in preparation for the second D-Day of a spiritual awakening.

World War One was known as the Great War; one thing was sure, great numbers of men died and only the Lord knows how many of them were lost forever. Some never had a chance or eternal hope of survival and neither do we without Christ, because our hope is in heaven, in Jesus Christ. Today, many believe that the greatest outpouring of the Holy Spirit is still to come, leading up into the end times as Joel prophesied (Joel 2:28-30), but in the meantime the spiritual war continues and millions go to a lost eternity. For many, hell is the truth seen too late, but each one of us is in a position to warn someone.

Chapter Twenty-Four

Unconditional Love

My trips to France were in preparation for the future, as the Lord led me deeper into a hidden life of intercession. But first, I was to learn to love the unlovable ones, with His unconditional love, because our spiritual victories can only be proved viable by the practical victories we have experienced in our daily lives. Consequently, over a period of about a year, I was introduced to many individuals who were homeless, whom I was called to help (James 1:27). Some refused all offers of help and others received all I offered.

Jesus said, "Then the King will say to those on His right hand, 'Come, you blessed of My Father, inherit the Kingdom prepared for you from the foundation of the world: for I was hungry and you gave Me food; I was thirsty and you gave Me drink; I was a stranger and you took Me in; I was naked and you clothed Me; I was sick and you visited Me; I was in prison and you came to Me.' "Then the righteous will answer Him, saying, 'Lord, when did we see You hungry and feed You, or thirsty and give You drink? When did we see You a stranger and take You in, or naked and clothe You? Or when did we see You sick, or in prison, and come to You?" And the King will answer and say to them, 'Assuredly, I say to you, inasmuch as you did it to one of the least of these My brethren, you did it to Me' " (Matthew 25:34-40).

One Sunday I had a Divine appointment with a tramp, a homeless man who walked from town to town during the year. He had walked from Manchester, in the north of England, and was on his way to London, in the south east. He had been living on the streets for eight years and had a routine of travelling to various parts of the nation, and when he came to my home town, the Lord decided to introduce me to him. Seeing his need, I invited him home for a wash, a meal and a change of clothes. Very few people ever talked with him, but as God showed me how to love him practically, he explained that his wife had had an affair with his best friend, and he turned to drink. This made him lose his job and his children were taken into care. He had lost all hope and I did my best to help him, but was it possible that all my motives were still wrong? There is a certain amount of pride in being the helper, instead of the helped, and the Holy Spirit showed me that I was unable to love him, in a pure selfless way, like Jesus.

After helping this man, I was led to a married couple with two children who were struggling. They had trodden a downward spiralling path into mental health issues and their home and garden was a terrible mess. I felt very sorry for them and did all I could to help them which continued for some years. However, I found the more I helped, the more ungrateful they appeared to be. I was very keen to help them, pray with them, give them Scriptural and prophetic guidance as the Spirit led me, but for some reason they were unwilling to help themselves, by taking the steps that the Lord showed them to get free.

These lost people, some homeless, helpless or hopeless were led my way by the Lord over many years. I would see them as I travelled, or shopped or wherever I went. 'Do not set your mind on high things, but associate with the humble' (Romans 12:16). In one sense, over the years I saw more of Christ in them than in some Christians I knew (Matthew 25:37-40). I am convinced one of these homeless men was an angel, because of his deep blue eyes, otherworldly stare and his need of nothing I could offer. 'Do not forget to entertain strangers, for by so doing some have unwittingly entertained angels' (Hebrews 13:2-3).

For many years, the Lord brought the outcasts, the homeless and the lowliest in society to my attention and after time, it became a struggle, when people accepted my help and returned for more, yet refused to help themselves. However, through this the Holy Spirit showed me the limits of my love. There seemed to be a never-ending stream of needs and I began to start avoiding some people whom I knew would try to consume much of my time, yet *refuse* to do their bit (Luke 16:10, 2 Timothy 3:7). Through my resistance to continually help them, the Holy Spirit showed me that my care and Christian love was conditional.

The Holy Spirit was trying to change my self-centred nature for His selfless giving nature. The Lord Jesus told us to love our enemies (Matthew 5:44), yet I was struggling to love friendly people whose needs seemed endless. I realised how limited my own love was and began to pray to receive a baptism of love, just like the man at the Bible College of Wales. I prayed for two years for the Holy Spirit to baptise me with His love, and replace my limited love with His unlimited mercy, and my prayer was answered unexpectedly when God sent me to South Africa.

Apartheid was the official government policy of racial segregation in South Africa, which led to white people being in charge and control of practically everything. Two years after this unjust system collapsed in 1994, and as the nation was on its first steps on the path towards seeking equality, I arrived in South Africa knowing not a single person.

My son came with me and as we sat in a café in Johannesburg, a black African man entered the establishment and placed an order. When I looked at him, the Holy Spirit told me to invite him to join us at our table. His name was Philemon and after explaining why I asked him to join us, he told us he was born-again. The Lord prompted me to say, "Have you received the baptism of the Holy Spirit?" He said, "No," and as he sat down at our table, we raised our hands and prayed, "Receive." He looked like he received a cold shower as the Holy Spirit came upon him and he shivered in joy. Thrilled with this new experience of God he asked for our contact details, but we had no pen. Another black man was watching and Philemon went to him, asking for a pen, and this man wanted to know what had just happened to him.

Philemon had to rush off to work and the man he spoke to came over saying, "Hi, my name is Daniel, I'm a saver of souls," as he slapped the bottom of his shoe and said, "Not soles!" Then he added, "I hear a great prophet of the Lord has come to South Africa," which I felt was taking it too far, but Philemon's testimony must have had a great impact upon him, because he decided to ask his boss for the night off from his work, so he could be with us. He pleaded with us to wait for him, as he sought permission and he soon returned with authorised leave of absence.

Daniel introduced us to some of his friends in one of their homes and the woman of the house invited us to a meeting in a few days time. Suddenly, the Holy Spirit came upon me in power, and I began prophesying beyond my control. Her husband was present and I said in a loud powerful voice, "What's the matter with you man? You keep gambling away the rent money! When are you going to take your responsibilities as a husband seriously? The only person you are fooling is yourself! You think I don't know when the pastor walks in the front door, you slip out the back? I know everything, I see everything." As the words and many more came out of my mouth by the power of the Holy Spirit, in my mind I was thinking, "I hope this is all right!" I was not in control and I knew nothing of the character and behaviour of this man. I was a stranger in this man's home and as I prophesied this man's wife looked on in astonishment and said, "You must have been living in my house to know all this," and she turned to her husband and said, "You've had it this time, God has caught you red-handed!" The Holy Spirit had not finished with this man, and I forcefully said, "By the time I return to this house (to take the meeting, which I had been invited to), you'd better repent, and put your life right with God, or you will be in deep trouble with the Lord!"

On the following day Daniel introduced us to Priscilla, who invited us to her house-church one evening to minister. My son and I were the only white people present, and these black Africans had suffered terrible and absolute discrimination by other white people during Apartheid, which had only recently ended. As I began to speak, I saw that a spiritual barrier had arisen in the minds of many of these women, because of the miserable way they had been treated by white people. I knew by the Holy Spirit that they could not receive the word I was to give because of the race divide in the nation, and so I asked the Holy Spirit what I should do. He said, "Go and kneel down in front of them and ask them to forgive you, for the harsh treatment they had received under the rule of your white European forefathers." The Scripture states: 'Go and humble yourself' (Proverbs 6:3), and when I did this, the strong man in the spiritual realm and in the hearts of these people was bound, and they forgave me, and a spirit of unity prevailed.

The atmosphere changed and suddenly the Holy Spirit moved and took the floor through me. I was led to offer to pray for all present and everyone responded. I was given a word of knowledge that there was a woman present who had been sexually abused by her male family members, and I asked the female leader of the group to stand with me, as I discreetly shared this with the woman I received the word for. As I shared, the female leader looked with astonishment that I was quietly dealing with this and said, "They've all been abused." I had no idea that sexual abuse was so prevalent and deemed acceptable by so many men in South Africa.

I was shocked by this revelation and felt the compassion of the Holy Spirit for all these women who had been abused. Now as I understood the situation, I told them that the doorway to deliverance and freedom was to forgive, as the enemy uses our unforgiveness to keep us bound (Matthew 18:28-35). The "torturers" which Jesus spoke about in verse 34, are evil spirits empowered by our unwillingness to obey the Lord's command to forgive, who come to steal our peace, joy and love, and torture our minds in bitterness with the memories of all the bad things that happened to us, and embitter us, as we think of what we would like to do to those who have wronged us.

I knew the Holy Spirit wanted all these women to be healed and I asked if they were willing to find grace in their hearts to forgive these men for their sinful abuse, and all responded in the affirmative. Together, the Holy Spirit moved upon them as they chose as one, to publicly forgive their abusers. The Holy Spirit moved in power and healed them of their horrific memories and I too was touched deeply by their tears, and the demons of abuse, shame and hurt left them, as they received freedom in Christ.

As I rejoiced at the freedom these women received, the Holy Spirit also showed me that I had built a wall around my inner man, to protect myself emotionally from the struggles and pains of life. This wall was built to keep pain out, but it had also hindered the work of the Holy Spirit to heal me from the years of abuse from my childhood, and this stronghold in my life collapsed too, because of the humility of these women. If they were prepared to humble themselves to be free, so was I!

Chapter Twenty-Five

A Baptism of Love

The following day in South Africa, we returned to the home of the gambling man, whom the Holy Spirit had rebuked through me. Initially he had joked and laughed the day before, but now after thinking about it, he said he was willing to put things right with God. I realised that this type of man could not be reached with a kind, gentle message of love, and this was the reason the Spirit rebuked him. In this context, I reminded him that dealing with God is not a game and it is a very serious: 'For our God is a consuming fire' (Hebrews 12:29). I told him if he was serious, he must get on his knees and repent. I was amazed as this hardened man fell to his knees in repentance before God, weeping and pleading for forgiveness. Then he asked his wife to forgive him and cried out to the Lord to help him be a better husband.

On the way to this meeting, I had seen a plaque in a shop, which stated: 'Those who pray together stay together,' and the Lord told me to buy it. Now I knew, this was the couple who should receive it, as a reminder and testimony to this day of repentance and restoration. This experience was important, because the next day they had to leave their home, because he had indeed gambled the rent money away.

There was also a young man present who asked for prayer and when I laid hands on him, he fell to the ground and lay motionless. The Holy Spirit then gave me an instruction, which I had never received before or since. He was laying still on the ground when the Holy Spirit said, "Cast your shadow over him and he will be healed." This was a big test of faith for me (Acts 5:15). I hesitated as I thought about this, when the Lord told me to fully explain to those present what I was going to do and why! All the people were watching and the man had his eyes closed, so there was no way that he could see what was happening. Additionally, we were indoors, so I had to search for the light source, a single bulb hanging down on a wire then

I had to find where my shadow was in relation to the light. I thought to myself, 'I don't even know what is wrong with this young man,' and the Holy Spirit told me to stop thinking about it and hesitating, as He said, "Do it and leave immediately." As my shadow went over his body (from his ankles upwards), he trembled as God touched him and after a short explanation, we left as God told us to. The Lord was showing me anew that if you are going to walk in this kind of anointing, you have to be completely obedient to Him every step of the way, even if He says, "Leave now!" This is what happened to Phillip the evangelist during the revival at Samaria, great things were happening, then he was told to leave and go into the desert (Acts 8:5-40).

South Africa was still very much in times of deep trouble, crime was exploding in the city centres and the streets were not safe in many areas, and yet on our visit, the Lord had protected us every step of the way. There were places we had been to which were no-go areas and we did not even know it. Whenever we left our hotel, a staff member gave us warnings about the dangers of being white people in a difficult area, and warned us not to go here or there, do not wear any jewellery, no rings, no watches, do not wear any fancy clothes and take no money with you! On the first day they advised us not to walk around outside. We informed the manager that we had a hire/rental car. Don't go out in that she stated, "When you need to go somewhere, tell us and we will order you a taxi, and the same taxi will bring you back at a designated time." This was during a time of major carjacking and a number of tourists had been killed, whilst the other related advice was, "Do not stop for anybody, do not pick anybody up, if there is somebody lying in the road blocking it, do not stop, (you will probably be mugged or shot), just drive over them!" We did use our hire car and thankfully, we did not come across anybody lying in the road.

Towards the end of our trip to South Africa, a black pastor warned us, "I advise you never to go into the park (this was near our hotel), you will certainly be mugged. Even I and many others refuse to go in there, I have been mugged there." We smiled at him and said, "We've been in that park everyday and no-one has ever come near us!" The Lord had protected us on this journey and we did not even know it! However, on one occasion, when we were on foot, the Holy Spirit informed us not to return on the same road that we walked up. On our way to the airport, I was excited, thrilled and overjoyed at all the Lord had achieved in South Africa.

Our eleven-hour night flight home was to be a time of sleep, but when I saw the woman sat next to me the Holy Spirit said, "Rejection." She was the first to speak to me and after pleasantries, I asked, "How long have you suffered from rejection?" Tears welled up and she replied, "How do you know?" I explained that the Holy Spirit had revealed it. "Do you mean God?" she inquired. "Yes," I said and she told me that a few days before this journey, she had been jilted by her fiancée just days before her wedding and was heading to London, to spend a few days with her friend. "In the hope of finding God," she said. "God has already found you!" I explained, as I shared the gospel and I left her to the Holy Spirit.

After many hours of the night flight, most people were sleeping and my two years of prayer for a baptism of love were suddenly answered. For hour after hour, as I sat in the seat, wedged in where I could not get away, I was flooded with God's love, '...The love of God has been poured out in our hearts by the Holy Spirit who was given us' (Romans 5:5). I began to sob inaudibly, as I broke-up on the inside and His Divine love flooded in. I can only explain what I felt was like liquid love, breaking down all the inner walls and defences; it was a holy love, so pure that it touched every part of me. It was not a gifting or empowering, this was a melting. The cold hard interior, sometimes like ice, melted away before God's presence. I felt transparent and vulnerable before the Lord God. I was afraid and overwhelmed by the Holy Spirit. I wanted to say, "That's enough," but I was unable to. It came in waves, until I felt transformed, renewed and this was my own personal revival to be more Christ-like. My limited love was now flooded by His limitlessness.

God is love and in 1 Corinthians 13 Paul explains what love truly is. The entire chapter is filled with wisdom and is worthy of diligent study. 'Love suffers long and is kind; love does not envy; love does not parade itself, is not puffed up; does not behave rudely, does not seek its own, is not provoked, thinks no evil; does not rejoice in iniquity, but rejoices in the truth; bears all things, believes all things, hopes all things, endures all things. Love never fails' (1 Corinthians 13:4-8).

All the fruit of the Holy Spirit – love, joy, peace, patience, kindness, goodness and self-control, all spring forth from His love (Galatians 5:22-23). In the past, I had relied on being strong and tough, warring in my own strength, but now the Holy Spirit taught me in a deeper way, that true spiritual warfare cannot be fought in the flesh, but only in the Holy Spirit through love. This lesson would be very important in the future, especially as the Lord showed me how many tares the enemy has sown amongst His people, in places you would never expect, just as Jesus taught (Matthew 13:24-30). I soon learnt that when you come face to face with a tare, what's in them, evil spirits, will recognise the Holy Spirit in you and will hate you for being God's channel. These evil spirits will hate you with a passion and may growl and threaten you. The natural response is to deal with the problem in the natural realm and hate them in return, but if you retaliate in the flesh, you will be defeated before you have even started. 'For though we walk in the flesh, we do not war according to the flesh. For the weapons of our warfare are not carnal but mighty in God for pulling down strongholds' (2 Corinthians 10:3-4). I share more on this later.

The experience of the flooding of the Holy Spirit into my life in a fresh way transformed me deep within. So many people have been touched by the Holy Spirit within church buildings and at house groups and laid on the floor in His presence, yet returned home the same; this was not the case with this encounter. He purged me deep within and changed my nature from the fleshly and carnal responses, towards being closer to what the Lord wants. When we landed at Heathrow airport in London, England, God's love had so changed me that I was still sobbing and unable to speak to my wife on the phone. She asked our son, "What's the matter?" My son replied, "I'm not sure, he slept most of the time." I was trembling for hours and unable to speak without whimpering or crying. This was all a part of God's good, pleasing and perfect will, as He led me deeper into intercession.

Chapter Twenty-Six

Intercession

From the day the Holy Spirit came to abide in me in 1989, He made it very plain that intercession was not prayer, as I understood it. Over the years I began to understand that intercession was always at the centre of all that the Holy Spirit led me into. I also noticed that very few people in our churches know or appreciate the difference between prayer and intercession. Prayer usually involves people telling God what they want, feel or think. Prayer often begins and ends with us trying to tell God what is the best thing we think He should do in any situation. Intercession is the opposite of this; it begins and ends with the Holy Spirit. Intercession does not involve looking inward at the self, but upwards towards God's will. It involves interceding for what the Lord Jesus wants, as we feel burdened with what the Holy Spirit feels, and as we discern what God thinks in any given situation.

Intercession is a Divinely given burden to be responsible for the effective outcome of any given situation, as directed by the Holy Spirit. Just as prayer is mostly focused on praying good ideas, which find their genesis in human reasoning, so intercession is interceding for God's will to be accomplished through the Holy Spirit. The two are very different and an intercessor can only pray as he or she is led by the Holy Spirit. This is the golden law of all intercession, as the Lord taught in John 15 and the apostle John explains in 1 John 5:14-15. If you wish to understand the difference further, read *Rees Howells Intercessor* by Norman Grubb (especially chapter 12, 'What is an Intercessor?'), *Samuel Rees Howells: A Life of Intercession* by Richard Maton, (especially chapter 41, 'What is Intercession?'), and *Revival Fires and Awakenings* by Mathew Backholer, (chapter 15, 'Ask and it Will be Given' and chapter 21, 'I Have Made you a Watchman').

When I began walking with God, no one I knew, understood the difference between prayer and intercession. It is clear in

Scripture, but unless the Lord shows you, you can never see it. Consequently, as the Holy Spirit led me, I found that intercession was at the very heart of all His dealings with me. He was continually encouraging me to allow Him to obtain higher places of authority, as I interceded.

Before an intercession began, the Holy Spirit would often give me a place(s) of abiding, as John 15 explains. This could mean fasting, changing my attitude, or giving etc., just as the Holy Spirit directed. This practical obedience would keep me focused throughout the intercession, as the Holy Spirit engaged the enemy in the spiritual realm and overcome him, by the power of Jesus' victory on the cross. This kind of intercession and abiding could continue for months or even years, until the Holy Spirit told me He had won through and gained a position of intercession.

If intercession could be likened to natural warfare, we all start off as trainees or recruits, and if we are willing and obedient, we will be led by our Teacher, the Holy Spirit, to go into war, win victories, gain our stripes and advance up the ranks. To have gained a position of intercession means you have won a battle and never have to re-fight it, subject to abiding, and the lessons learned can be applied in other spiritual battles. The further we go with the Lord, the varying the degrees and stages in abiding. The deeper the oneness with the Holy Spirit and His will, the greater the power of the risen life of Christ can operate through us, and further positions of spiritual authority will be gained.

Perhaps you are beginning to see how prayer and intercession are very different, just as I learnt in my walk with God. In all the intercessions the Lord led me into, I realised that everything was akin, related by the blood of Jesus, to the completion of Jesus' Every Creature Commission (Matthew 28:19-20, Mark 16:15). In other words, all the burdens were like branches linking into God's Vine, which pulsates with His will to reach all people with the gospel of Jesus Christ.

The intercessions I was led into would involve carrying a burden and abiding in Him daily, enduring until victory. I would identify with those I interceded for, and at times, agonise and suffer as they did, until the Holy Spirit gained the victory through me over the enemy. Intercession is costly and must not be devalued by some romantic notion; intercession can and does break people. Crucifixion of the old self always precedes intercession; the old man has no play in the spiritual warfare of the new. The intercessor is like a grain of wheat, which falls to the ground and dies, and becomes buried, before it germinates, grows and comes into fruit (John 12:24).

The Lord led me into many intercessions and victories have been gained to His glory, and each time, the Lord took me a step further and deeper into His victory of the cross over all the powers of the enemy. The Holy Spirit then led me into my next engagement when He spoke to me through His Word about Molech. Molech was the detestable god of the Amorites and like all false gods, behind him are evil spirits. 'The things which the Gentiles sacrifice, they sacrifice to demons and not to God' (1 Corinthians 10:20). Molech is a demon and as a demon he is thirsty to kill, steal and destroy life (John 10:10). The Amorites worshipped Molech by sacrificing their children to this demon on their altars (Leviticus 18:21, Leviticus 20:1-5, 1 Kings 11:4-7). God has warned His people not to sacrifice any of their children to Molech, and by doing so, the name of the Lord would be profaned. The sixth commandment must not be broken, "You shall not murder" (Exodus 20:13).

The demon called Molech was disenfranchised in the West, when Christianity spread and the ancient practice of sacrificing children was forbidden; but the demon itself never died, and has always sought a new way to remerge into the modern world to take innocent lives. Molech wants the death of the innocent and does not mind if we call it child sacrifice on altars, or abortion. Today, many nations in the world, including nations which were once openly Christian, have prostituted themselves to Molech and he has returned to take children, in a new form, but the end result is the same. Devaluing and consuming of human life and an empowering of a demon god.

God forbids His people to follow the path of unbelievers. 'They even sacrificed their sons and their daughters to demons and shed innocent blood...and the land was polluted with blood. Thus they were defiled by their own works and played the harlot by their own deeds' (Psalm 106:37-39).

Pregnancy and all lives are precious to God, because He is at work in the mother's womb (Psalm 139:13). All life is created in God's image (Genesis 1:27), and the fruit of the womb is a gift from God (Psalm 127:3). When a family goes through the tragedy of a miscarriage they say, "We lost our baby," and most parents will grieve for the loss of their child, especially the mother, but when a child is unwanted the same people can say, "It's only a foetus, get rid of it." The only difference in the situation is the spiritual stronghold in the mind, which must be cast down (2 Corinthians 10:5). God says of our nations, "They have no pity on the fruit of the womb" (Isaiah 13:18). To take the life of an unborn is a sin, even if you are the father who has insisted on the abortion, or abandoned the woman when she became pregnant, which resulted in an abortion, the man is just as culpable as the woman. This needs to be confessed and forgiven, because God already has a plan for the lives of the unborn in their mothers' wombs. 'Your eyes saw my substance, being yet unformed. And in Your Book they were all written, the days fashioned for me, when as yet there were none of them' (Psalm 139:16).

The loss of any young life to God is a source of great pain, whether the humans involved want that life or not. For my family, the Lord allowed us to go through a situation that helped teach me the value of life in the womb. A few years before, whilst I was away serving the Lord, my wife had a threatened miscarriage and I returned home immediately by train. In the carriage, I poured the whole of my being into prayer for many hours, until victory prevailed. As I sat on the train giving thanks and glory to God, the Holy Spirit kept repeating, "First fruits, first fruits." I know the voice of the Holy Spirit, but this was different. Why was He repeating Himself? His tone of speech was not the same. I phoned a friend and asked him to meet me at the station, so I could arrive home as soon as possible. When I entered the house, I learned that my wife and I had lost the baby. We were devastated. We would of course, get over it, millions have to and do.

Our baby had not been born, but we grieved because we lost our child. Through this devastation, I began thinking about the millions of babies that are killed through abortion. The Holy Spirit was so tender and gracious towards me at this time, but I had not understood why. He explained to me that He was leading me into an intercession regarding abortion in the United Kingdom. I also learned much later, how an intercessor in the USA was called to the do the very same thing. This personal miscarriage was a first fruit of intercession and the baby was to be given back to the Lord, placed on His holy altar, so no flesh could claim the glory for any future victories.

As the Holy Spirit led me, I asked Him to show me what my place of abiding would be. He told me that for the first six months, part of my abiding was to give myself to a time of separation for fasting and prayer. 'Do not deprive one another except with consent for a time, that you may give yourselves to fasting and prayer' (1 Corinthians 7:5). Abortion is often the result of lust or money concerns dominating decisions, and so I was also to believe God for £1,500 ($2,400) to be shared equally in three amounts: For the Jews, the Gentiles, and the unborn. These amounts would be a sign that God would empower the intercession.

I was placed on one meal a day, for forty days, which caused unwanted attention. Generally speaking, only those close to me would know about my position in Christ and my place of abiding. I found it to be a sad fact that in Christian ministry there is too much loose talk, which costs spiritual victories (James 1:26). When the Holy Spirit does something outstanding, the temptation is to share it far and wide before the correct time, when often we must be silent (2 Kings 18:36).

Praise the Lord for all those who have gone before, who left us their testimonies of their lives with Jesus; but for those who share of their exploits far too early in their walk with God, or with the wrong motives, you can bring the wrong kind of attention to yourselves from demonic forces. When God calls you to submarine warfare, it is a foolish mistake to turn yourself into a lighthouse, for all the enemies of God to set their targets against! In addition, if you bring glory to yourself, you may lose the anointing you once had and begin to stagnate.

Praying in the money I needed to give away was the easy bit, as the Holy Spirit through me had already gained a position of grace, or "a gained place of intercession," as Rees Howells would say, for finances. This meant the Holy Spirit could always call upon the grace of faith in that area at any time He chose. One third of the money was sent to a ministry, which enable Jews to leave Russia and go to Israel. Another third was given to a Christian organisation that helps women who were thinking about having an abortion to make a pro-life choice. The final third was given to a Christian TV ministry, who had produced a programme highlighting the Scriptural view to what abortion truly is, and how the evil spirit called Molech, is feeding off these human sacrifices to modern convenience, careers, promiscuity, prosperity and of choice etc. We hear much of the 'right to choose' but what of the right to life for the unborn child, who will speak for him or her?

'Deliver those who are drawn toward death, And hold back those stumbling to the slaughter' (Proverbs 24:11). 'Open your mouth for the speechless, in the cause of all who are appointed to die' (Proverbs 31:8).

During the intercession, the Holy Spirit told me that under no circumstances was I ever to engage Molech by name or bring any accusations against him. When dealing with demonic beings, this attitude is both wise and biblical (Jude 9). Each day I engaged in praying in tongues and allowed the Holy Spirit to take over and do His work as Romans 8:26 explains. It was certainly not easy and in all my years of intercession, this turned out to be the most costly. If the enemy cannot touch you directly, he will look for someone close to you to work through and he found a willing applicant and participant in one close friend.

Through my fasting and places of abiding, I had lost a lot of weight and this caught the attention of others. I had also walked as a Nazirite for six months on another occasion (Numbers 6, Judges 13:5), which got many tongues wagging! While these types of intercession were ongoing, I was very much hidden away. Due to many factors, my mind was under constant attack from the enemy who knew no bounds as the accuser of the brethren (Revelation 12:10). It was a constant bombardment of lies, deceit and deception. At the height of the intercession for the unborn, there was one day when I was interceding in tongues for six hours.

By the end of the six months, I was really unsure of the outcome and on the last night of the intercession, I was alone with Holy Spirit in an attitude of prayer. My wife had gone to bed and I was meditating on all that had happened over the past months. Had I not received the baptism of love previously, I would have been unable to complete this intercession because of the conflict within and without.

As I watched the hands on the clock reaching midnight, to signify the end of this six month intercession, I was glad that it was drawing to an end; as I'm not sure I could have taken much more spiritual and emotional attack. As the two hands met and became one at midnight, the Holy Spirit asked me, "Do you know what has been achieved through this intercession?" I replied, "No, sorry. I lost the plot weeks ago under all the attacks. Please forgive me." The Holy Spirit said, "Would you like to know?" I replied, "Yes," and I will always remember that voice of compassion when He said, "From this day forth, the devil can never kill any baby in its mother's womb, in the United Kingdom, who has been set apart to serve Me." Now I knew that all the future apostles, prophets, evangelists, pastors, teachers etc., and all those who have been called and set apart for God's work of service from the United Kingdom, for the purpose of building up the Body of Christ, would be saved by the Lord from Molech (Ephesians 4:11-12). These unborn, set apart to serve God, would now be saved and the enemy could not have them (Ephesians 2:10). By being bound, the enemy could not stop the harvest of souls that they will reap for Jesus Christ! The Holy Spirit saved these unborn children, their future children and their spiritual offspring, and their offspring, and so forth!

After all the trials of the last six months, I burst into tears and fell to the ground, where I laid for some considerable time. Frequently I have heard others ask, "Why does God allow this?" Maybe because He is waiting for someone the Holy Spirit can work through, to bring about His Kingdom here on earth, as He desires. The devil tried to kill me while in the womb and God has worked in and through me, to help stop it happening to others, and this was only the start.

Chapter Twenty-Seven

Spirit of Addiction

Jesus said, "Assuredly, I say to you, whatever you bind on earth will be bound in heaven, and whatever you loose on earth will be loosed in heaven. Again I say to you that if two of you agree on earth concerning anything that they ask, it will be done for them by My Father in heaven. For where two or three are gathered together in My name, I am there in the midst of them" (Matthew 18:18-20).

Jesus taught that His disciples (which includes His obedient followers today), have been given authority to overcome all the power of the enemy and nothing will harm them/us (Luke 10:17-19). So where are the strongholds of the enemy? Well, I was about to learn that they can be all around us.

We are told many times in the Bible that the physical land can be defiled and in the unseen spiritual dimension, sin gives the enemy strongholds to bind people (Leviticus 18:28, Jeremiah 3:9), and keep them under his power (John 14:30). The unseen spiritual opposition in the heavenly realms exercises power over people, as these demonic principalities exploit their legal right to lord it over people under their control. 'You once walked according to the course of this world, according to the prince of the power of the air, the spirit who now works in the sons of disobedience' (Ephesians 2:2).

Some Christians believe they can simply shout or bang their drums in their churches to breakdown these strongholds, but unless they are directed by the Holy Spirit, these acts are nothing more than the manifestation of confidence in the flesh. Only the Holy Spirit knows what key must be used to unlock the demonic strongholds where we live, and only He can lead us to effectively undermine and demolish these demonic strongholds.

However, it is possible to live unaware of the spiritual war raging where we live, and this happened to me. Over a period of time, I sensed something was wrong and the reassuring calm of the Holy Spirit's presence was not the same. I was still learning to walk in the gift of discernment, but in my spirit I seemed to understand all was not well, but could not work out what it was or why. Had I grieved the Lord in some way? I examined my spiritual life in the light of God's word, the Bible, and I was not in any deliberate sin, as far as I knew.

In any relationship there are times when there is an atmosphere, so you must ask the other person, "Is everything ok?" As I am sure you know, this kind of question can bring forth all kinds of mixed reactions – some good, others not so good. Whenever you ask such a question you must be prepared for a response and whenever you ask God the Holy Spirit a question, you must prepare yourself for the answer, and get ready to respond to it. It is sinful to ask the Spirit of God a question, receive a direct reply and then do nothing about it. Sadly, churches do this all the time with prophecy.

The Holy Spirit is the revealer of mysteries, and one of the great joys I learnt when dealing with Him, is that He is always honest and He cannot lie. He is the Spirit of Truth and will guide you into all truth, and will tell you what is yet to come (John 16:13). Jesus said, "It has been given to you to know the mysteries of the Kingdom of heaven, but to them it has not been given" (Matthew 13:11).

God the Father, God the Son and God the Holy Spirit know the past, present and future and will warn us of what is to come, if only we will truly believe and listen. "I am the Alpha and the Omega, the Beginning and the End," says the Lord, "who is and who was and who is to come, the Almighty" (Revelation 1:8).

The Holy Spirit was doing His best to get my attention through my unease, to warn me of future events, which would come to pass. But there are times when we are too busy for our own good and the good of others. Our minds are often on so many things that the Holy Spirit, who speaks in a small still voice, cannot be heard (1 Kings 19:12).

When I took the time and the effort to be still and enter again into His rest, He impressed upon my mind the thought that drug dealers would be moving into the area, where we live and meet as a Church. After prayer and fasting for further clarification, I was shown the exact road, close to where we reside, where the enemy sought to enter. In response we started prayer walking this road, claiming it in the name of Jesus Christ and partaking of the Holy Communion, from one end of the road to the other, declaring the Lordship of Jesus. We were directed to place elements of the communion in each property, as a sign to the principalities and powers.

This was not a routine we practiced in all spiritual warfare, but instead we were led by the Holy Spirit in each case. Prayer and intercession, with practical abiding or acts of obedience, play an important role, as the Spirit leads, to weakening the demonic chains over areas, and then His light will pierce the darkness. Great ideas, following the examples of others, or doing what you did last time will have no effect if the Lord does not lead. If we try to copy others, we will be like Israel sending the Ark of the Covenant into battle, when the Lord remains in the camp (1 Samuel 4:1-11). The power was not in the Ark of the Covenant, or in 'the thing' we did last time, but in obedience to God Almighty!

As I gave some thought to all the Lord was revealing to me, I was reminded that this road, which the enemy wanted to attack, was part of the 'high ground' which leads to a local viewpoint that overlooks the surrounding area for miles.

In years past, this road had three churches only a stone's throw away, in each direction. In the past, this land had been reclaimed for Christ, but now some of it had slipped into enemy hands. One of these churches was built shortly after a man received a miraculous healing at an open-air outreach, when an evangelist prayed for him. Up until then, this man had to wear a full length leg iron frame, to support himself. Another church belongs to the Salvation Army and they once held regular meetings at the viewpoint, before marching back to their place of worship, declaring the Lordship of Jesus over the area. Today, only the meeting place for the Salvation Army remains as a public place of worship.

With the turning of the tide of Christian spiritual dominion in the heavenly places in the area, the enemy began doing all he could to reclaim this ground, and the nation as a whole. He does this soul by soul, family by family, street by street, town by town, city by city, nation by nation – unless he is stopped!

God warned us that the enemy was trying to move in and after prayer walking around the streets, and discreetly partaking of Communion all around, we believed we had the victory and thought no more of God's warning. The land had been reclaimed, we thought and we moved on. But then two years later, the Holy Spirit told me that a spirit of addiction was now ruling over the area! This came as a real shock and surprise to me; I truly believed we had dealt with this and had not given it any further thought.

As always, when I am unsure of a situation, I ask the Holy Spirit to confirm it to me, in a way that I can truly understand. The very next day, I saw a Christian woman who lived nearby and found that she had become an alcoholic. Then I learnt that some drug dealers had moved into a flat in the very road we had prayed over. The police knew these men had moved into the area, but they had no evidence to convict them of dealing.

As I sat reading my Bible in my front room, I was also able to see drug dealers supply a man who had a young family, and an alcoholic collapsed outside our church, with all her bottles clanging on the ground. In another provocation from the enemy, a young man who was once a Christian began throwing the remains of drugs over my fence. It seemed like the enemy was trying to provoke us with his power, or was it just the Holy Spirit showing us what was happening? We had been caught napping – taking a spiritual sleep. There was once a Christian witness in many homes in the area, but one by one, the enemy was taking them, and others.

Then the Lord showed me, having claimed this ground two years before, we should have continued to proclaim the Lordship of Jesus over this area. We had not done this and were caught off guard. The local Church should in part, be the watchman and a centre for intercessory prayer in whatever area they live. As they are led by the Holy Spirit in prayer, and witness, they keep the spiritual hedge of protection strong (Job 1:10), and like Nehemiah, rebuild the walls and keep them effective for keeping the enemy at bay (Nehemiah 6:15-7:3).

Led by the Holy Spirit, we began to bind this strong man, the spirit of addiction and pull down the stronghold. In the name of Jesus Christ we overcame him by the blood of the Lamb and the word of our testimony (Revelation 12:11). It took eighteen months to get the victory and as we did our part, the local community also did theirs.

We bound the strong man in the heavenly realms and the community was empowered both to see, and provide the police with relevant information to help them in their war against drugs. We were given the assurance by the Holy Spirit that we had been given the victory and one week later, the police informed all the local residents that they had completed a successful search warrant, at the address of the drug dealers, and they were evicted from the area and dealt with.

What was interesting about this time of spiritual warfare, was that two days before the police raid, the Christian woman who had been bound by the demons of alcoholism called at my house, where we meet as a church, and asked me to give her a lift in my car, to the off-license. I knew she wanted to buy alcohol and I could not share in her sin, so I refused. Instead, we contacted a friend of hers who came to help her back to her house.

Had I fallen for this trick of the devil, eighteen months of intercession would have been wasted and the victory lost. Satan was attempting to get me to undermine my principles of abiding, by encouraging and enabling a believer to remain bound by the spirit of addiction. It was a trick of the enemy and the Lord enabled me to overcome. Satan often tries to trick us with the Gibeonite deception, desiring us to make a treaty with an enemy of God (Joshua 9:1-15, 2 Samuel 21:1-2).

In another case, a friend of mine who was an elder, shared the following. Very late one night his pastor received a phone call from a widow who was in a desperate state of mind. He agreed to visit her at home, as part of his duties of pastoral care. His wife said to him, "Do not go on your own and take an elder with you." He took his wife's advice as godly wisdom, and when they arrived, the woman opened the door and was completely naked!

Both men agreed, had either of them been alone, temptation may have overcome them. Let those who have ears to hear, hear what the Holy Spirit says to the churches (Matthew 11:15, Revelation 2:7). We have two eyes and two ears, we need to watch, listen and then act. The devil, as his name depicts, is evil, and we live in evil times, because demonic spirits will do all they can to kill, steal and destroy the Church. We are not permitted the liberty of spiritual sleep, to stand by and watch it happen.

Chapter Twenty-Eight

The Saddest Revelation of All

Once again, I am going to share some hard testimonies, but they reveal how good God is and how He desires to bless us, but our disobedience (and rebellion) hinders this. I shared earlier how the Holy Spirit had gained an intercession through me for finances, which He could call upon any time He chose to (chapter 18). I learnt from Rees Howells that there is a golden rule concerning finances, and this is, you can only prevail upon the Lord to give larger amounts of money towards His work, which you have had already given, or proved willing to give, if you were able to.

One day, through a series of unexpected Divine appointments the Lord led me to connect with a missionary. He was struggling financially and I was told by the Holy Spirit to believe for £500 ($800) a month, for twelve months, to help support him abroad. The Holy Spirit showed me He was giving this man a lifeline, to give him the time to get close to God, and begin seeking the Lord for his daily bread (Matthew 6:11, Philippians 4:19). Like many in his generation, he had relied on the generosity of Christians, who had supported him for decades, and as this was 'safe support,' he did not need to rely on the Lord. Now God wanted him to draw close to Him and begin to live by faith, financially and spiritually.

For my part, I had the burden of fasting, praying and practical abiding of believing, in order to be able to pray in the money needed on a monthly basis. The burden once carried by many, was on me alone. This I did without question and the Lord was faithful. It was a great relief to this man that I helped him. Then, as the twelve months were coming to an end, I contacted the missionary to share a word that the Holy Spirit had given me for him. He listened and said, "I will need to pray about this." To which I replied, "Did you pray about receiving the money every month?" "No," he said. In my heart, I asked the Lord, 'What are you trying to teach me in this?'

I was again introduced to another full-time Christian worker and after sharing a meal with him, I offered to pray a blessing upon him, based on Jesus' teaching. The Lord said, "He who receives you receives Me and he who receives Me receives Him who sent Me. He who receives a prophet in the name of a prophet shall receive a prophet's reward. And he who receives a righteous man in the name of a righteous man shall receive a righteous man's reward" (Matthew 10:40-42).

This man said, "All I want is the good, pleasing and perfect will of God," and I was very impressed at this statement. Nonetheless, as we stood together and prayed, the Holy Spirit came down in power on me. As I fell down under the weight, I cried out, "Oh my Lord, how I wish my brother was receiving this." I could not truly understand what had happened; why had the Holy Spirit bypassed the man I was praying a blessing on and touched me? By now the reader must be aware that God's good, pleasing and perfect will is for all believers is to be transformed into the image of His Son, the Lord Jesus Christ, which is a work of the Holy Spirit (Romans 8:29).

As I thought about this, I asked the Lord, "What are you trying to teach me through this?" A few weeks passed and I heard from this man, that he was also in great financial need. Knowing that I had gained a position of intercession for finances, he asked me to pray for the money to come in. It was a large amount and I asked the Holy Spirit, "Am I at liberty to pray for such an amount?" The Holy Spirit said, "Yes." The money soon came, much to my surprise and it came in one amount. I quickly passed this on to the man and he was very much comforted.

Sometimes I struggled as I tried to understand what the Holy Spirit was teaching me through these life lessons. Then, the Spirit made it plain. In the first case of the man who needed the £500 ($800) a month, I was shown that many in ministry do not know the Holy Spirit or His way of provision. Now, as their supporters withdrew their help because of retirement or other issues, they struggled having never learnt to be close to the Holy Spirit and pray in the money.

The second man also chose to reject the Holy Spirit when He came down in power, despite the fact that this was God's good, pleasing and perfect will for him, to conform him into the image of Jesus Christ. Only the Holy Spirit can make us live like Jesus and only He can make Jesus' victory real in our lives. But it was not just anyone who was trying to bless him, it was God the Holy Spirit, who had chosen the moment to come upon him, and he chose to reject Him! (Acts 8:21).

For me, the saddest revelation of all was that both were willing to accept the money when I prayed it in, and gave it to them with no strings attached, but they hardened their hearts when the Holy Spirit had something else to share with them. I believe the answer to their desperate needs was given to them, through me, to enable them to receive the challenging words of full surrender to the Holy Spirit, which I had for them. The Lord seemed to always prepare the way for His revelation to be given, by proving that I was the Lord's servant. As the Scriptures state: 'For our gospel did not come to you in word only, but also in power, and in the Holy Spirit and in much assurance, as you know what kind of men we were among you for your sake' (1 Thessalonians 1:5).

In my experience, the majority of those who claim to be disciples of Jesus Christ, want Him for His blessings *only* and then want Him to leave them alone, so they can get on with 'His work,' in the way they want, which is in reality, *their* work and not His! They believe that having a Bible with directions, and supporters to pay their bills means they do not need to draw near to the Holy Spirit and obey His voice. Very few have any desire to *fully* lay down their lives, as living martyrs, to give up all they want in order to allow the Holy Spirit to live through them to do His work, of reaching the world with the gospel. They only love Him in measure, for what they can get out of Him. If you truly love Him, you will give Him *all* your heart, soul, strength and mind. Then you will be able to claim, in truth, that your body is a temple of the Holy Spirit.

If you are challenged by this, that's ok, because I was very challenged when the Holy Spirit tried to reveal this to me. It is far easier for the flesh to sit in a church and pretend to be blind to all that is going on, than to allow the Spirit to open your eyes and ask you to carry the burden. Ever since my conversion, I have never understood the apathy, self-centredness and contentment with rituals and tradition in churches. It was a difficult lesson for me to learn, that the Lord is ever battling with His Church, urging it to repent, pray and obey, but like Israel of old, many do not want to hear (Mark

8:18). We continue in religious rituals and tradition with the Lord, and think that accomplished musicians can imitate the anointing. We sing of our deep commitment to God and full surrender, and call it worship, whilst we know in our hearts the words we sing are not true! The Lord said through Isaiah, "To what purpose is the multitude of your sacrifices to Me? I have had enough...when you come to appear before Me, who has required this from your hand, to trample My courts? Bring no more futile sacrifices" (Isaiah 1:11-13).

One of the saddest examples of our commitment to meetings, for the sake of meetings, was when the Holy Spirit placed a burden on my heart to get the leaders of our church together to repent and seek God for a Christian revival. We began to meet, to pray and word got out, and month by month, pastors from other areas began to attend, until most of the Bible-believing leaders in our area were meeting each month for the sole purpose of praying for revival. In the first meetings we were on our knees repenting, confessing our lack of power and need for Him to come in revival power, but as more senior pastors began arriving, they began to take over and the nature of the meetings changed dramatically. I remember clearly the day when the original purpose of the meeting was sidelined, when in this meeting with all the pastors, an elder said, "When are we going to repent?" Then the senior pastor who had now taken charge, without anyone's approval, said, "Repent? What for?" In my heart, I knew I was to be silent, but in my mind, I said, "For our powerlessness, for our indifference, for ignoring the Holy Spirit, and for our half-hearted commitment to Jesus' teaching on the cost of discipleship."

We have, as churches, resisted the will of our Head, Jesus Christ, and rejected the leading of the Holy Spirit. Our nation has not seen an awakening for more than a century, despite the fact that God wishes all men to be saved and has promised to pour out His Spirit on all flesh![1] Who is the problem? It is us! We don't want to pay the price. Billions are going to hell and we say, "What's that got to do with me? When's the next meeting going to start?" Instead of carrying burdens from the Holy Spirit (Romans 8:26), we preach on God giving us temporal blessings whilst many with itching ears, love these self-centred messages (2 Timothy 4:3-4). We ignore the Lord's warnings on distractions and worldliness, as

Christians have become indistinguishable from non-Christians (Luke 12:15, Luke 14:18-24). We read 2 Chronicles 7:14, but never actually get around to humbling ourselves, truly praying and turning from our wicked ways in repentance. Even when we meet for national days of prayer, the time is mostly taken up with celebrity speakers and with new bands and songs.

These may be hard lessons to learn, and hard teaching[2] to digest, but unless we learn them, we will never be able to move forward in God. The prayer meetings for revival, which began with repentance were soon transformed into a social time, as the pastors talked about new songs to be learned, celebrity preachers coming to the area and the work in their churches. The original purpose of praying for revival with repentance was forgotten and the Holy Spirit was grieved. The state of the Church, the Spirit showed me, is not much different from the testimony the Lord gives in Revelation 1-3.

Chapter Twenty-Nine

Where the Lord Provides

In all my experiences with God, I found that the Lord is ever seeking to teach His children to listen and abide with the Holy Spirit. Only He knows what the work is, how it is to be done and when. Therefore, without Him, we are simply wasting our time. This lesson was impressed on me time and time again, and as ever, the Lord wanted to share this with all who have tender hearts willing to heed His voice.

As I have shared, the Lord would lead many people to my home and one couple arrived, who had a served the Lord for years, who had a need for £4,000 ($6,400). This couple had been brought up within Christendom to believe that you raise money by solicitation: going to churches and Christians, where you explain your vision (or your perceived call) and ask for financial partners (regular financial gifts or a one-off sum of money). Rees Howells and many others had been taught that the arm of the flesh is very long, and if God is truly behind a work, you must trust in Him alone to provide. The nation of Israel trusted in the might of Egypt on a number of occasions (instead of trusting God), yet it was just a broken staff of reed which splintered into their hands! (2 Kings 18:21, Isaiah 36:6). Therefore, I said to this couple, "If it is of the Lord, He will provide, but if not, you should stay at home."

I told them again that their *desire* to go is *not* the call. I said they need not worry about God's way of provision, for, "The Lord is more than able to provide through prayer and fasting." As they listened to me, they said, "Will you pray about it?" "Yes," I replied, "I will ask the Holy Spirit." Much to my surprise, the Holy Spirit told me that I was to be responsible to pray in half of the money. They were encouraged by my commitment and were very tempted to go back to the old plan of asking people to support them, instead of trusting in the Lord and in Him alone.

This was an intercession, and as usual, the Holy Spirit gave me His terms and conditions for the prayer to go-through, which I call my abiding. The Holy Spirit said to me, "I will make you one with them," which meant their needs became my needs, and in a spiritual way, I shared the burden with them. I was to be just as responsible to pray in the money as they were. I told them, "You're faith must be in God and not in others." To make sure they did not trust in the hand (or arm) of the flesh, I said, "Under no circumstances are you tell anyone else," in order to gain influence over them to give. "That will be very difficult," they confessed.

In my experience I found it is one thing to be burdened to pray for *your* own needs and quite another to feel the burden of *another*, as you intercede for their needs. In such a situation, you have to carry a double burden, one for yourself and one for them, and if you fail on your own, the problem is just your own, but when interceding for another, you cannot fail and leave them in the lurch – without support or assistance! The burden was very real.

After a month of prayer, I phoned this couple to tell them I had received a gift of £1,000 ($1,600) towards the total. They were both very pleased that money was coming in, but confessed they had not had any answers themselves. The following day, I went to the bank to pay the money in, and as I stood in the queue, the Holy Spirit said, "If you take one of the paying in slips with you by faith, tonight I will add another £1,000!" I picked up the slip and by the end of the evening, the money I received was doubled! That evening, I phoned my friends and shared the good news, and they were silent for a while, saying, "We have still not received anything and to make matters worse, we just learnt we need another £1,000." "Oh, it will come," I said, and that was end of our conversation.

As I thought about this, I said to myself, "I have done my bit and prayed in half of the money, now the rest must be up to them." But suddenly the Holy Spirit picked me up on my less than charitable statement. "What do you mean, the rest is up to them? Have I not made you one with them?" I knew I was wrong and apologised to the Lord, and began praying for a further £500 ($800), which was the half of the new additional money which was required.

For some reason, it was very hard for me to pray in the £500, and when it came in, I felt much happier. I was now free and had prayed in half of all the money needed, including the additional money for the unexpected expenses. "No," said the Holy Spirit, as He rebuked me, "you are not free. I have made you one with them and you will not be free until every pound (euro or dollar) has come in."

This intercession was very different from all previous ones and was far from over. By now, the couple had received some gifts, so I rejoiced with them, but there was still a substantial shortfall. Then, to my surprise the Holy Spirit said, "You are no longer to pray for the balance." I asked the Holy Spirit, "Why?" And He replied, "Because I have made you all one in Me." I was baffled by this statement, but the Holy Spirit was now about to teach me something new, when He said, "You are not to ask me to deliver you, when you have the means to meet that need yourself." I was not pleased and said, "But I do not have the money," to which He replied, "Yes you do." As I thought about where this money was, the Holy Spirit said, "It's in the Lord's Account, you have more than enough." (The Lord's Account was where money for ministry was banked, ready for each trip or mission as directed by the Holy Spirit). I was not happy and protested by saying, "But that is the money I have prayed in for my next trip to America." Then the Holy Spirit asked, "When are you going?" I replied, "In July." Then the Holy Spirit said, "When are they going?" "In June," I said. "First need, first call," the Holy Spirit told me and added, "We are all one in Spirit and in truth; their need comes before yours; take of what we have and use it for them, then I shall supply for your need in plenty of time."

Through this incident, I learnt another valuable lesson. If it is in your power to help another and you have the Holy Spirit's *approval,* do it. Then, when you have a true need yourself, He will meet it also. He met my need for America and He still meets my needs (Philippians 4:19). Through all these experiences, I was learning that the time is coming when those who are in full-time ministry, will have to look to the Lord God and His Holy Spirit in all matters, and all the work of the Holy Spirit relates back to the Every Creature Commission, that all would be given an opportunity to hear and respond to the gospel (Matthew 28:18-20, Mark 16:15). Every one who claims to serve the Lord will have to choose His way or their own, and those who rely on man (Isaiah 36:6), so they can do their own work, may well go bust!

As I mentioned earlier, we gave our home to God and He said He would use it for His glory (chapter four). This was no theoretical surrender of our rights, as our home belongs to Him and the Lord has used it for decades. For years, it has been a house-church, plus homeless families have stayed in this home, and tramps have been welcomed. We still meet as a church and Jesus is the Head, as the Holy Spirit guides us by the gifts of the Spirit and through His Word.

Many big churches have to spend all their money on the up-keep of their buildings, whilst the apostles met in people's homes or public places, and preached (Acts 8:3, Romans 16:5, Philemon 2). This enabled them, and us, to give far more into the work of preaching the gospel around the world. In this commission, we were told by the Holy Spirit that we must begin to believe for finances for Bibles for our brothers and sisters in Christ in other nations, who are too poor to afford one themselves. Within a week of this guidance, money began to arrive. First, came £1,000 ($1,600), followed by £500 ($800), for which we thanked and praised the Lord, giving Him all the glory. Then one day, £10 ($16) came for this work and I was so thrilled, and did not commit the sin of despising the day of small things (Zechariah 4:10).

We had not received any gifts for a while, so I was full of praise and thanksgiving for this additional gift, which would enable a few believers to have a Bible. Then the Holy Spirit whispered to me and told me He had been testing me, to see if I would be just as joyful over this small amount, as I was the larger. He told me, "Because you have rejoiced over the £10, you can claim £10,000 ($16,000)." I immediately believed and we all had great joy as the money came in. First, came £1,000, then £500, then another £1,000, then £350, until we reached the £10,000. We had received the thousand-fold and much more besides (Matthew 19:29), and it continues on today, a never-ending flow of oil to reach those who need it most (2 Kings 4:2-6). Jesus Christ said to His disciples, in relation to the hungry multitude, "You give them something to eat" (Matthew 14:16). We too, are called to help give the living bread, the Word of God to hungry souls (Deuteronomy 8:3, Matthew 4:4).

On another occasion, the Holy Spirit showed me He wished to provide through me fully, for a Bible College student, whom He was calling into full-time ministry. Was I willing? Yes and I knew He could do it through me. A year later, the Lord told me He wished to support another full-time worker from the same College. In addition, if they ever needed a home in the United Kingdom, God's house, my home, was available as long as they had need of it. This also kept me in touch with what was going on around the world, as they travelled on the Lord's work. The Holy Spirit continues to provide for all their needs daily, as He has for more than a decade. They too have been called to support full-time Christian workers in other parts of the world, as the chain of grace continues to others.

In all of this, the Holy Spirit was working through me to gain even higher positions of intercession, by faith, in and for others. Like many others, I have been deeply troubled with the way a few in Christian media raise support. Is it possible that a tare has somehow, slipped in unnoticed and lured others in to adopt their ways? Jesus warned this will happen (Matthew 13:24-30). A tare can be a lure, something which entices, a bate, with the power to attract others. They beckon you and draw you towards them – to ensnare you. They seduce you to their will – they are decoys of temptation. A decoy is something or someone, used to entrap others or distract their attention. What happened throughout Israel's history was written down for our benefit. 'Now all these things happened to them as examples, and they were written for our admonition, upon whom the ends of the ages have come. Therefore let him who thinks he stands take heed lest he fall. No temptation has overtaken you except such as is common to man; but God is faithful, who will not allow you to be tempted beyond what you are able, but with the temptation will also make the way of escape, that you may be able to bear it' (1 Corinthians 10:11-13). Presumption is to take God for granted; and a tare or a weed will do this, as it is a plant growing where it is undesired.

George Müller, J. Hudson Taylor, Rees Howells, Samuel Rees Howells and many others were led down the path of abiding surrender, as they looked to God alone in the quiet of the prayer closets, which Jesus taught in Matthew 6:5-8. God has promised to provide all our needs, if we do His will, His way. To hire professional fundraisers, rather than to abide, fast and pray, looking alone to God to provide, brings shame on the name of Jesus Christ. It's a mockery for all to see.

I am reminded of a man of integrity, the founder of a Christian TV channel who was approached by a professional 'Christian' fundraiser who stated he could raise millions for the channel – for a fee of fifty percent! This fundraiser was not hired by this TV channel. 'Therefore, since we have this ministry, as we have received mercy, we do not lose heart. But we have renounced the hidden things of shame, not walking in craftiness nor handling the word of God deceitfully, but by manifestation of the truth commending ourselves to every man's conscience in the sight of God. But even if our gospel is veiled, it is veiled to those who are perishing' (2 Corinthians 4:1-3). If you wish to know more, please read, study and meditate on Jesus' teaching in Matthew 6.

Presumption is a sin that many in Christian leadership commit. After all this time, I can still hear what a missionary, who was out of touch with God, said to me, "It's very simple, all God has to do is send the money and I'll get on with the work!" This is the sin of presumption. 'And Moses said, "Now why do you transgress the command of the Lord? For this will not succeed. Do not go up, lest you be defeated by your enemies, for the Lord is not among you. For the Amalekites and the Canaanites are there before you, and you shall fall by the sword; because you have turned away from the Lord, the Lord will not be with you." But they *presumed* to go up to the mountaintop. Nevertheless, neither the ark of the covenant of the Lord nor Moses departed from the camp. Then the Amalekites and the Canaanites who dwelt in that mountain came down and attacked them, and drove them back as far as Hormah' (Numbers 14:41-45).

The sin of presumption means stepping ahead of the Lord, outside of His will, hoping to achieve the general directive, which the Lord has given, and it is sought by the power of the flesh, instead of by the leading of the Spirit. "But the person who does anything presumptuously, whether he is native-born or a stranger, that one brings reproach on the Lord, and he shall be cut off from among his people. Because he has despised the word of the Lord, and has broken His commandment, that person shall be completely cut off; his guilt shall be upon him" (Numbers 15:30-31).

For some, pride in the call is often the reason for their fall. The right attitude to have is this: 'Keep back Your servant also from presumptuous sins; let them not have dominion over me. Then I shall be blameless and I shall be innocent of great transgression' (Psalm 19:13). We must accept God's work, His commands and commission, which must be carried out exactly as He says, and in His timing. On the reverse side, when the Holy Spirit tells us not to go somewhere, or to cease socialising with someone (or a group), or not to attend a particular event – we must also heed His command.

'Do not be like the horse or like the mule which have no understanding, which must be harnessed with bit and bridle, else they will not come near you' (Psalm 32:9). 'If we live in the Spirit, let us also walk in the Spirit' (Galatians 5:25).

In spiritual warfare, you dare not, put your own interpretation on what He says. If you are really serious about serving the Lord, in whatever way He chooses, you would be wise and well advised to read, study and meditate on 1 Kings 13, the man of God from Judah. Fast and pray, asking the Holy Spirit to show you what it's all about. Don't ask others, He wants to teach you, if you are willing to learn. Not everyone in the Body of Christ has a teachable spirit and it is not unusual to come across full-time Christian workers without the Holy Spirit, who seem to think they know all there is to know, based upon their studies of books on theology etc. Jesus would say to them, "Are you not in error, because you do not know the Scriptures, or the power of God?" (Mark 12:24).

Chapter Thirty

Power and Resistance

In all my Christian life, I had been involved with lively churches, which moved in the gifts of the Holy Spirit, and was surprised when the Holy Spirit sent me on a four thousand mile round trip, with the express purpose of sending me to a very traditional church. This church, without the Holy Spirit was in terminal decline. It had lasted decades and was on the road to closure. To my surprise, the Lord showed me He had a plan to save and revive it. He showed me and others, what His plan was and how He would lead it back into health. The church took several steps in the right direction and it was beginning to grow.

After being there for a while, I was invited to be part of the small leadership circle. The Lord showed me I must fix the maintenance problems of the building, spending my time doing painting and other practical jobs. In addition, I began to teach the people how to welcome and receive the ministry of the Holy Spirit. One surprised visitor, knowing the traditions of the church said, "The Holy Spirit has come here too!"

After years of preparing the ground, fixing the building, teaching the people, prayer, repentance for the past and cleansing the building etc., we received prophecies and directions of God's plan for the church. We sensed we were on the path towards a revival, God would get the glory, Jesus would be exalted, the Holy Spirit would be given His rightful place, the congregation would be revived and many would get saved. The confirmation of this belief took place one evening, when in the leader's meeting, an unusual event took place.

As the leadership meeting was closing, where we had discussed and planned the services ahead, the Holy Spirit came upon me and I was led into prolonged prayer, seeking God. I felt compelled to fall to my knees; the others were bent double, sat in their seats. There were only three leaders present in the meeting, but suddenly, as I knelt down in reverence, a fourth unseen Person entered the room. The atmosphere changed and none felt able to look up. The Holy Spirit, dare I explain, stepped in and it felt like He was walking amongst us. We were silent when He came in and the minutes became hours in His presence and we stayed till past midnight.

One of these leaders was a very traditional man, who had avoided all supernatural encounters with God, and chose this church because of its rituals and safe religion, and yet, even he was humbly touched by this encounter. As this fourth Person walked about in the room, this traditional Christian was touched by Him and suddenly all the pain left his body.

As I had been praying for revival for over a decade and was called to help prepare this church for God's outpouring, I expected the pastor would be thrilled at this encounter, but he was greatly unhappy that his routine had been changed. To make sure this never happened again, he decided to re-schedule our leadership meetings to a time where it was impossible to linger in God's presence again. Why did he not want to welcome God in our midst?

A little time later, the Holy Spirit moved in His gifts during a prayer meeting, and the pastor made it very plain that he had no wish to take the church in that direction. Then, the church received a prophecy from an elder of another church, who was related to our church secretary. The pastor refused to share it with the members of the church, despite it all being a positive word about the fellowship growing in numbers, through the work of the Holy Spirit. Then when the pastor was pressed by the Holy Spirit, who was seeking to move the church on, he finally confessed to a few leaders, that the only reason he became the pastor of this church was to top-up his final few years of income to gain his full pension!

One day the Holy Spirit spoke to me about this pastor and said, "Go to his house immediately," and when I arrived, he told me he had been praying for God to send someone. I found him with his head in his hands and he confessed, "I'm afraid that when I go home to heaven, I'll be meeting a stranger." For forty years, this man had preached and been the pastor of many churches, but he never truly cultivated his relationship with the Lord, and the Holy Spirit was a stranger to him. For decades people looked to him and all he had to give them, was what he had read from books.

I have included this testimony and the following, not to discourage anyone, but to explain how only the Holy Spirit can reveal the true situation in any church. The most discouraging situation is to live in deception and be deluded, and this is why the Spirit of Truth must reveal the truth in any given situation (John 14:17).

In all the troubled churches the Lord sent me into, and they were of differing denominations, I noticed a two-fold manifestation of His will. First, He would use me to bring healing, deliverance, prophetic words and encouragement. By these and more, the Lord would show by works of power that I was His servant and could be trusted as such. Second, after the pastor or elders had seen God working in and through me to their benefit, the Holy Spirit would reveal His plan, which was not always easy, and then they had to make a choice to obey God or reject His revealed will. Additionally, every prophetic word, which gave direction would be accompanied by several confirmations, from unconnected sources.

In another church I was called to, I found out that the previous pastor had been lured into adultery by a tare and was expelled by the church. Whilst the new pastor was being sought, the numbers plummeted and one Sunday by chance, an out-of-work pastor *happened* to walk in, or so they thought. As innocent people, they did not realise that the pastor happened to walk in on several churches without a leader, and managed to find the elders each time and explained his line of work. They saw a Divine appointment, without considering that it could be a devilish one, (see Nehemiah 2:10, 19, Nehemiah 13:4-9, Matthew 13:24-30).

This man was invited to become the pastor and two years past without any growth. At this point, I was led by the Holy Spirit to join this church because God had a work He wished to do there. After being there for a while, the pastor knowing my walk with God asked my advice if we should participate in a nationwide evangelistic campaign. He asked me to pray about it, and the Holy Spirit showed me how He would supply two full-time evangelists and two part-time evangelists to evangelise the whole area, at no cost to the church!

The pastor was living rent-free in the manse, with a good expenses package, and as he did not receive a wage, every penny (cent) counted. Nevertheless, he was happy for things to remain the same, without the evangelism taking place, as he was running his own business, as well as the church. This was the work of a tare, a wolf in sheep's clothing; refusing to see the local area evangelised because of the fear that the fellowship should grow from a new source. He had no reason to fear these evangelists because the work of an evangelist and a pastor are distinct, and complementary in the Church (Ephesians 4:11-15). These evangelists were going to give the shepherd (who was actually a hireling) a boost to the church, by new members and additions into the Kingdom of God.

In every church service there were prophecies and tongues given, but it was clear that by rejecting the revealed will of God, they had opened themselves up to the flesh, or worse, and now most of these manifestations were not inspired by the Holy Spirit. In a hope to display that all was well, the pastor would lead the meetings and manipulate others to prophesy or speak in a tongues. Several times he urged one of his weaker elders by saying, "You've got a word, please give it now," and the elder looked confused, and said, "No." The pastor replied, "Yes, you have." "No," insisted the elder. "Yes, you have!" the pastor insisted, and the elder crumpled and said, "Ok." Then tried to give a tongue or a prophecy out of his mind. It was very evident because he stumbled, struggled and was confused.

When these inconsistencies continued, the words that were spoken were *always* about everything being ok and that revival was soon to come, with no reference to the decision to reject the will of God to evangelise the area. One day, one of the men who had been there a very long time prophesied, "There's sin in this church, terrible sin," and I thought, 'That rings true and must be dealt with.' Nevertheless, the pastor refused to acknowledge the word or be reminded of it. The pastor had rejected God's plan to reach the area. After some years, the Holy Spirit told me to leave, because He had already left and the church closed a few years later (Revelation 1:20, Revelation 2:5), so no more people could be duped or deceived.

In another church, in a town far from where I live, I was invited to preach on two different Sunday services. I was warned that disunity had broken out, which had led to a split. What I found out is, that often it is not what they tell you, but the *things they fail to tell you* which causes the problems. The elder who had invited me to preach had been in his position for more than thirty years, but the congregation wanted a full-time pastor, not the enduring leadership of this elder, and those with him. Twice in recent years, he had interviewed two prospective preachers to be the pastor, and both times, he was the person who decided they were not suitable, but invited each one in their turn to be the church evangelist. Both candidates agreed, believing the Lord had opened the door, but both felt the overwhelming sense that this elder did not want them there, even after seeing conversions and a small but significant growing congregation, so they left. This routine of one man controlling took place for more than thirty years!

This elder recognised my calling and asked if I could pray and discern the will of the Lord, and like Jeremiah, when I gave it to him, he was not pleased (Jeremiah 42:20-21). The Holy Spirit told me that he should leave and let the others, whom God had sent, to get on with the work! Nevertheless, he insisted that he was the only person who could make this church viable, despite all the decades of failure.

Some months later, I received a phone call from this elder's wife, seeking to know exactly the word I was given by the Holy Spirit for him. When she heard it, she said, "That's not what he told me." Then she told me what had happened to him, after he had rejected the direction of the Lord. The elder was now close to a breakdown because the church had shrunk further to less than a handful and themselves. Yet the elder was still unwilling to let go, because, as I realised, he was a tare who for more than three decades had exercised full control over that church, as numbers dwindled.

The Lord sent me to another church to serve in the fellowship and the pastor said, "Your exactly what we've been praying for. We've been asking the Lord for a prophet and intercessor, and He's sent you." Over the next year, when this pastor and his wife faced any crisis, the Lord led them to me, and I was able to minister prophetic words, direction and helped them with deliverance. Once again, the Lord used me to help them and this prepared the ground for them to receive direction from the Holy Spirit.

On three occasions, this pastor came round my house. Each time I testified that the Holy Spirit had spoken to me, having told me that he was coming and what I was to share with him. On all these occasions, I asked him to spare the time to listen to what the Holy Spirit had given me for him; after all, it was the Holy Spirit who sent him! The Lord told me to remind him about his first calling, but he always told me that he was too busy to listen. Why did he treat the leading of the Holy Spirit with such informality and indifference? Eventually I said to him, "Why did you become a pastor, because your calling was to be an evangelist?" He later confessed this was true, but he chose not to have the time to receive the word God gave me.

As this man was unwilling to receive the word of the Lord, he continued as the pastor in his own flesh, and the church struggled from bad to worse. I saw the Lord trying to reach out to him, but he had stopped up his ears. In the end, he had a breakdown, as he worked nights to pay his bills and led the church in the week. Was this the work of a tare? No, this was rebellion and selfishness, the flesh uncrucified.

At another church in an affluent area, a young homeless man slept in the church porch at night to keep dry and out of the wind. Some of the congregation were concerned, but not for the right reasons, and raised the cry, "What can we do?" Large glass doors were made to order, at a considerable cost and hung in place, shutting off the porch from anybody who wished to shelter there.

At one church I attended for some time, I was invited along to see how the Alpha Course worked and to assist and share. For this church, it was a social event, a night out with a free meal from a highly qualified chef, rather than a friendly way to introduce people to Jesus Christ. One of the church members boasted that she had been on the Alpha Course five times! Another member gleefully stated that this church was the only evangelical one in the diocese, yet the Holy Spirit was not permitted to operate, was not wanted and the majority of those who attended were sadly not born-again, and had not passed from death to life, they were unregenerate.

An elder, responsible for evangelism had a great burden for the prostitutes that hung around outside the church he attended. The elder was so concerned that he spoke one evening to the congregation about this delicate situation, who was going to reach them with the good news? Later, the minister was approached, "I'll deal with it," he said, and spoke to one of the woman members about it. The following week all the prostitutes were gone, and the week after that, "Where are they?" the elder asked the minister, "Why have they not been invited into the warmth and given (a cup of) tea?" "Oh, I dealt with it, the ladies told them to move on!"

As I was tucked away in the hidden life, it did not hinder the work of the Holy Spirit from leading people to me. From time to time, strangers would be guided to my home and contact me by Divine appointment. One day, a pastor from Africa was walking down my road, a complete stranger and he came knocking on my door. He said, "Every time I have passed this house I felt the Holy Spirit prompting me to knock this door." He managed to find the confidence to knock and was pleased to find I was a believer, who was sold-out to God to serve Him full-time. The Holy Spirit gave me a prophecy for him and when I prayed with this brother, the Holy Spirit overpowered him, and all this took place within ten minutes of his arrival!

I was invited to speak to him and his friends a few days later at a church meeting and the Holy Spirit moved in great power. One woman testified that she had never known anything like it. She said since that day when the Spirit came upon her, "I've had my own personal revival for days!"

Once again, I saw the pattern of the Holy Spirit – first He would demonstrate His power and then the person He was trying to speak to, would acknowledge this power. This happened every time and then the Lord would give them a word (which they did not want to receive), but was necessary for true discipleship (Proverbs 3:11-12, Hebrews 12:4-12).

One day I was with this African pastor and I shared with him that God was giving him the opportunity to receive the Holy Spirit as a Person, to indwell him, possess him, lead him and guide him. This was the next step deeper in God's will, which the Lord wanted him to take. Like Ezekiel, the Holy Spirit is ever desiring to take us deeper into Him (Ezekiel 47:1-6), but in every step, there is a further identification with the cross, before we take a further step into Christ's resurrection. 'That I may know Him and the power of His resurrection, and the fellowship of His sufferings, being conformed to His death' (Philippians 3:10).

After I shared the *full cost* with this African pastor, which Rees Howells and others have paid to have this close walk with God, he went home and I heard nothing from him. Then one day he sent me an email explaining that he was too busy building his ministry, and he could not devote that amount of time to get to know God the Holy Spirit. Once again, this was rebellion against God. It was the manifestation of the selfish uncrucified flesh resisting the will of God, in order to promote 'my' ministry (3 John 9-11).

In many of these situations, the Holy Spirit in me was so deeply grieved that I felt tormented by it myself. Peter wrote about people who lived in or taught error (2 Peter 2) and cited Sodom and Gomorrah as an example: 'And delivered righteous Lot, who was oppressed by the filthy conduct of the wicked (for that righteous man, dwelling among them, tormented his righteous soul from day to day by seeing and hearing their lawless deeds)' (2 Peter 2:7-8).

These hard lessons, which I learnt in different churches, took place over decades. I was pleased to learn how God reaches out to His people, but shocked how they often reject Him. Of the ancient people of Israel, the Lord said, "I have stretched out My hands all day long to a rebellious people, who walk in a way that is not good, according to their own thoughts" (Isaiah 65:2). 'Woe to those who go down to Egypt for help, and rely on horses, who trust in chariots because they are many, and in horsemen because they are very strong, but who do not look to the Holy One of Israel, nor seek the Lord!' (Isaiah 31:1). And, ' "Woe to the rebellious children," says the Lord, "Who take counsel, but not of Me and who devise plans, but not of My Spirit, that they may add sin to sin" ' (Isaiah 30:1). In my experience, this testimony is also true of churches, who are dismissive and complacent concerning the Every Creature Commission (Matthew 28:18-20, Mark 16:15), and think of church as a social club, instead of a house of prayer for all nations (Isaiah 56:7, Luke 19:46). Too many pastors and teachers ignore Jesus' teaching on the cost of discipleship and seem content to go on with religious routines, as if God did not notice. The body, if it can, has tried in many places to disconnect itself from the Head (Romans 12:3-8). Yet, I have found in almost every church, chapel or mission hall etc. that there are a few people, who have a good heart and are desperate to go further with the Lord, but don't know how.

Chapter Thirty-One

Go West – America

It pleased the Holy Spirit to hide me away for a time in a small Baptist church, tucked away down a backstreet. It had only a handful of elderly people, mostly retired, and they were faithful with the same light that their fathers and grandfathers had received. They loved their traditions and even wanted to have a church meeting to vote on what colour the walls in the church hall should be (after years of neglect), which my son and I had volunteered to paint. It had been the same colour for more than six decades. They also loved to bake cakes and sell them to the people of the world at a financial loss, in an attempt to raise money for missionaries!

They were good people, but people who had been taught tradition and many were not born-again. They had no real experience of the work of the Holy Spirit and when I returned from my trips serving the Lord, they would always inquire if I had a nice holiday!

It was at this time, one Sunday evening that I was in the pulpit, very high up in this old traditional church building, where they liked the speaker to be, whilst the majority of the people still sat at the back, struggling to hear, then something happened. That night I noticed a couple who slipped in towards the end of the service. The Holy Spirit sent them to tell me that there was an outpouring of the Holy Spirit in Pensacola, Florida, USA, and I was instructed to go there as soon as I could arrange it. The first thing I did was to ask the Holy Spirit if this was from Him and if so, to make the finances available. By the time I went to bed that night, two people had contacted me, both offering me £500 ($800) each. This was a very clear message to me to go and I was there six weeks later.

Three years previously, the Holy Spirit had spoken to me about going to the United States of America. He had shown me very clearly that I was to go to a small town called Mount

Horeb, in a particular state. It was named after the mountain in the Bible, which is first mentioned in Exodus 3:1. 'Now Moses was tending the flock of Jethro his father-in-law, the priest of Midian. And he led the flock to the back of the desert, and came to Horeb, the mountain of God.' While I was still believing the Lord for the finances for this trip, I was led by the Holy Spirit to go to Wales and visit my dearest sister in Christ, Peggy Coulthard, (trained under Rees Howells), who by now was being cared for in a rest home for the elderly. When I arrived the very first thing she said to me was, "You look like a man who is about to emigrate to America."

Peggy's days on earth were drawing to a close and her mind began to wonder, and she got things mixed up. Please be careful dear reader, if ever you come across an elderly man or woman, sat in the corner of God's house, sleeping or acting odd, or unconventional. What you see, is due in part to the fall and banishment from the Garden of Eden (1 Corinthians 15:42). They are very much alive in spirit, but their mind and memory can be confused at times. The man or woman at the corner of God's house may have led millions to Christ in revival or through evangelism; the other may have been the intercessor whom the Holy Spirit used to birth it in their younger days.

Peggy had been an answer to my prayers and she also picked up in her spirit that I was going to the USA, but in her mind, she thought I was emigrating. Based on this one sentence, my family and I all went together. It turned out to be a real break. The Holy Spirit did of course use me and on the Sunday, we visited a very large church. The man on the door discovering that we were English, told a few people and we received a very warm welcome. Part way into the service the minister stopped preaching and said, "I believe the Lord wants the man from England to come to the front and speak." Before I had left for America, I had purchased a pair of sandals in a sale and as the label stated they were in my size, I never tried them on in the shop. At home, when I did try them on, they did not fit me and the Holy Spirit told me they had to travel with me to the USA and He would show me who they were for.

As I began sharing from the front why we had come, the Holy Spirit said, "The sandals are for the pastor." Therefore, I asked my son to get them for me from our hire/rental car and proceeded to share with the pastor, and his flock, that the Holy Spirit wanted the pastor to wear them, as the sandals of the gospel of peace (Ephesians 6:15). The Holy Spirit was concerned that they had been through a difficult time as a church and things had not been handled as the Bible states. To avoid it happening a second time, they must all walk in the gospel of peace, which surpasses all understanding, and loving one another as Christ loved them.

The pastor came forward and tried the sandals on, and they fitted him perfectly, which was a relief to me, because they acted as a confirmation to the word I had given him, and therefore the word was accepted as from the Lord. I also shared about the time we had lost a baby through a miscarriage and that the Word of God says, "God is not a man, that He should lie, nor a son of man, that He should repent. Has He said, and will He not do? Or has He spoken, and will He not make it good?" (Numbers 23:19). After I had finished speaking, a man ran up to me thanking me for all I had shared regarding our miscarriage. This man then placed a hundred dollar bill (£62) in my hand stating, "You will never know how much you have changed my life. Forgive me, I must get home as soon as possible and tell my wife."

My son had a chat with one of the church members who made a disparaging comment about the prophetic word I gave, saying, "I didn't have a clue what he was on about." This often happens when people come to church to be entertained; but if you turn up to meet God, having prayed for the speaker, in all probability you will receive something. Nevertheless, if you turn up in the flesh, as many do, you will be disappointed and confused when God speaks, as this man was.

While I was in England, preparing for my first trip to the USA, the Holy Spirit told me that I would meet some Amish believers, and I did one morning, in the lobby of our motel. An Amish woman was selling some cushion covers etc., and I noticed the quality was very high. The woman asked, "Would you like to purchase anything?" and I replied politely, by saying, "No," but the Holy Spirit whispered, "Yes you would." Therefore, I turned to the woman and she asked, "Have you changed your mind?" "Yes," I said, and I purchased three cushion covers, at the cost of about $30 (£19). I handed over a hundred dollar bill. The woman had no change. The Holy

Spirit whispered, "You don't need any change," so I told the woman, "Please keep it all." She smiled, in the same way as Peggy had, and exclaimed, "Praise the Lord! He promised me He would provide for me!" "What do you mean?" I inquired. "I have come here to see a chiropractor," she said, "but I did not have all the money I needed for the appointment, and the Lord told me to make an appointment and He would provide all I needed and He has."

As I reflect on this, I realise that a man in the church in which I shared gave me $100 (£62) and I gave the same amount to this Amish woman, who clearly had a strong relationship with the Lord and was sensitive to the Holy Spirit. As ever, I was a channel through whom the Lord could pass His money to others.

A few days later, the pastor of the church we visited, invited my family for breakfast and he was wearing the sandals the Holy Spirit had provided for him. They had received a clear word, and had made attempts to follow it, but did they have a full heart to pay the full price to have an outpouring of the Holy Spirit in their church or area? This pastor introduced me to a man the church had employed to arrange the Christmas nativity celebration. I was surprised, because it was only July. They told me they wished it to be, "The biggest and the best ever," and it turned out this man was a professional organiser, who travelled once a week to them, all expenses paid. All this was very new to me, using the Lord's money to entertain the flock. Did this have anything to do with fulfilling Jesus' Every Creature Commission?

The Holy Spirit had another surprise for me, because it was Peggy who had planted the idea of 'emigration' into my mind; I had not sought the Lord to confirm if it was His will or not. It turned out that it was not God's will for us to emigrate, but the Lord allowed me to continue to believe this, to teach me a lesson that I would never forget. Every word must be tested, and we must never step ahead of the revelation God has given us, even if a great man or woman of God gives us a direction, without it being tested and approved by the Holy Spirit. Of course, this will only work if you know the Holy Spirit personally and can hear His voice. Nevertheless, the Lord allowed this idea of emigration to reside in my mind, in order to help test me, to see if I was willing to leave my own nation and the people I was familiar with, like Abraham had to (Matthew 19:29, Luke 14:33). On a secondary point we must also be careful of a 'Gibeonite deception,' this was where Joshua and the elders took what was said as being ok and correct, *without inquiring of the Lord* and the Gibeonites deceived them (Joshua 9:3-27).

It is our responsibility to always check with the Holy Spirit to confirm or deny any leading we receive from another (1 Corinthians 14:29-33). Remember the man of God from Judah was misled by an old prophet and it cost him his life (1 Kings 13). If we spend our lives looking for others to direct us into God's will, instead of cultivating a strong relationship with the Holy Spirit, we may well end up starting out in the Holy Spirit, but ending up in the flesh.

Now back to my trip to Pensacola, Florida, USA, a few years after my first trip to America. I had been sent to Brownsville Assemblies of God, where there was an outpouring of the Holy Spirit, which led to millions of people visiting the church, as God changed many lives.[1] Some people queued from 4:30am, for a seat in the 7pm service! The meetings here were powerful because God was moving and therefore they became controversial. Satan never allows God to save so many souls and to change and touch people's lives, without calling forth his 'hidden' tares to fight. There are sleeping religious spirits in many who are planted in churches to oppose all those who are called to visit or welcome the Holy Spirit in such a way.

All who have read the history of Christian revivals and awakenings will know that Satan always opposes God's work and it is always controversial, as it was in the apostles' day, just like on the day of Pentecost (Acts 2). So how can we know if some new move is from God or not? Is it a Divine visitation or a demonic delusion? If you want to know if something is from God, ask yourself: are people repenting and turning to Jesus Christ, are they reading their Bible more, spending more time in prayer, living more Christ-like lives, embracing the cross and holiness, or are they having a knees-up, running wild and living for self?[2] Ask the Holy Spirit to show you. Don't follow the advice of religious people, who may or may not be in touch with God, because it may be the blind leading the blind (Matthew 15:14).

The internet is ablaze with people who are being used by Satan to oppose all the work of the Holy Spirit (who glorifies Jesus Christ), as the devil vents his hatred and bitterness through them. As Jesus said, "You will know them by their fruit" (Matthew 7:16). In all these internet posts, including social media, your mobile/cell phone, books, or guidance being given by word of mouth, do you witness the fruit of the Holy Spirit – which is love, joy, peace, patience, goodness, long suffering and self control (Galatians 5:22), or the fruit of Satan – division, jealousy, hatred, strife, restlessness, pride, bitterness, misery and accusation, etc.? The devil's prime occupation is accusation! (Revelation 12:10).

Far too many have walked outside of God's fold of obedience, that the only way they can feel better about their backsliding heart is to accuse others of being worse! 'An ungodly man digs up evil, and it is on his lips like a burning fire' (Proverbs 16:27). Some look *only* for the negative, amidst so much positive, and *only* talk, write or emphasise the negative as a means to denounce the whole. They reject and denounce the majority because of a minority (or a single event/incident).

Those in leadership must highlight error, mistakes and bad doctrine when it arises, to protect the flock, but the spirit in which we speak or write, can testify which spirit operates in us – the Holy Spirit, the flesh or demonic spirits. Is it to edify and correct in meekness and love or just to denounce and tear down? As Jesus said, "You do not know what manner of spirit you are of. For the Son of Man did not come to destroy men's lives but to save them" (Luke 9:55-56). 'To whom have you uttered words? And whose spirit came from you?' (Job 26:4).

God moved mightily in the Brownsville Revival (1995-2000) in Pensacola, Florida, as the gospel of Jesus Christ was preached. Around four million people came and heard Steve Hill's Christ-encompassing, cross-embracing messages of repentance and holiness, as tears rolled down his face. The Holy Spirit was outpoured and it became one of the longest continuing revivals in a single location in the last two centuries. It was not a series of evangelistic campaigns, but a true outpouring of the Holy Spirit, and when God comes amongst His people things will happen. Most people who left the church sanctuary went away desiring a closer walk with God and more of Him, others who were led into repentance and met the Saviour had their lives changed forever.

We received a very warm welcome from the staff of Brownsville church, and as I thought about what was happening at Brownsville, compared to what happened to the church I had visited when in America on a previous trip, I wondered, 'Why has the Holy Spirit chosen to visit here and not the other church? Was it because God found a man and others with him, willing to pay the full price for God's glory to come down, rather than to be entertained?' One got a revival, which changed lives and swept people into the Kingdom of God, the other got an expensive nativity play.

Chapter Thirty-Two

Re-Crossing the Jordan

Out of all the people that the Lord God led out of Egypt, who were twenty years old or above, only two crossed the Jordan River into the Promised Land. Why? Because they had a different spirit from the rest, like the leaders at Brownsville, Pensacola, had a different spirit from many others I had met (Numbers 14:24). The Lord said, "Surely none of the men who came up from Egypt, from twenty years old and above, shall see the land of which I swore to Abraham, Isaac, and Jacob, because they have not wholly followed Me, except Caleb the son of Jephunneh, the Kenizzite, and Joshua the son of Nun, for they have wholeheartedly followed the Lord" (Numbers 32:11-13).

It is a metaphor when I say, "God is preparing a new generation to re-cross the Jordan and reclaim the ground the enemy has taken from us, while the Church in the West has been sleeping." What is the purpose of the Church? Are we to keep on meeting, for the sake of meeting? Is our commission to entertain? Should our prayer meetings be shallow and led by our own ideas and fears? Should they be a wish list to God of what I or we want? Why do so many churches and the Christians in them feel lost and directionless?

When the Holy Spirit took possession of Rees Howells' surrendered body in the early twentieth century, the Lord taught him how God is ever trying to reach out to the world with the gospel. At the end of 1934, Rees Howells received the Every Creature Vision, a revelation from God that Jesus Christ's last command to the Church had still not been obeyed, two thousand years after His ascension![1] Jesus told His disciples that "every creature" must be given the chance to hear and respond to the gospel, and whoever believes will be saved. As a sign to all, accompanying the preaching of the gospel would be the power to deliver people from demons, healing of the sick, supernatural protection and the outpouring of the Holy Spirit, which would include the gift of tongues being given to believers (Mark 16:15-18).

Jesus Christ was not crucified and raised again to life so we could have a dead religion! The Lord did not call people to Himself so we could get bored and tired of empty religious rituals! God called us and has a destiny for us all (Ephesians 2:10). He wants us to surrender our lives to God, fully and completely (Romans 12:1-2), so the Holy Spirit can live through us, to reach the world with the gospel of Jesus Christ! God wants to empower us and transform us into the image of His Son (Romans 8:29). Paul explained it like this: 'For the Kingdom of God is not in word but in power' (1 Corinthians 4:20). Do you have the power of God operating in your life? God does not have a special plan for important people only, but for all Christians. Do you want to live a life in the Holy Spirit? Do you want to be made a branch in the Lord's vine? Would you like to experience Divine appointments and power for God's glory?

Rees Howells responded, "Yes" to all those questions and committed himself, in the Holy Spirit, to a lifetime of Holy Spirit led intercession. One of his great burdens was to see the Every Creature Commission completed, and for this to take place there needed to be a release of finances to fund missionaries. What is certain from his life, is that the Holy Spirit gained an intercession through Rees Howells, his son Samuel, and the team of intercessors at the Bible College of Wales (1924-2004), for the men, women and finances, which will be needed, to complete the Every Creature Commission.[2]

Rees Howells had a vision of 10,000 men and women who would respond in full to the Holy Spirit's invitation to surrender all to Christ, and allow the Holy Spirit to live His life through them. He had the assurance that such people would be raised up, and *you* could be one of them. What will their lives be like? These are the ones that the Holy Spirit will call and enter, as He did with the apostles and others down the generations. He will form them into a spiritual army of Christian warriors, marching in love, one by one, into every spiritual battle, which the Lord leads them, by prayer and intercession until victory has been gained.

The Church is not a social club and our commission is not to entertain, or to meet together with no vision or purpose – we are called to reach the world with the gospel. To do this, intercessors must go ahead in spiritual warfare, as Paul explained: 'To the intent that now the manifold wisdom of God might be made known by the Church to the principalities and powers in the heavenly places, according to the eternal purpose which He accomplished in Christ Jesus our Lord' (Ephesians 3:10-11).

All who are called into this life of intercession will be formed into the image of Jesus Christ, by the Person of the Holy Spirit living in them, and they will walk in the light as overcomers. "What is an overcomer?" you ask. When the Lord Jesus Christ invited Rees Howells to surrender his life, so God the Holy Spirit could live in and through him, the Spirit said to Rees. "On no account will I allow you to cherish a single thought of self, and the life I will live in you will be one hundred percent for others. You will never be able to save yourself, any more than the Saviour could when He was on earth. Now, are you willing?" That evening a friend asked Rees Howells if he could testify if he had accepted the Lord's challenge and the Holy Spirit challenged him, "How can you do that? You have seen the position of the overcomers, but you have not yet entered it. I have been dealing with you for five days; you must give Me your decision!"[3]

An overcomer is a person who has made a full and unconditional surrender of his or her self to the Lord Jesus, and has invited the Holy Spirit to live His life through him or her for the glorification of Jesus. They do not live for self, they live for Christ. Everything they are and own belongs to the Lord, and they can testify with Paul, in truth that: 'I have been crucified with Christ; it is no longer I who live, but Christ lives in me; and the life which I now live in the flesh I live by faith in the Son of God, who loved me and gave Himself for me' (Galatians 2:20). An overcomer is a person who can sing, "I surrender all," or any other worship song or hymn of full devotion, without their conscience telling them that they are singing lies and calling it worship. It is a mockery to sing of such a surrender, when one remains in full possession of all one is and am, the syndrome of *me, myself and I* is sin.

These overcomers, the 10,000 and perhaps more, which Rees Howells interceded for, will not be religious, by any stretch of the imagination, and they will appear to some, to be very different than other believers. This is because they will be and need to be. Many Christians have become one with the world and those who are one with God are a threat to them. This is why Paul warned: 'Do not be conformed to the pattern of this world' (Romans 12:2), and Christ came to 'deliver us from this present evil age' (Galatians 1:4). We cannot be one with a world, which is in rebellion against the will and standards of God. Jesus said, "The world hates you" (John 15:19), because your light shines upon their evil deeds. Jesus said, "For everyone practicing evil hates the light and does not come to the light, lest his deeds should be exposed" (John 3:20).

The overcomers I am referring to will not be regular church goers as you think, satisfied with empty ritual or the status quo. They will know there is more and will want more of God; perhaps this is you? Contrary to popular belief, we are not serving God when we meet without Him, just for the sake of meeting, to do what we do once again. Jesus said, "The wind blows where it wishes, and you hear the sound of it, but cannot tell where it comes from and where it goes. So is everyone who is born of the Spirit" (John 3:8). In other words, the ways of the Holy Spirit in people's lives will be an affront to religious people, who hope if they turn up for a Sunday meeting, and tick a few boxes on prayer, worship and Bible reading, that God is pleased.

The apostle Paul wrote: 'And He [Jesus] died for all, that those who live should live no longer for themselves, but for Him who died for them and rose again' (2 Corinthians 5:15). Is this your testimony, you live for God and not for yourself?

God spoke to Amos to warn the Lord's people that He hates religious rituals, devoid of true worship (Amos 5:21-23). God used Isaiah to tell the people, "To what purpose is the multitude of your sacrifices to Me? ...Bring no more futile sacrifices.... Your appointed feasts My soul hates. They are a trouble to Me, I am weary of bearing them" (Isaiah 1:11-14). In these passages the Lord tells us how troubled He is by empty religious rituals, devoid of true surrender. They trouble God, just as the empty religion of the Pharisees and Sadducees troubled Jesus. The Lord knew those two sects were very religious and respected in society, but all their religion was a sham (Matthew 23:14-36).

If you welcome the Holy Spirit to lead you and live through you, it will be a challenge to many. Over the years, some have called me a spiritual gipsy because of the way the Spirit led me to speak His word in many churches, others said I was doing the devil's work or was deceived, when I was led to call for repentance. Very few could see that the Holy Spirit had an itinerant ministry for me, because there were few who could speak His word, or were bold enough to speak it, when needed. The Lord sent me to help others and He taught me in every situation He sent me to. He used me to help others and he trained and refined me in the process, and when some of these churches rejected the Holy Spirit, the Lord left them to their own work until it closed. For me, it was on the job training, as opposed to being sat down and bombarded with sermon after sermon, with no action.

I was told more than once by church members that I was not really committed "to our church" because I did not attend every single meeting. Perhaps they were right; I was not committed to "*their* church" because I am committed to the true Church of Jesus Christ. Little did these people know that as they were meeting and witnessing yet another re-run of a powerless meeting from the past, that God was working in and through me and others, at the very same time, elsewhere. Whilst religious traditions prevailed, the Holy Spirit was at work. You might ask, "Why did you not tell them what the Holy Spirit was doing elsewhere, whilst they were meeting?" My only reply is to confess that my life is not my own and the Holy Spirit in me, is not answerable to any religious man or woman, or a religious spirit. Jeremiah was pressed to conform to a broken religious system, but he was in touch with God and could not. I was not told to try to explain or justify my actions to them, because it is the Lord who vindicates. Whilst many were meeting for the sake of meeting, the Holy Spirit was reaching out throughout the world, and I felt sincere sympathy for those who did not realise that their endless meetings did not glorify God, because He was not welcome.

In the last days the true Church and the false church are separating even further apart. The true Church will be deeply concerned to meet the conditions of discipleship, set forth by Jesus Christ in the Gospels, and will welcome the Holy Spirit in their midst to do His work. The true Church will live with eternity in mind and will set its mind on the things of God (Colossians 3:2). Meanwhile, the false church will outwardly be religious, but will say in its heart, "Don't bother us with Jesus' teaching on the cost of discipleship; He didn't mean that teaching was for us anyway. We've been called to be blessed and we don't want anything to interfere with the comfortable lives we're seeking to live. And, we don't want any of that fanaticism which happened with the Wesley's or Evan Roberts in those revivals; that's all over now. God doesn't speak today. Come on everybody, let's sing hymn 252, I surrender all."

The Holy Spirit is the Spirit of Truth and teaches all that Jesus taught (John 14:17, John 16:13-14). But there is one very big difference; the Holy Spirit will live out the teaching of the Bible in and through those He is invited to enter, in each and every situation He leads them into. The truth is this, the Church with all its best evangelistic efforts, including the forgotten Decade of Evangelism is still having little or no impact upon communities. Churches are shrinking and shutting, instead of thriving in the Holy Spirit. This is a sign of God's judgment for disobedience, for a Church that does not reflect its Master, or obey Him, is no longer a lampstand for all to see (Revelation 1:20, Revelation 2:1).

Why did God show Rees Howells that 10,000 people would surrender all to Him and He would live through them? Because, the Holy Spirit working in and through overcomers, in revival or awakenings, will achieve more in the lifetime of the Holy Spirit's outpouring, than we can achieve in all our lifetimes of effort and fleshly planning! "This is the word of the Lord to Zerubbabel: 'Not by might nor by power, but by My Spirit,' says the Lord of hosts" (Zechariah 4:6).

To be led by the Holy Spirit means we cannot struggle and strive to enter into the calling God has for us. We must obey Him in all things and that is the only call. With the changes that took place because of the Charismatic Renewal and the subsequent outpourings of the Holy Spirit, with the gifts of the Spirit being made manifest, there was for some a tendency to still operate in the flesh, to struggle and strive, by whatever means, to be seen. The last day overcomers will be the opposite in spirit to those who strive to be in the limelight. They will do their best not to bring attention to themselves, because they will point to Jesus Christ alone, for the glory of God. 'For I determined not to know anything among you except Jesus Christ and Him crucified' (1 Corinthians 2:2).

Chapter Thirty-Three

The Overcomers at Work

One evening I was walking along a beach when I noticed a lump of jagged rock, which was once part of the cliff rock. It had broken away with a landslip and had been rolling around in the surf. There are times when the Holy Spirit speaks without words and this was one such time, and I knew I was to pick up the lump of jagged rock. The Lord said four times to Jeremiah, asking, "What do you see?" as He spoke to him through nature (Jeremiah 1:11). This white rock that I picked up was about the size of a man's hand, and as I proceeded along the shore, I found three more rocks, each one smaller, and smoother in looks and touch, than the one before. The last one had been transformed from the large rock substance that I first found, into a smooth pebble, measuring 4 cm in diameter. Time and tide, working with the elements had taken a large, jagged piece of rock, which once fell from the cliff and in the process of time, turned it into a smooth, useable pebble. This reminded me of how the Holy Spirit can take a rough person, that the devil once controlled and shouted through (2 Timothy 2:26), and turn him or her into something that has been refined by God's fire, and becomes fit for purpose, that He can speak through. The Lord is the Master Potter and we, like clay, must be remoulded into Christ's image (Jeremiah 18:2-7). The Lord will not force us to change, we must invite Him to change us, and accept it when it is hard, as our natural selfish nature, is replaced for His Divine selfless nature.

Today, in this generation the Lord God is seeking to raise up and release men and women, like the first disciples, to walk in the power of the Holy Spirit, as Jesus did on earth. The Lord is seeking a return to New Testament Christianity and this is what truly inspired me when I first became a Christian. I was told that the same Holy Spirit who worked in Jesus and the apostles, is working in the world today, and we are to expect the same results. All these decades on, I can look back upon years of Divine appointments, set in the midst of my regular routines. These testimonies, which I have shared and others I have not told, should not be exceptional, but should be part of what it means to be a Christian. Signs, wonders, miracles, gifts of the Spirit, are all part of normal Christianity; religion without power is what is abnormal and is a sign of spiritual decay, decline or even death.

Some of the people God is raising up, I believe, will experience the most unusual miracles like the apostles witnessed. Passports and visas will not hinder some of them, as they will be transported by the Holy Spirit, when necessary, as Philip was, from one place to another. 'Now when they came up out of the water, the Spirit of the Lord caught Philip away, so that the eunuch saw him no more; and he went on his way rejoicing. But Philip was found at Azotus. And passing through, he preached in all the cities till he came to Caesarea' (Acts 8:39-40). It was the same with Ezekiel: 'Then the Spirit lifted me up, and I heard behind me a great thunderous voice: "Blessed is the glory of the Lord from His place!" ' (Ezekiel 3:12).

Many true believers are praying for and looking forward to the promise of a global revival and awakening, as Joel prophesied this outpouring in the last days when God pours out His Spirit (Joel 2:28-32), a final ingathering of the harvest before Jesus Christ comes again. However, let us not forget that Satan will not let God move in power without a fight. For some, it will be revival or riots, like the days of John Wesley, whilst others will be led to cast their shadows over the sick, like Peter and people will be healed to glorify Jesus Christ (Acts 5:15-16). Our brethren in China and other parts of the world know what it means to be persecuted and this is a sign of the end times, as well as, signs, wonders and miracles accompanying the preaching of God's word.

If you think the end time outpouring of the Holy Spirit will be days of ease, as heaven comes to earth, then remember what happened in the apostles' days! The outpouring of the Holy Spirit led to great troubles, as well as joy (Acts 13:48-52). The Lord told us He did not come to bring peace, but a spiritual sword, separating the clean from the unclean, the saved from the rebellious (Matthew 10:34-39). Into this mix, the devil will do all he can to bring confusion, by introducing counterfeit measures, as the Scriptures declare: 'The coming of the lawless one is according to the working of Satan, with all power, signs and lying wonders, and with all unrighteous deception among those who perish, because they did not receive the love of the truth, that they might be saved. And for this reason God will send them strong delusion, that they should believe the lie, that they all may be condemned who did not believe the truth but had pleasure in unrighteousness' (2 Thessalonians 2:9-12).

This great outpouring of the Holy Spirit, with deceptions taking place in other areas, will lead, as all revivals do, to another thrust of missionary endeavour to reach every creature with the gospel.[1] In some regions of the world there are unreached tribes of people living in jungles who are protected by law from outside contact.[2] They have no immunity from "Western diseases" and contact with these untouched tribes, as history has proved, can wipe out large numbers of each tribe. To combat this, the Holy Spirit will call intercessors to pray for overcomers, who in turn will visit them, in the power of the Holy Spirit and speak to them in their own tongue, to share the good news of Jesus Christ with them, with signs following. The Holy Spirit's Presence in and over them will stop any germs or diseases attacking those with whom they share the gospel.[3] Sadly, a few in the enthusiasm of their own flesh, will go out and step ahead of their calling, by raising up their own support without the Lord, and will go on to dissipate the call by working on their own ideas. Some may well make contact with those unknown, but without the Holy Spirit's guidance and the miracles He supplies, they may well introduce them to the devil's diseases (John 10:10).

Signs and wonders on their own will not be a sign of the truthfulness of the last day servants of God, because, "If they do not speak according to this word, it is because there is no light in them" (Isaiah 8:20). The Bible will be your guide to test and discern, in the Holy Spirit who is from God or man, so you must get to know your Bible now!

Those who have been called and sent forth by God will have the fruit of the Spirit bearing fruit in them. The devil cannot counterfeit love because it is the fruit of the Holy Spirit, but he can and will produce counterfeit gifts in his vessels, sent to lead people away from Christ. This is why Jesus warned of false believers, "Beware of false prophets, who come to you in sheep's clothing, but inwardly they are ravenous wolves. You will know them by their fruits. Do men gather grapes from thornbushes or figs from thistles? Even so, every good tree bears good fruit, but a bad tree bears bad fruit. A good tree cannot bear bad fruit, nor can a bad tree bear good fruit. Every tree that does not bear good fruit is cut down and thrown into the fire. Therefore by their fruits you will know them. Not everyone who says to Me, 'Lord, Lord,' shall enter the Kingdom of heaven, but he who does the will of My Father in heaven. Many will say to Me in that day, 'Lord, Lord, have we not prophesied in Your name, cast out demons in Your name, and done many wonders in Your name?' And then I will declare to them, 'I never knew you; depart from Me, you who practice lawlessness!' " (Matthew 7:15-23).

If you accept the call to be a last days overcomer, the Holy Spirit will set a guard over your heart and tongue, and you will be expected to meet God's high standards of holiness. God said, "Be holy for I am holy" (Leviticus 11:44), and Jesus said, "Be perfect" (Matthew 5:48). Be warned, if you are called, chosen and commissioned to go, guard your tongue (Numbers 12:1-16, James 3:1-12). Once again, you will be well advised and wise to read, study and meditate on these Scriptures.

The Holy Spirit is very sensitive and He will leave you if you are not careful (Psalm 51:11). Most churches do not know who they are dealing with, when they casually speak of the Holy Spirit. I have seen on more than one occasion, film footage of Kathryn Kuhlman whilst ministering on a platform, crying and pleading with the people not to grieve the Holy Spirit (Ephesians 4:30), because He was all she had. If He is grieved, He will leave.

Today, some in ministry have left the narrow road, with its small gate and chosen the broad road, with its wide gate (Matthew 7:13-14). They have trusted in all of man's methods and this has grieved the Holy Spirit, and in so doing, they are struggling financially. They have agreed overdrafts, which is akin to paying a tithe to the devil; taking money from believers and siphoning it from God's Kingdom, to give to the world. The overcomers which the Holy Spirit will enter will receive all they need, as long as they are doing His work, His way, in His time frame, and they will live sacrificially like the apostles (1

Corinthians 4:9-13). Remember some of those recalled in the Holy Spirit's hall of faith, were the ones rejected and despised on earth, suffering great hardships for the Lord (Hebrews 11:35-40). 'Therefore let us go forth to Him, outside the camp, bearing His reproach. For here we have no continuing city, but we seek the one to come' (Hebrews 13:13-14).

Who is the Holy Spirit? Even though at times, there can be a special closeness to Him, as you abide with the Holy Spirit, you must never forget He is God. Paul warned: 'Do not grieve the Holy Spirit of God' (Ephesians 4:30). Anything you say, any vow or promise you make, He will remember. We have all known times when we have been so jubilant that we have spoken out without thought to what we said. He is so tender and loving, but also very strict about what we say or claim. We are human. He is not. He knows our motives and where they are rooted.

The Holy Spirit has a sense of humour, but He dislikes all unreality. It is pointless to say to Him about some vow or promise, "I meant it at the time," because He knows that if we do not fulfil what we stated, we never did truly mean it. Whenever I have said to Him, "I love you Lord," He will smile so graciously and tenderly, because we only love Him in measure, but are not aware of it ourselves.

We are God's children and at times, act like young children who say to their father, "I do love you daddy," but what motives can hide behind such statements! Have they broken something? Do they want something? You cannot, dare not, treat the Holy Spirit like a human being, for He is not human. He is God's Holy Spirit, a Person, with His own will, which far exceeds yours. Peter said to Ananias, "Why has Satan filled your heart to lie to the Holy Spirit? ...You have not lied to man, but to God" (Acts 5:2, 4). He is strict, but He can also melt you in an instant, with His love, which is so pure and holy that it penetrates every part of your being.

It is my own personal belief that you can never truly come to know and fully understand the Third Person of the Trinity and His ways. If you have invited the Holy Spirit to introduce Himself to you, you will be *ever* learning and getting closer to Him, if you obey; but He ever remains God and we are only human. The Holy Spirit is continually doing all He can to reveal Jesus to us and bring Him glory, so the Spirit Himself will always be beyond us. Jesus said, "However, when He, the Spirit of Truth, has come, He will guide you into all truth; for He will not speak on His own authority, but whatever He hears He will speak; and He will tell you things to come. He will glorify Me, for He will take of what is Mine and declare it to you. All things that the Father has are Mine. Therefore I said that He will take of Mine and declare it to you" (John 16:13-15).

There have been occasions in my life when the Holy Spirit has drawn close to me and every time, I felt like Isaiah did. "Woe is me, for I am undone! Because I am a man of unclean lips and I dwell in the midst of a people of unclean lips; for my eyes have seen the King, the Lord of hosts" (Isaiah 6:5). I can tell you of one special time, when I felt Him touch my arm as we walked together late one night, in fellowship. How afraid and yet protected I felt by His presence. I dared not look up.

Who is the Holy Spirit? He is God on earth, here and now, the agent of revival, and in the light of Jesus Christ, we are transparent before Him. Fifty-one years ago, from the time I write, I walked with a small chain in my hand to hurt another, for all the wrong reasons; today, I walk with Him, as part of a great chain of grace, that reaches all over the earth. This chain of God's grace and mercy, joined link by link by those surrendered and filled with Him, can be used to save others who are bound and chained here on earth.

As Isaiah prophesied of the Lord Jesus, "The Spirit of the Lord God is upon Me, because the Lord has anointed Me to preach good tidings to the poor; He has sent Me to heal the broken-hearted, to proclaim liberty to the captives and the opening of the prison to those who are bound; to proclaim the acceptable year of the Lord and the day of vengeance of our God. To comfort all who mourn, to console those who mourn in Zion, to give them beauty for ashes, the oil of joy for mourning, the garment of praise for the spirit of heaviness; that they may be called trees of righteousness, the planting of the Lord, that He may be glorified" (Isaiah 61:1-3).

What are we living for? To obey the Lord Jesus Christ, as the Holy Spirit reveals His will to us! What is the Lord's ultimate will? That the Every Creature Commission may be fulfilled! "As I live," says the Lord God, "I have no pleasure in the death of the wicked, but that the wicked turn from his way and live..." (Ezekiel 33:11). 'For this is good and acceptable in the sight of God our Saviour, who desires all men to be saved and to come to the knowledge of the truth' (1 Timothy 2:3-4).

Jesus said, "Go into all the world and preach the gospel to every creature. He who believes and is baptised will be saved; but he who does not believe will be condemned. And these signs will follow those who believe: In My name they will cast out demons; they will speak with new tongues; they will take up serpents; and if they drink anything deadly, it will by no means hurt them; they will lay hands on the sick, and they will recover" (Mark 16:15-18). Jesus said, "All authority has been given to Me in heaven and on earth. Go therefore and make disciples of all the nations, baptising them in the name of the Father and of the Son and of the Holy Spirit, teaching them to observe all things that I have commanded you; and lo, I am with you always, even to the end of the age" (Matthew 28:18-20).

Chapter Thirty-Four

The Challenge

God is looking for men and women after His own heart, who will do His will (Acts 13:22). Being obedient to the Holy Spirit is not always popular, but it is very effective, and most rewarding, as the following people have testified in Scripture: Matthew, Mark, Luke, John and Paul, to name only five from the New Testament. In modern history, there are many the Lord Jesus used, like: Jonathan Edwards, John and Charles Wesley, George Whitefield, William Wilberforce, Lord Shaftsbury, George Müller, Charles Finney, Billy Bray, C. H. Spurgeon, Florence Nightingale, D. L. Moody, J. Hudson Taylor, William and Catherine Booth, Maria Woodwood Etta, Evan Roberts, Amy Semple McPherson, Rees Howells, George and Stephen Jeffreys, Kathryn Kuhlman, Samuel Rees Howells, Jean Darnell, Reinhard Bonnke, Luis Palau, Steve Hill and _____. I have left a space for your name, if you are willing to be made willing? In addition, there is a warning of the personal cost: You will know sleepless nights, you will be assailed on occasions with doubt, fear, discouragement, intimidation and oppression. If it happened to Elijah and Jeremiah, it can happen to us (1 Kings 19:1-4, Jeremiah 9:2). If you are called and have decided to sign up to the school of the Holy Spirit, you may not be in the limelight of willing souls who have won many to the Lord, with signs and wonders confirming the preaching of the gospel; instead, like me and thousands of others, you may be hidden away for a season. One thing is for sure, if you become a true messenger of Jesus Christ you will be opposed.

Orville Gardener said, "When a prophet is accepted and deified, his message is lost. The prophet is only useful so long as he is stoned as a public nuisance for calling us to repentance, disturbing our comfortable routines, breaking our respectable idols, shattering our sacred conventions."[1]

G. D. Watson (1845-1924) was a Wesleyan Methodist minister and evangelist. He wrote: 'If God has called you to be really like Jesus He will draw you into a life of crucifixion and humility, and put upon you such demands of obedience, that you will not be able to follow other people or measure yourself by other Christians, and in many ways He will seem to let other people do things which He will not let you do.

'Other Christians and ministers who seem very religious and useful, may push themselves, pull wires, and work schemes to carry out their plans, but you cannot do it, and if you attempt it, you will meet with such failure and rebuke from the Lord as to make you sorely penitent.

'Others may boast of themselves, of their work, of their successes, of their writings, but the Holy Spirit will not allow you to do any such thing, and if you begin it, He will lead you into some deep mortification that will make you despise yourself and all your good works.

'Others may be allowed to succeed in making money, or may have a legacy left to them, but it is likely God will keep you poor, because He wants you to have something far better than gold, namely, a helpless dependence upon Him, that He may have the privilege of supplying your needs day by day out of an unseen treasury.

'The Lord may let others be honoured and put forward, and keep you hidden in obscurity, because He wants to produce some choice fragrant fruit for His coming glory, which can only be produced in the shade. He may let others be great, but keep you small. He may let others do a work for Him and get the credit for it, but He will make you work and toil on without knowing how much you are doing; and then to make your work still more precious He may let others get credit for the work you have done, and thus make your reward ten times greater when Jesus comes.

'The Holy Spirit will put a strict watch over you, with a jealous love, and will rebuke you for little words and feelings or for wasting your time, which other Christians never feel distressed over. So make up your mind that God is an infinite Sovereign, and has a right to do as He pleases with His own. He may not explain to you a thousand things which puzzle your reason in His dealings with you, but if you absolutely sell yourself to be His love slave, He will wrap you up in jealous love, and bestow upon you many blessings which come only to those who are in the inner circle.

'Settle it forever, then, that you are to deal directly with the Holy Spirit, and that He is to have the privilege of tying your tongue, or chaining your hand, or closing your eyes, in ways that He does not seem to use with others. Now, when you are so possessed with the living God that you are, in your secret heart, pleased and delighted over this peculiar, personal, private, jealous guardianship and management of the Holy Spirit over your life, you will have found the vestibule of heaven.'[2]

There is no glory for the flesh in this kind of life, but God is well pleased and you will learn to be His friend. Jesus said, "No longer do I call you servants, for a servant does not know what his master is doing; but I have called you friends" (John 15:15). Do you want to be a true friend of God?

As there is no glory for man, you may ask, "Why did you publish your testimony?" The answer is simple – God told me to! I knew the lessons the Lord taught me should not be lost, and even before the millennium I began to share my story with a publisher, on the understanding that on my promotion to glory, they may wish to publish some or all of it. I never wanted to publish this account whilst I was still living.

My reluctance to have my life story in print whilst I was still alive was also the start of another battle. My unwillingness to publish anything had become an unexpected stronghold, which I was not going to let go off. The handful of people close to me, who knew what the Holy Spirit had been doing through me over the years, kept saying, "You should do it now." This was a message I received several times by the few trusted people who are near me and the ministry. Nevertheless, I felt unable to bring myself to do it. I was always obedient to God's instructions, but I struggled with this one. I was reminded by the Holy Spirit, how when the time came for Rees Howells to lay down His life and body to the Holy Spirit, he had, 'To be willing to be made willing,' by the Holy Spirit. I too was made willing and overnight my attitude changed. I was now willing and I became enthusiastic to recall the wonders of the Lord on a notepad and by dictation.

Chapter Thirty-Five

Three Shocks and a Tare

If you accept the call to be an overcomer, filled with the Holy Spirit and emptied bit by bit of self – you will receive greater revelation and many shocks. The flesh life will fight for its life and the only answer is crucifixion with Christ, death to self. In addition, your eyes will be opened and like Jeremiah or Ezekiel, you will see the true spiritual condition of God's people. Religion wants everything to be 'nice' and 'easy,' but a Holy Spirit led life, walking in the Spirit means participating in spiritual warfare, which the Church is called and commissioned to participate in (Ephesians 3:10-11, Ephesians 6:10-18). The Holy Spirit not only shows us how to pray, but also exposes falsehood to bring repentance, forgiveness and grace – if it is accepted by those who are guilty.

Jesus was betrayed by Judas (Luke 22:21), one of His apostles (Matthew 10:2-4), so we should not be surprised when someone close to us does the same. Unfortunately I was. The subject of tares, for some, will be difficult and complex to understand. If God has members of the Body of Christ, who are truly committed to Him, then it follows that the devil will have counterfeited the same (2 Corinthians 11:14). The Bible calls these people tares or weeds (Matthew 13:38). The apostle John warned: 'Little children, it is the last hour; and as you have heard that the Antichrist is coming, even now many antichrists have come, by which we know that it is the last hour. *They went out from us, but they were not of us*; for if they had been of us, they would have continued with us; but they went out that they might be made manifest, that none of them were of us' (1 John 2:18-19).

You may be familiar with the term church plant, or church planting; the apostles planted churches, as do some missionaries. Tares are devil plants. Satan plants them in churches, fellowships and in Christian ministries etc. Jesus explained it in a parable. He said, "The Kingdom of heaven is like a man who sowed good seed in his field; but while men slept, his enemy came and sowed tares among the wheat and went his way. But when the grain had sprouted and produced a crop, then the tares also appeared. So the servants of the owner came and said to him, 'Sir, did you not sow good seed in your field? How then does it have tares?' He said to them, 'An enemy has done this.' The servants said to him, 'Do you want us then to go and gather them up?' But he said, 'No, lest while you gather up the tares you also uproot the wheat with them. Let both grow together until the harvest and at the time of harvest I will say to the reapers, 'First gather together the tares and bind them in bundles to burn them, but gather the wheat into my barn' " (Matthew 13:24-30).

'Then Jesus sent the multitude away and went into the house and His disciples came to Him, saying, "Explain to us the parable of the tares of the field." He answered and said to them, "He who sows the good seed is the Son of Man. The field is the world, the good seeds are the sons of the Kingdom, but the tares are the sons of the wicked one. The enemy who sowed them is the devil, the harvest is the end of the age, and the reapers are the angels. Therefore, as the tares are gathered and burned in the fire, so it will be at the end of this age. The Son of Man will send out His angels, and they will *gather out of His Kingdom* all things that offend, and those who practice lawlessness and will cast them into the furnace of fire. There will be wailing and gnashing of teeth. Then the righteous will shine forth as the sun in the Kingdom of their Father. He who has ears to hear, let him hear!" ' (Matthew 13:36-43).

As a general rule, tares are so deceived and deluded, that they are not aware of it. This is why tares can think they are part of God's Kingdom, when all their actions prove they serve another (1 John 2:15-17). As they deceive others, so they are deceived themselves: 'Impostors will grow worse and worse, deceiving and being deceived' (2 Timothy 3:13). Tares arise when 'religious-minded' people give their will over to the will of evil spirits; and just as the Holy Spirit seeks a body to live in and work through, so does the devil, through antichrist spirits. These spirits are literally antagonists of Christ, enemies of the Lord and Christianity; but they live and work through people who, outwardly at least, are not against Jesus Christ or Christianity. These weaker antichrist spirits who find homes in rebellious religious people are part of the preparation for the Antichrist and the false church (2 Thessalonians 2:3). Jesus is coming back to reign for a millennium on earth, and Hitler with the Nazi regime, and others, wanted to have their own counterfeit millennial reign.

Jesus warned that in the last days, there will be wars, famines, pestilences, earthquakes and great persecution (Matthew 24:6-10). Then the Lord said, "Many will be offended, will betray one another and will hate one another. Then many false prophets will rise up and deceive many. And because lawlessness will abound, the love of many will grow cold" (Matthew 24:10-14). The Lord clearly states in verse 10, that *many*, not a few, will turn away, *betray* and *hate others*. In verse 12, the Lord tells us *the love of many will grow cold*, many, not the few.

In 2 Thessalonians 1, reference is made concerning Jesus' second coming. It will not happen until the rebellion, falling away or apostasy occurs. This is the deliberate rejection of God's truth; and from it will emerge a true Church and a false church, filled with people like you and me, one will be on the Lord's side, another on the devil's side; and yet both will be outwardly religious (1 Timothy 1:19-20, 2 Timothy 4:10). Jude explained that these religious people will be spiritually empty and will produce terrible fruit (Jude 12-13).

Only the Holy Spirit knows those who are Christ's wheat or the devil's tares, but if the Holy Spirit is not welcomed in any building or meeting of believers, how can they claim that it is God's house? If the body of a man is dead without its spirit, then it follows that a church without the Holy Spirit is also dead. In addition, if you reject the Holy Spirit, then you are more vulnerable to receive other spirits!

Over the years, I had three great shocks when the Holy Spirit spoke to me about my close friend. We had been friends for decades and I was meditating on second Thessalonians, concerning the man of lawlessness mentioned in 2 Thessalonians 2, which is another reference to the Antichrist, who will oppose God and set himself up in God's temple. Verse 7 of the same chapter tells us that the secret power of lawlessness is already at work in the world.

We know terrible times will be coming to the true Church and to prepare for this battle, we have been told to watch out for those who cause divisions amongst us, because they are not serving the will of the Lord Jesus Christ, but their own sensual appetites. 'Now I urge you, brethren, note those who cause divisions and offences, contrary to the doctrine which you learned, and avoid them. For those who are such do not serve our Lord Jesus Christ, but their own belly, and by smooth words and flattering speech deceive the hearts of the simple' (Romans 16:17-18). This is what lawlessness is, serving one's own will instead of the will of God, it is rebellion.

I was shocked when the Holy Spirit warned me that my close friend felt contemptuous of me. I defended him, "Never." When I told my friend the exact thing the Holy Spirit had said, he denied it all and by his smooth talk and flattery, what was in him deceived me. I accepted the lie and believed what I wanted to believe, what I was comfortable with. I did not wish to face the truth. I had rejected the truth and it cost me dearly for many years to come. The Holy Spirit cannot and will not lie. Once again, the Holy Spirit was so gracious towards me.

In a Contemplation of David (a psalm), he wrote: 'The words of his mouth were smoother than butter, but war was in his heart; his words were softer than oil, yet they were drawn swords' (Psalm 55:21). David wrote of those 'who speak peace to their neighbours, but evil is in their hearts' (Psalm 28:3).

The second shock was unveiled as the Holy Spirit showed me that my close friend was wedded to the world, and was being used by Satan to undermine my call and ministry. We are called to be wedded to Jesus and the will of God, as His Bride, the living Church. He is the Groom. But when I learnt that he was wedded to the world, I thought, 'Oh, this explains so much.'

The apostle John wrote: 'Do not love the world or the things in the world. If anyone loves the world, the love of the Father is not in him' (1 John 2:15). The apostle Paul wrote: '...You also have become dead to the law through the Body of Christ, that you may be *married to another* — to Him who was raised from the dead, that we should bear fruit to God' (Romans 7:4). 'For I am jealous for you with godly jealousy. For *I have betrothed you to one husband,* that I may *present you as a chaste virgin to Christ*' (2 Corinthians 11:2). 'He died for all, that those who live should live no longer for themselves, but for Him who died for them and rose again' (2 Corinthians 5:15). 'You were bought at a price; do not become slaves of men' (1 Corinthians 7:23).

The third and greatest shock stunned me for a moment, when the Spirit told me that my close friend "is a tare, a tool in the hands of the devil." That helped explain all the problems he caused, and why he did all he could to hinder me obeying God. The Lord showed me that if I was willing, He would teach me more in order that I might share it with others. As part of my teaching, I was led to visit the graves of Rev. Duncan Campbell, Evan Roberts, Sir Winston Churchill, David Lloyd George, T.E. Lawrence, Viscount Montgomery, Rees Howells and Florence Nightingale. All these people knew who their enemies were. Some were spiritual or political, others military or ideological and others were infections and diseases. But the secret was, and still is, knowing who your enemy is. The Bible tells us this (Nehemiah 2:10, 19, Nehemiah 13:4-9).

Many times in the Scriptures God warns of tares and the enemy within, especially as the great spiritual battles ensue, like the end time battles. "Do not trust in a friend; do not put your confidence in a companion; guard the doors of your mouth from her who lies in your bosom. For son dishonours father, daughter rises against her mother, daughter-in-law against her mother-in-law; a man's enemies are the men of his own household" (Micah 7:5-6). Jeremiah the prophet heard the Lord God say, "Everyone take heed to his neighbour and do not trust any brother. For every brother will utterly supplant and every neighbour will walk with slanderers. Everyone will deceive his neighbour and will not speak the truth. They have taught their tongue to speak lies; they weary themselves to commit iniquity. Your dwelling place is in the midst of deceit. Through deceit they refuse to know Me" (Jeremiah 9:4-6).

The Lord Jesus Christ did not come to bring harmony, but to lead us to war in His Kingdom, to destroy the works of the enemy and to set people free from the power of Satan. The Lord said, "Do not think that I came to bring peace on earth. I did not come to bring peace but a sword. For I have come to 'set a man against his father, a daughter against her mother and a daughter-in-law against her mother-in-law,' and 'a man's enemies will be those of his own household.' He who loves father or mother more than Me is not worthy of Me. And he who loves son or daughter more than Me is not worthy of Me" (Matthew 10:34-37).

In all warfare, people have to choose what side they will be on. Jesus said, "Do you suppose that I came to give peace on earth? I tell you, not at all, but rather division. For from now on five in one house will be divided: three against two, and two against three. Father will be divided against son and son against father, mother against daughter and daughter against mother, mother-in-law against her daughter-in-law and daughter-in-law against her mother-in-law" (Luke 12:51-53).

Slowly but surely, it was as if spiritual scales were dropping off my eyes. Tares are sons and daughters of the evil one, sown by the devil (Matthew 13:38-39). They are assigned to oppose God's servants and to do all they can, to discourage, dishearten, depress or even destroy! Judas was a disciple and the Lord spent a whole night in prayer before he was chosen (Luke 6:12-16), but Judas still betrayed him for thirty silver coins, and even Satan himself entered him (John 13:27). This man loved money more than Jesus. Judas had been taught by Jesus that, "No one can serve two masters; for either he will hate the one and love the other, or else he will be loyal to the one and despise the other. You cannot serve God and mammon" (Matthew 6:24). Judas was wedded to the world and would fellowship with the devil, instead of with the Lord.

The devil who is the tempter, will search out those who are not fully committed to Jesus Christ in churches and Christian homes, to draw them away from God and back to the world, as the Lord explained in His parables (Matthew 13:19-23). Jesus said, "For where your treasure is, there your heart will be also" (Matthew 6:21).

Demonic forces will do all they can to get you to fellowship with demons, through sin, knowing that the Holy Spirit will depart from you (1 Timothy 4:1). King David, a man after God's own heart knew the danger of this and prayed, "Do not cast me away from Your presence and do not take Your Holy Spirit from me" (Psalm 51:11).

Samson was so deceived that he was unaware that the Lord had left him (Judges 16:20). The Holy Spirit departed from King Saul, as an evil spirit from the Lord tormented him, and even those around him could see and understand what was going on (1 Samuel 16:14-23). It's the same today; demons have infiltrated the Church, just as the apostles said they would (1 Timothy 4:1). These devils are doing all they can to destroy it or at least make it powerless, from within. Lot was tormented in his righteous soul by the lawless deeds he saw and heard in Sodom and Gomorrah (2 Peter 2:7-8), and so are many God fearing Christians in their churches!

The Holy Spirit was so grieved in me on occasions, in some churches or Christian fellowships, by what He and I observed, that I was compelled to speak to the pastor or leaders. I have lost count of the number of times when they replied by saying, "If you are looking for a perfect church, don't go in, you will spoil it." There is some truth in this saying, but it is also a mockery to maintain a status quo which is unacceptable to the Lord, who is holy and commands His Church to be so (1 Peter 1:15-16).

Jesus has made it very plain, as the Groom, what He wants His Church, His Bride to be like. 'Husbands, love your wives, just as Christ also loved the Church and gave Himself for her, that He might sanctify and cleanse her with the washing of water by the word, that He might present her to Himself a glorious Church, not having spot or wrinkle or any such thing, but that she should be holy and without blemish' (Ephesians 5:25-27).

The individuals of the Body of Christ are all grafted into God's vine and in John 15, Jesus tells us that God the Father is the Gardener, who prunes out the dead wood in the vine, and puts it on the fire. During the 1904-1905 Welsh Revival, so many people came to put their faith in Jesus' death and resurrection that they had to build or enlarge chapels, mission halls and church buildings to gather the harvest. In time, some of the people returned to their own godless ways and many of the religious people returned to their own pious rituals and traditions. As they did, the Holy Spirit departed, the numbers fell and today all over Wales, and the United Kingdom, you will find empty buildings that were once houses of worship, former chapels, churches and mission halls. Now they are homes, offices, mosques, nightclubs, restaurants and shops etc., (Revelation 1:20, Revelation 2:5).

Already the devil has his eyes on those who can be groomed from religious Christians into his tares (Isaiah 29:13, Isaiah 46:12), to challenge what God is going to do in the greatest harvest the world has ever seen. Satan had his tares ready in Israel to oppose the coming of the Messiah, the Lord Jesus Christ (Mark 7:6-13). The Pharisees and Sadducees were religious men who claimed they were waiting for the Messiah, but they were the one's who opposed and rejected Him, and sought to kill Him! Jesus said to the Pharisees, "You seek to kill Me, because My word has no place in you. I speak what I have seen with My Father and you do what you have seen with your father." They answered and said to Him, "Abraham is our father." Jesus said to them, "If you were Abraham's children, you would do the works of Abraham. But now you seek to kill Me, a Man who has told you the truth which I heard from God. Abraham did not do this. You do the deeds of your father... You are of your father the devil and the desires of your father you want to do. He was a murderer from the beginning and does not stand in the truth, because there is no truth in him. When he speaks a lie, he speaks from his own resources, for he is a liar and the father of it" ... Then the Jews answered and said to Him, "Do we not say rightly that You are a Samaritan [a grave cultural insult] and have a demon?" (John 8:37-48).

In the case of Jesus, those who served the devil made the same accusation against Him! If the true Church is going to counterattack this threat, it is imperative that the Holy Spirit be released in and through those members of the Body of Christ He has called to be His channels, through whom He can work. The man or woman at the front reaping the harvest cannot fight these battles on his or her own.

In more recent times, some churches have come some way towards what the Lord requires, with leadership teams. In 1 Corinthians 12:13-30, Paul gives teaching to this end. There has to be a spirit of unity, both in the Word and in the Holy Spirit, as verses 13-14 express. The Body of Christ (each individual member), not just the man at the front, must know the Word of truth, the Bible, and the Spirit of Truth. John explained: 'Now by this we know that we know Him, if we keep His commandments' (1 John 2:3). You cannot obey His commands if you do not know them and this is the trouble with the Church, which is made up of many members including you and me – those who have repented and forsaken their former lives of sin, confessed Jesus Christ as their Saviour and Lord, and live for Him. The Lord declared through the prophet Hosea, "My people are destroyed for lack of knowledge" (Hosea 4:6), and, "Let us pursue the knowledge of the Lord" (Hosea 6:3).

You must know the Word of God which has been given to us in the Bible, and you must also know the Holy Spirit and His will. The Sword of the Spirit is the Word of God (Ephesians 6:17). This Word, under the direction of the Holy Spirit is living and powerful (Hebrews 4:12), and it can change your life and of those around you!

Tares are well trained in the art of lies, deceit and deception. Most will cloak or cover their words with enough truth to make what they say (or do) palatable. If you meditate on God's Word the Holy Spirit will reveal Jesus' good, pleasing and perfect will to you. Jesus Christ said that all who respond to the gospel must be taught, "To observe all things that I have commanded you" (Matthew 28:20). If you are willing to observe all He teaches, you will grow in the grace of God and get to know the Holy Spirit; if you do not, you may be cut out of the vine and cast into the fire! Jesus said, "If anyone does not abide in Me, he is cast out as a branch and is withered; and they gather them and throw them into the fire, and they are burned" (John 15:6).

The Holy Spirit made it very plain to me that when I turned my back on Him as a young teenager, the enemy assigned a tare to me, which was my future close friend. He was sent into my life to hinder God's work in it. Tares love the world. John commands: 'Do not love the world or the things in the world. If anyone loves the world, the love of the Father is not in him. For all that is in the world – the lust of the flesh, the lust of the eyes, and the pride of life – is not of the Father but is of the world. And the world is passing away, and the lust of it; but he who does the will of God abides forever' (1 John 2:15-17). Because tares love the world, the spirit of the antichrist abides in them (1 John 2:18, 2 John 7). Like the people of Judah in the Old Testament, these tares do not give all their hearts to God, but only in pretence and this opens them up to devils/evil spirits (Jeremiah 3:10). These tares are religious and just go through the outward motions, they are double-minded and unstable in all they do (James 1:7-8).

Chapter Thirty-Six

The Form and Nature of Tares

From your very first meeting with some tares, they can radiate the nature of a kindred spirit. This is because they have a powerful spirit of delusion/deception in them and over them. Naturally, it is counterfeit and the opposite of meeting someone who walks with the Holy Spirit in them and over them. There are times when some people have to be handed over to Satan (1 Corinthians 5:5, 1 Timothy 1:19-20), but is only done under the direct instruction of the Holy Spirit.

All evil spirits/demons are at their heart, antichrist and antichristian (Revelation 16:14). The man of lawlessness, which Paul has written of (2 Thessalonians 2:1-12), is yet to be revealed; but he will be a person who has given himself over to Satan. As already mentioned, a tare will have an antichrist spirit abiding in them and working through them.

Paul warned the pastor Timothy: 'Now the Spirit expressly says that in latter times some will depart from the faith, giving heed to deceiving spirits and doctrines of demons' (1 Timothy 4:1). He also warned him of religious people, having a form of godliness, but they deny its power. 'But know this, that in the last days perilous times will come. For men will be lovers of themselves, lovers of money, boasters, proud, blasphemers, disobedient to parents, unthankful, unholy, unloving, unforgiving, slanderers, without self-control, brutal, despisers of good, traitors, headstrong, haughty, lovers of pleasure rather than lovers of God, having a form of godliness but denying its power. And from such people turn away!' (2 Timothy 3:1-5).

Paul warned Timothy that some preachers will turn from the truth and teach fables instead of biblical truth. 'For the time will come when they will not endure sound doctrine, but according to their own desires, because they have itching ears, they will heap up for themselves teachers; and they will turn their ears away from the truth, and be turned aside to fables' (2 Timothy 4:3-4).

John the apostle told the Christians that false spirits will be operating in churches, with false prophets, who are really people committed to the world! We are told we must test the spirits by discerning the message that is shared. Many of these false prophets or teachers etc., will exhort worldly concerns and reject the teaching of the apostles. 'Beloved, do not believe every spirit, but test the spirits, whether they are of God; because many false prophets have gone out into the world. By this you know the Spirit of God. Every spirit that confesses that Jesus Christ has come in the flesh is of God, and every spirit that does not confess that Jesus Christ has come in the flesh is not of God. And this is the spirit of the Antichrist, which you have heard was coming, and is now already in the world. You are of God, little children and have overcome them, because He who is in you is greater than he who is in the world. They are of the world. Therefore, they speak as of the world and the world hears them. We are of God. He who knows God hears us; he who is not of God does not hear us. By this we know the spirit of truth and the spirit of error' (1 John 4:1-6). The apostle Paul warned that some people whilst claiming to be Christian have a lower regard for the Bible than other books, or *their* culture, or *their* philosophy that they prefer to exhort, as they preach 'another gospel' and a 'different Jesus' (2 Corinthians 11:3-4, Galatians 1:6-9).

The devil has a chain of command, similar to a pyramid style of top down leadership. Satan remains at the top and below him are principalities and powers, ruling spirits, evil spirits/demons. This structure was taught by Paul and at their heart, all of them are little antichrists and messengers of Satan (Ephesians 6:12-13).

God has those whom He has set apart from birth and the devil makes it his business to find out who these people are, so he can oppose and harasses them. A tare, that is a person who may be religious but has given themselves over to these evil spirits, even unaware, will have fellowship with demons. They will talk to them. Their bodies will become a counterfeit temple, which the demons work through.

These demons can only live in that body by agreement. They abide in them because in the spiritual world they have a

- 204 -

legal right (Revelation 12:10). The devil and his demonic hordes are legalists, they know what their rights are, according to the principles set forth at the beginning of time and they will insist on claiming all that is theirs and adhering to them. In the book of Job, this righteous man is put to the test, when Satan tries every legal trick in the book to get him to sin (Job 1:9-2:10). The high priest Joshua was also subject to a demonic legal attack and the court of heaven rules in Joshua's favour (Zechariah 3:1-5); a similar situation happened to King David (1 Chronicles 21:1). All these men overcame Satan, but tares give in to him (even unknowingly) and align themselves and their will to his!

The demons in the bodies of tares will have every right to be there, because they were welcomed in, usually unbeknown, but they are there by agreement. They cohabit together. The human and the demon spirits in them live together (Luke 22:3), like a husband and wife, but this is a counterfeit union. You cannot cast them out because the tare is in agreement with them. At the end of the age, Jesus taught He would gather "out of His Kingdom" all those who are lawless and offend Kingdom standards (Matthew 13:24-30, 36-42).

The Lord said, "Therefore as the tares are gathered and burned in the fire, so it will be at the end of this age. The Son of Man will send out His angels and they will gather out of His Kingdom all things that offend, and those who practice lawlessness, and will cast them into the furnace of fire. There will be wailing and gnashing of teeth. Then the righteous will shine forth as the sun in the Kingdom of their Father. He who has ears to hear, let him hear!" (Matthew 13:40-43).

When the Holy Spirit abides in you, Jesus said, "He will eat with you and you with Him" (Revelation 3:20). It is the same with tares and demons; only they do the same as a counterfeit. They become good friends, or so the tare is deceived into believing.

It is highly unlikely that a tare in a church, fellowship or ministry etc., will agree to receive deliverance, but should they, as the host of these demons, you can be sure that the strong man (the ruling spirit who controls them all) will send out one or two lesser, minor demons, to deceive you into thinking the job is done. After sending them out, this ruling spirit will welcome them back later, as the person returns to fellowship with these spirits. As Jesus said, "The last state of that man is worse than the first" (Luke 11:26).

As part of this great deception, a person who is a tare may assist others in casting out demons in other people, as long as the focus does not turn to them (Acts 19:14-17). Jesus taught that people would claim to be His disciples who were not. They would do wonders and cast out demons, yet they do not know Jesus Christ as they "practice lawlessness" (Matthew 7:22-23). The tare will also have a religious spirit, which enables them to hang around the Lord's people, to feed off their spirits and to learn all they can about those who are truly serving the Lord. They do this so that they can direct soulish prayers towards them, which are gratifying to the flesh and demonic in nature (James 3:14-16).

These people may have a spirit of lawlessness operating in them, which means they will always be a law unto themselves. They may have a spirit of rebellion, which is the sin of witchcraft (1 Samuel 15:23). They may have a spirit of selfishness (me, myself and I), and they will have an independent spirit; which will never be truly subject to another because they prefer to be self-reliant.

Tares are more often than not seeking attention one way or another, because they are motivated by their own sense of self-importance. The more time you give to a tare only tends to feed and empower the antichrist spirits in them; the tare misinterprets your actions and is emboldened to keep coming back for more. All the time and attention a tare receives is perceived as acceptance as part of the Body of Christ, as is their behaviour when it is clearly not acceptable to do and say such things as a tare would. Because of the tare's ungodly traits and actions it is imperative that you are led by the Holy Spirit and not your emotions which can be very misleading. Jesus always spoke the truth and faced others with it, and we must do the same. Jesus said, "If you abide in My word, you are My disciples indeed. And you shall know the truth, and the truth shall make you free" (John 8:31-32).

The devil wishes to deceive the true Church, by working through tares in the hope he can set up a counterfeit church, within the real, and outside of the real, that can be used to steal/poach real believers into and dampen their faith. This is the counterfeit bride which Jesus taught on, which Satan is raising up (Mark 13:22). This is an expression of female rebellion which will not submit to God, as John warned (Revelation 2:20, Revelation 17:1-18). It is the personification and embodiment of rebellion, by being wedded to the world, instead of Christ. This is a representation of wickedness, the unseen force in all the earth; which seeks ever to be hidden further and deeper away (Zechariah 5:5-9). These tares will fully embrace the Antichrist when he comes.

Paul does not teach that being a true member in Christ's Church will lead to a life of ease, because we are invited into a war, where we are to wrestle with evil spirits through prayer and intercession. 'For we do not wrestle against flesh and blood, but against principalities, against powers, against the rulers of the darkness of this age, against spiritual hosts of wickedness in the heavenly places' (Ephesians 6:12).

Tares are hosts of antichrist spirits here on earth, who have direct communication with spiritual hosts of wickedness in heavenly places. They are spiritual spies who inform the powers of darkness about believers that are serving the Lord, or about the wider work of the Body of Christ, through a faithful church and obedient ministry etc., which is a threat to Satan's kingdom (Matthew 25:41).

One way or another, tares are committed to bring division, and as I have said before, it is impossible to fight tares in the power of the flesh (2 Corinthians 10:3). The demons in them will do all they can, by any means, to provoke you into sin. The true servant of the Lord must always operate in love, because God is sovereign; He is in control of all things and all things are under His control. As Jesus explained, God has allowed tares to be sown amongst His people and He told us that we too must be aware (Matthew 13:28-30). Consequently, do not be surprised if God allows a tare to continually provoke you, because it will produce in you the fruit of the Holy Spirit and will teach you additional lessons on spiritual warfare (2 Corinthians 12:7). When you come under attack by a tare, if you remain in Christ, abide in His love and walk in the light as He does, you will be taken into greater paths of victory.

Be warned, a tare will go to any lengths necessary to gain victory over his or her prey. They are soul partners with Satan and his will. They are by nature two-faced, double-minded, and masters of deception. If called to, they will use their bodies to manipulate others into sin, those of the opposite sex, or those of the same sex – all to destroy God's work.

For the majority of Christians, spiritual warfare is a hidden mystery and so is any tare amongst them. It is the very nature of spiritual warfare to be clandestine. These tares are like obstinate children; stubborn, self-willed and unyielding. They like to form an alliance, but not by the Spirit of the Lord, as Isaiah declared (Isaiah 30:1). They are rebellious, deceitful and unwilling to listen to the Lord's instructions. They despise seers, prophets and visions, which God gives of what is right and holy. They want only to hear pleasant things, not the truth which they hate, because the Holy Spirit is shining a spotlight on them and their work, and they despise being confronted by the Holy Spirit.

As tares are sown into God's Kingdom and pretend to be true disciples of Jesus, they will generally honour God with their lips, but their hearts are far from Him (Isaiah 30:8-16). These tares desire the praise and approval of others, and will seek ways to get it, even through inordinate affections. They are driven from within and strive for acceptance, and believe that everyone has a price at which they can be bought, just as Judas, one of the twelve disciples was bought for thirty pieces of silver/thirty silver coins. They will go to great lengths over periods of time to ensnare others. They are often devoid of any peace and are tormented. They seek out the attention of others by doing good works 'for the Lord' (Amos 5:21), purely to make themselves feel better and in a similar fashion to the Pharisees, to inwardly say, "Look at me," to get outward praise and public recognition (Matthew 6:5).

All true born-again Christian believers know that in repentance and rest, they will find the peace and joy of their salvation. In quietness and confidence will be their strength (Isaiah 30:15); but tares will have none of this. Tares will not surrender or accept defeat and the Body of Christ, the living Church needs to wake up to this fact, and deal with all that is demonic in their ranks (Ephesians 3:10).

A word of warning, do not overreact and begin a witch-hunt in the flesh, this is not being led of the Spirit. A true tare will be more than eager to assist you to wage war and bring false accusation against others, which will only add further confusion, paranoia and disunity.

The demons that ensnare a religious person to become a tare have had thousands of years to perfect their art of deception. Without the guidance of the Holy Spirit, who uncovers their deception, the Church is helpless. Tares are made up of a nest of demons that can vary considerably. Every nest will have a strong man or ruling spirit, a religious spirit and an antichrist spirit, including a host of others. Each nest is tailor-made to plant next to an individual who serves Christ, or a church or a ministry, to discourage, dissolve or destroy them/it. I repeat on purpose: they are well trained and are planted by demons that are of a higher order than they are. Jesus met a man who was possessed by a demonic strong man called Legion, and this strong man was in control of thousands of devils in this one man, enough to drive around two thousand pigs down a steep place, into the sea to their destruction! It said to Jesus, "My name is Legion, for we are many" (Mark 5:9).

Tares are a law unto themselves, as the apostles found (3 John 9-11). On the outside, because of their striving religious spirit they may appear at first, to be an answer to prayer because they are keen to be seen in the ministry of helps, yet for all the wrong reasons. They have perfected the image of servanthood, with the purpose of getting into the inner circle, and into positions of influence or control. More often than not, they will go the extra mile, appearing considerate and are often the first to think of giving cards or presents to people, and taking an interest in others, to gain information.

To gain acceptance and mastery, they are so devious that they may continue unseen for years, working hard, contributing, whilst all the time the enemy is embedding them into the ministry for the right time of his choosing. Nevertheless, the true believers will discern that on the inside, they are rebels and always will be, and the prophets who speak up to warn of them must be heeded.

Just like spies during the Cold War period, these tares are like terrorist sleeper cells, waiting for years to be in the right place at the right time to undermine God's work. Like Islamic extremists, these people can appear to be just another friendly person, but suddenly they awake after years to cause havoc. Tares may be great tithers and even give offerings, they may teach or lead prayer groups, because they have learnt to be all things to all men – but they are big trouble!

The last thing we need right now are church buildings full of Christians, who believe this, that and the other, but never do anything – but meet regularly. What is required, are disciples of Jesus who will be filled with the Holy Spirit and obedient to Him, operating in the gift of discernment, to see what the enemy is doing. With the coming of the Antichrist in the future, those without the Holy Spirit in our churches will be at the devil's mercy, because he has no mercy, and they may even welcome him. Satan has already planted scoffers in churches, sent to undermine faith and belief in God's revelation for the last days (2 Peter 3:3).

As ever, to gain victory over tares, we must walk in the Holy Spirit, accept His gift of discernment and wisdom, and walk in God's love. The Holy Spirit taught me that I can only gain victory over the tares by always operating in His love, then you can shut them up, shut them down and shut them out – excommunication from God's work. Elisha the prophet knew how to deal with tares in God's house, as he would never look at them or notice them. Elisha said, "As the Lord of hosts lives, before whom I stand, surely were it not that I regard the presence of Jehoshaphat king of Judah, I would not look at you, nor see you" (2 Kings 3:14-15).

Chapter Thirty-Seven

Beware of the Visit-Tare (Visiting Tare)

'Then Jesus sent the multitude away and went into the house. And His disciples came to Him, saying, "Explain to us the parable of the tares of the field." He answered and said to them, "He who sows the good seed is the Son of Man. The field is the world, the good seeds are the sons of the Kingdom, but the tares are the sons of the wicked one. The enemy who sowed them is the devil, the harvest is the end of the age and the reapers are the angels. Therefore as the tares are gathered and burned in the fire, so it will be at the end of this age. The Son of Man will send out His angels, and they will gather out of His kingdom all things that offend, and those who practice lawlessness, and will cast them into the furnace of fire. There will be wailing and gnashing of teeth. Then the righteous will shine forth as the sun in the Kingdom of their Father. He who has ears to hear, let him hear!' (Matthew 13:36-43).

There is a truth that Christians in most denominations are agreed upon, that we are living in the last days, the end times (Matthew 24, Mark 13, Luke 21). When it comes to tares/weeds, it is a very different story. In all my years, outside of my own Christian walk and ministry, I can only recall once hearing a pastor mentioning a tare, and that was briefly in passing. With the last days comes the end time harvest, with the sons of the Kingdom growing alongside the sons of the evil one, as Scripture states. Jesus made it very plain in this parable (Matthew 13), that there will be an end time harvest, and with it, the end of the age, when Jesus will send out the angels to separate the good from the evil, and "they will gather out of His kingdom" all things that offend.

While large sections of the Church have been sleeping in the dark with their eyes closed, the devil has sown his tares. The tares are ready and waiting for the next spiritual awakening, a heaven-sent revival when the Holy Spirit will come upon a dead Church and revive it. The devil, anticipating this move of

God, has already planted many of his tares, who will rise up and oppose the work of the Holy Spirit at this time. So like watchman on the city walls, be on your guard and on the lookout for the visit-tare (2 Samuel 18:24). The visit-tare is a tare that drops in as a visitor on a dead or dying church, to be used by Satan to destroy it. In all probability, this church will have already had a visit, by the Holy Spirit, in the body of an overcomer, who was sent to show them God's plan for them.

God's plan for all churches has already been revealed. Plan A, is the narrow path that leads to the resurrection life in Christ Jesus (John 10:10, Acts 1:8), to be conformed into His image (Romans 8:29), to accomplish His mission – wrestling principalities and powers (Ephesians 3:10-11), and fulfilling the Great Commission (Mark 16:15). However, if they have already rejected the true light of His Word and the work of the Holy Spirit, then they have been made ready, by lying, deceiving spirits, to embrace the deception of the wide path that leads to destruction (1 Timothy 4:1). You have been warned. You will suffer what you tolerate.

At one time the Holy Spirit led me into a dead and dying church that was tucked away down a backstreet. When the congregation and the pastor expressed they had no desire for the Holy Spirit's power working there, He departed and instructed me to leave also. But waiting in the wings was a tare that the devil had planted. When the pastor retired, the tare came forward and offered 'to help,' in anyway the person could, and within a few months, all the leadership team had become subservient to the will of this tare! Even future pastors, could do nothing without this person's approval! To the undiscerning visitor today, it is just another church struggling to stay alive. To the discerning, it is a counterfeit body, without the Holy Spirit, and is dead.

As I have said before, remove a man's spirit and his body dies, remove the Holy Spirit from the Body of Christ, the Church and it dies also. You can keep a human body on a life-support machine for years and it looks as if the person is sleeping. It's the same with a dead church, you can keep it going, aided by money and give it the appearance of life, but in truth, it is already dead. Nobody wants to pull the plug on a life-support machine, but the devil, working through a principality, working through tares, are more than happy to counterfeit the appearance of life, through a dead church fellowship. This false church will lead many to a lost eternity and stop others from entering into God's good, pleasing and perfect will for their lives, which is to be conformed into the image of His Son Jesus (Romans 8:29). The will of God for His Church is for it to have His life in them, in all its abundance (John 10:10), by the power of the Holy Spirit living in them (Acts 1:8, Acts 10:38), but the tare wants to control all and resist the will of God the Holy Spirit; this leads us to the Jezebel spirit.

From the outset, let me make it plain. The Jezebel spirit is a spirit without gender and will target any willing man or woman to work through. The Jezebel spirit is a principality that operates through witchcraft, in the form of intimidation, manipulation and domination; aided by spirits of lies, deceit and deception. Jezebel is an unseen enemy, which influences every demon that works in and through tares/weeds. It has a true hatred of God-given male authority and hates prophets, intercessors, overcomers, and all the true servants of the Lord, with a passion unknown by most Christians.

Principalities are spiritual forces of evil, having strongholds over nations, people groups or geographical areas etc. These evil spirits are invisible to the human eye and can only be seen when you are 'in the Spirit' (Ezekiel 3:14, Ezekiel 37:1, Revelation 1:10). Such times are few and far between, and only comes to pass as the Holy Spirit wills. Therefore, it has pleased the Lord to use others on the earth at different times, to give us all an insight to the true nature of that spirit, which gives us a better understanding of how they operate, see 1 Kings 18:13-19, 1 Kings 21:5-11, 2 Kings 9:7, 22, Revelation 2:20-24.

Tares/weeds, the demons in them and all controlling spirits over them must all be confronted and overcome by the Church (Ephesians 3:10-11). This was the pattern of the Lord Jesus and His disciples. 'Then the seventy returned with joy, saying, "Lord, even the demons are subject to us in Your name." And He said to them, "I saw Satan fall like lightning from heaven. Behold, I give you the authority to trample on serpents[1] and scorpions, and over all the power of the enemy, and nothing shall by any means hurt you. Nevertheless do not rejoice in this, that the spirits are subject to you, but rather rejoice because your names are written in heaven" ' (Luke 10:17-20). For further study on the role of the Church binding, defeating and overcoming principalities and powers, see also Matthew 18:18-20, Colossians 2:9-15, James 2:17-19 and Revelation 12:10-11.

When first confronted, a tare/weed will more often than not, take a submissive stance, exhibiting an appearance of genuine concern for any misunderstandings (Acts 8:18-24). However, it will be only a matter of time, when the tare/weed will have to be challenged by those in a position of authority over them (3 John 9-11). *Then* you will begin to experience the full force of the Jezebel spirit against you.

The principality Jezebel will control, manipulate, intimate and dominate all the demons that make up the demonic nest in the tare/weed. It will terrorise them (oppress by fear), to bring about its own counterfeit wicked will, by doing all they can to control, or destroy the person or the ministry of the ones it preys on. Tares/weeds are tormented to achieve their goal and hate genuine true repentance, for they know it is the golden key to true freedom.

Be warned, when you declare war on tares/weeds, Jezebel will declare war on you, and you will discover some of your friends, family, and brethren alike, will begin to turn against you, and oppose you (1 Kings 19:1-4). However, you must stand firm in the full armour of God, with the Holy Spirit, in the name of Jesus Christ, washed in His blood and gain the victory over all your foes. Further warnings, you cannot live an unholy life and war against the devil's demonic hordes. Do not go beyond your remit, your God-given authority; be led by the Holy Spirit at all times, and at every stage of the warfare.

A word of warning in your enthusiasm to defeat the enemy. Do not rush in – to attempt to bind some principality or power and pull down its stronghold without the clear leading of the Holy Spirit and His designated authority to do so, which is very rare in truth, much rarer than many believers might think.

Authority in spiritual warfare is gained by a good knowledge of the Holy Scriptures, through the Holy Spirit, through holy living and practical experience gained over time. You may read a book on spiritual warfare and have a head full of knowledge, but without any practical experience, you will be very vulnerable to a backlash of attacks (sudden and adverse). If you are truly led by the Holy Spirit to take a special interest in spiritual warfare, then the principalities and powers of darkness will take a special interest in you. Spiritual warfare is not for the faint or half-hearted or double-minded (Acts 19:15).

In the days that we live in, we come across more and more individuals who believe what they want to believe, they believe what they are comfortable with, or believe in half-truths; when quite clearly (to many others), they believe in the wrong half! Through no fault of their own, they were encouraged to pray a prayer of commitment to Christ, but have not *truly* repented of their sins, (and forsaken them) or turned away from their old lifestyles, and most have no intention of doing so (Matthew 7:23). They are not truly born-again, they do not have the Holy Spirit living in them, they have not passed from death to life. Some of them who are bound by demonic strongholds have not received deliverance, and most have only a very basic knowledge of the Bible – they are biblically illiterate. Yet, they have been taken into church membership and are prime targets to be taken in and turned into tares (or lured into a cult).

As a deacon, I was attending a church meeting to discuss a maintenance project which would benefit our congregation. This would mean a considerable investment. I had attended this place of worship for several years and was surprised when a man that I had never seen or met before kept interrupting those who were sharing about the benefits of such a project. He became more and more opposed to the idea. Eventually, I rose to my feet and challenged him as to what right did he have to have an opinion on the matter? I was shocked to find out that he was a member! However, I pointed out to him that as he had not attended a single service in over two years, and did not financially contribute to the church, he should sit down and remain silent, which he did. This man was a tare. It turned out he would turn up from time to time and cause trouble.

What about Simon, the former sorcerer who was 'saved' during the revival at Samaria? Under the ministry of Phillip the evangelist, Simon believed in Jesus Christ, was baptised by Phillip and followed him, being amazed at the miracles and signs that were manifested under the ministry of anointed

Phillip (Acts 8:5-13). Peter and John, the apostles from Jerusalem, heard of the great work in Samaria and went to them so that the brethren in Samaria might receive the Holy Spirit. Simon saw that the Holy Spirit could be imparted by the laying on of hands and wanted to buy this gift! Peter rebuked him, "Your money perish with you, because you thought that the gift of God could be purchased with money! You have neither part nor portion in this matter, for your heart is not right in the sight of God. Repent therefore of this your wickedness, and pray God if perhaps the thought of your heart may be forgiven you. For I see that you are poisoned by bitterness and bound by iniquity" (Acts 8:18-24).

To the countless number of hard-working, faithful pastors and ministers who are kept so busy to notice everything going on in their fellowship and have no wish to add another burden to their already overburdened list of things to do, this is one thing you *dare not ignore or brush aside* (Jonah 1:6, Romans 13:11-12). Why? Because Jesus spoke about it and explained it in the simplest way, through a parable. Would you ignore a cancerous growth in your own body? Of course not. So why ignore one in the Body of Christ? (2 Corinthians 6:15). You must act early to have any real chance of victory, with limited loss or damage to the flock. Every church fellowship will be visited by a wolf in sheep's clothing and if the watchman is not standing in the gap, and watching over the flock, they will be in peril.

The Great Commission must be fulfilled and one of the Church's job functions is to send forth more labourers into the harvest field, to see the unreached reached; from every tribe, nation and tongue, coming to Jesus Christ and living for Him. However, we are in a war, but we stand on the side of victory, so take up the sword of the Spirit, the Word of God, and fight as the Holy Spirit directs. We must all give, go, pray and intercede as the Spirit leads, to glorify Jesus Christ.

Thank you for reading this book, please write a short (or long) review on your favourite review site, and give a shout-out on social media – thank you.

Social Media
www.facebook.com/ByFaithMedia
www.instagram.com/ByFaithMedia
www.youtube.com/ByFaithMedia and www.twitter.com/ByFaithMedia

Appendix A

Demons/Evil Spirits

In relation to demons/evil spirits, Christians and godly people can have, be oppressed, or be under the influence of them (Job 26:4, Mark 1:23-24, 39, Acts 5:3, 2 Timothy 2:24-26, James 3:14-16).

- A 'distressing spirit *from the Lord* came upon [King] Saul' because of his persistent rebellion against the Lord (1 Samuel 19:9). See also 1 Samuel 16:14-15.
- The 'devil put it into the heart of Judas Iscariot' to betray Jesus, one of the Twelve Disciples! (John 13:2).
- A 'daughter of Abraham' crippled for eighteen years, bent over, kept bound by a spirit of infirmity (Luke 13:10-17). Abraham's children are known as believers (Luke 19:9-10, Galatians 3:7-9), and the implied reference by Jesus was that she believed.
- Peter said that Satan filled Ananias' heart so that he and his wife lied to the Holy Spirit. They were numbered among the believers (Acts 4:32-35). They sold a plot of land and *claimed* to have given all the money to the church, but kept some. Both were judged by God and died instantly within hours of each other (Acts 5:1-11).
- Satan desired to sift Peter as wheat (Luke 22:31-32), and he did deny the Lord three times! And repented.
- Demonic forces can attack Christians – hence why Paul said we should have on the full armour of God and take the 'shield of faith' by which we 'will be able to quench all the fiery darts of the wicked one' (Ephesians 6:1-17).
- The apostle Paul received visions, revelations and had been taken up to the third heaven (2 Corinthians 12:1-2). To keep him humble he was given 'a thorn in the flesh, a messenger of Satan to buffet me, lest I be exalted above measure' (2 Corinthians 12:7-10).
- Satan stopped Paul and others from visiting the church at Thessalonica. Paul wrote: 'We wanted to come to you, even I, Paul, time and again – but Satan hindered us' (1 Thessalonians 2:18).

Demonic bondage can range from mild to severe and can cause hardness against the Good News (2 Corinthians 4:4), sinful behaviour (2 Peter 2:1-12), as well as apostasy and false doctrine (1 Timothy 4:1, 1 John 4:1-3).[1]

Appendix B

The Holy Spirit

The Holy Spirit led the apostles to reach the world. They did not follow their own plans and devise wonderful ideas; they prayed, fasted and sought the Lord.

- Jesus said, "For the Holy Spirit will teach you at that time what you should say" (Luke 12:12).
- 'The Spirit said to Philip, "Go near and overtake this chariot" ' (Acts 8:29).
- 'Now when they came up out of the water, the Spirit of the Lord caught Philip away, so that the eunuch saw him no more; and he went on his way rejoicing' (Acts 8:39).
- "Then the Spirit told me to go with them, doubting nothing. Moreover these six brethren accompanied me and we entered the man's house" (Acts 11:12).
- 'Then one of them, named Agabus, stood up and showed by the Spirit that there was going to be a great famine throughout all the world, which also happened in the days of Claudius Caesar' (Acts 11:28).
- 'As they ministered to the Lord and fasted, the Holy Spirit said, "Now separate to Me Barnabas and Saul for the work to which I have called them" ' (Acts 13:2).
- 'So, being sent out by the Holy Spirit, they went down to Seleucia, and from there they sailed to Cyprus' (Acts 13:4)
- 'For it seemed good to the Holy Spirit and to us, to lay upon you no greater burden than these necessary things' (Acts 15:28).
- 'They were forbidden by the Holy Spirit to preach the Word in Asia...they tried to go into Bithynia, but the Spirit did not permit them' (Acts 16:6-7).
- "The Holy Spirit testifies in every city, saying..." (Acts 20:23).
- 'They told Paul through the Spirit not to go up to Jerusalem' (Acts 21:4).
- 'When Agabus had come to us, he took Paul's belt, bound his own hands and feet, and said, "Thus says the Holy Spirit, 'So shall the Jews at Jerusalem bind the man who owns this belt and deliver him into the hands of the Gentiles' " ' (Acts 21:11-12).
- "The Holy Spirit spoke rightly through Isaiah the prophet to our fathers..." (Acts 28:25).[1]

Sources and Notes

Preface
1. See *The Trumpet Sounds for Britain, Vol. 2* by David E. Gardner, pages 132-134.
2. See *Rees Howells Intercessor* by Norman Grubb, Lutterworth Press, 1952, chapters 34-36.
3. Rationing in Britain was phased out during 1953-1954, eight years after the end of WWII.

Chapter 1
1. Dripping was the fat that had dripped off cooked meat and was left to harden and used as a spread.
2. The copper was a large washing vessel used to heat the water, and the copper stick was not small!
3. *The Lewis Awakening 1949-1953* by Duncan Campbell, The Faith Mission, Edinburgh, Scotland, 1954, page 31.
4. Psalm 139:13-16 speaks of God creating a baby in its mother's womb. 'Your eyes saw my substance, being yet unformed. And in Your Book they were all written, the days fashioned for me, when as yet there were none of them' (Psalm 139:16). Samson's life work was preordained by God before he was even conceived and this was relayed to the mum to be (Judges 13:5). See also Job 10:8-9a, 11, Psalm 71:6 and Isaiah 49:1.

Chapter 5
1. In the Bible, God reveals the names of many demonic beings. A spirit of jealousy (Numbers 5:14), familiar spirit (1 Samuel 28:7), lying spirit (1 Kings 22:22), spirit of haughtiness (Proverbs 16:18-19), perverse spirit (Isaiah 19:14), spirit of slumber (Isaiah 29:10, Romans 11:8), spirit of heaviness (Isaiah 61:3), spirit of harlotry (Hosea 5:4), foul spirit (Mark 9:25), spirit of infirmity (Luke 13:10), deaf and dumb spirit (Mark 9:17-29), spirit of divination (Acts 16:16), spirit of bondage (Romans 8:15), spirit of the world (1 Corinthians 2:12), spirit of death (1 Corinthians 10:10, 15:26), seducing spirit (1 Timothy 4:1), spirit of fear (2 Timothy 1:7), spirit of antichrist (1 John 4:3), and the spirit of error (1 John 4:6). From *Holy Spirit Power* by Paul Backholer, ByFaith Media, 2013, page 114.
2. Devils, demons, evils spirits and unclean spirits are synonymous, they are generally, one and the same, and are referred to as such in different Bible translations.
3. For an overview of deliverance and ministry, see chapters 40-41 and 49 in *Extreme Faith, On Fire Christianity* by Mathew Backholer, ByFaith Media, 2013.
4. For an overview of spiritual and hereditary sins, sins of the forefathers/generational curses, see chapters 47-48 in *Extreme Faith, On Fire Christianity* by Mathew Backholer, ByFaith Media, 2013.

Chapter 6
1. Disciples of Jesus Christ are called to offer their bodies as living sacrifices (Romans 12:1), be led of the Spirit and walk in the Spirit (Romans 8:14, Galatians 5:18, 24-25). Christians should act in the power of the Spirit (John 14:12, Acts 1:8). For the leadings of the Holy Spirit, read the book of Acts, and *Holy Spirit Power, Knowing the Voice, Guidance and Person of the Holy Spirit* by Paul Backholer, ByFaith Media, 2013.

Chapter 8
1. From *How to Plan, Prepare and Successfully Complete Your Short-Term Mission* by Mathew Backholer, ByFaith Media, 2010, pages 25-26.
Chapter 9
1. *Living Together God's Way* published by Scripture Gift Mission.

2. For more about heaven-sent revivals, see *Revival Fires and Awakenings* by Mathew Backholer, ByFaith Media, 2009, and *Revival Answers, True and False Revivals* by Mathew Backholer, ByFaith Media, 2013.

Chapter 10
1. Who can stand in the Presence of God? Psalm 76:7, Revelation 1:17a.
2. For a biblical understanding of heaven, what it beholds and the glories beyond, see *Heaven, A Journey to Paradise and the Heavenly City* by Paul Backholer, ByFaith Media, 2013.

Chapter 12
1. See *Rees Howells Intercessor* by Norman Grubb, Lutterworth Press, 1952, and www.ReesHowells.co.uk.
2. See *Holy Spirit Power, Knowing the Voice, Guidance and Person of the Holy Spirit* by Paul Backholer, ByFaith Media, 2013.

Chapter 13
1. See *Revival Fires and Awakenings* by Mathew Backholer, ByFaith Media, 2009, chapter 9, for an account of the Hebridean Revival (1949-1952), and the DVD *Great Christian Revivals* by ByFaith Media, www.ByFaithDVDs.co.uk.

Chapter 14
1. The plural for shofar is shofars, whilst shofroth is also acceptable usage.

Chapter 15
1. The islands of Lewis and Harris are connected and whilst they are two islands, they can be referred to as the Isle of Lewis and Harris.

Chapter 16
1. In genuine revival, there are diversities of operation by the Holy Spirit, but the essential features are the same. The Holy Spirit may come as a dove or as a refiner's fire, like falling dew or an earthquake amid thunder and lightning! For more details on this subject with case examples from revival Church history see *Revival Answers, True and False Revivals* by Mathew Backholer, ByFaith Media, 2013, chapter 20.

Chapter 17
1. Part 6 of *Extreme Faith, On Fire Christianity* by Mathew Backholer, ByFaith Media, 2013, has multiple references to the devil (and demons) as a legalist who has 'legal rights,' but only if we relinquish them by our sin, or the sin of others, especially those in leadership. Zechariah 3:1-5 is a strong case example.

Chapter 19
1. For further biblical studies on demonised land, principalities and powers see *Extreme Faith, On Fire Christianity* by Mathew Backholer, ByFaith Media, 2013, chapter 50, 'Demonised Places/Territorial Spirits.' There are other chapters on spiritual warfare and deliverance from demons within the book.

Chapter 21
1. For an overview of the blood of Jesus Christ, its power, effects and benefits for believers see chapter 35 of *Extreme Faith, On Fire Christianity* by Mathew Backholer, ByFaith Media, 2013.

Chapter 22
1. For accounts of revivals and awakenings in Britain, America and other places of the world see *Revival Fires and Awakenings: Thirty-Six Moves of the Holy Spirit* by Mathew Backholer, ByFaith Media, 2009, and *Global Revival, Worldwide Outpourings, Forty-Three Visitations of the Holy Spirit* by Mathew Backholer, ByFaith Media, 2010.

Chapter 28
1. God desires all men to be saved (Ezekiel 33:11, Matthew 18:14, 1 Timothy 2:3-4), and has promised to pour out His Spirit on all flesh (2 Chronicles 7:14, Isaiah 44:3, Joel 2:28-29, Acts 2:16-21).
2. The Bible is full of hard teaching which kicks against our flesh: loving our enemies, taking up our cross, turning the other cheek, walking in the fruit of the Spirit etc. Just read the Sermon on the Mount (Matthew 5-7). The Bible also contains a number of denunciations, calls to repentance or hard messages for people to wake up, change, go in God's direction and do His will. See Isaiah 58, Joel 1:13-14, Joel 2:1, 12-17, John the Baptist's message (Matthew 3:1-10), Jesus' message (Matthew 3:17), Peter's sermon (Acts 2:14-40), Stephen's sermon (Acts 7:1-54), and the apostle Paul upset a lot of people by his godly preaching! (Acts 13:42-52, Acts 17:1-14).

Chapter 31
1. An account of the Brownsville Revival (1995-2000) can be found in *Revival Fire, 150 Years of Revivals* by Mathew Backholer, ByFaith Media, 2010.
2. For a fuller explanation of this, with a case example see chapter 23 of *Revival Answers, True and False Revivals* by Mathew Backholer, ByFaith Media, 2013.

Chapter 32
1. See *Rees Howells Intercessor* by Norman Grubb, Lutterworth Press, 1952, chapter 30, and *Samuel Rees Howells: A Life of Intercession* by Richard Maton, ByFaith Media, 2012, chapters 7 and 13.
2. For the history of the Bible College of Wales (1924-2011), see *Samuel, Son and Successor of Rees Howells* by Richard Maton, ByFaith Media, 2012. Samuel Rees Howells passed into glory in 2004.

Chapter 33
1. See *Global Revival, Worldwide Outpourings* by Mathew Backholer, ByFaith Media, 2010, notably chapters 5-7.
2. Especially in the Amazon jungles of Brazil and its bordering countries where unreached tribes have been spotted from the air, or seen along the riverbanks.
3. For a case example of protection from germs, and transportation in the Spirit see *God's Generals: Why They Succeeded and Why Some Failed* by Roberts Liardon, Albury Publishing, 1996, pages 182-185.
3. *Rees Howells Intercessor* by Norman Grubb, Lutterworth Press, 1952, chapter 5.

Chapter 34
1. *It's Time For Revival* by Gwen Shaw, Engeltal Press, 1988, page 56.
2. Original book source unknown, though in the public domain.

Chapter 37
1. For a greater understanding of Jesus' words, "I give you the authority to trample on serpents and scorpions" (Luke 10:19), see Job 26:13b, Psalm 91:13, Mark 16:18 and Acts 28:3-5.

Appendix A
1. From *Extreme Faith, On Fire Christianity* by Mathew Backholer, ByFaith Media, 2013, chapter 49.

Appendix B
1. From *Holy Spirit Power, Knowing the Voice, Guidance and Person of the Holy Spirit* by Paul Backholer, ByFaith Media, 2013, page 52.

www.ByFaith.co.uk
www.RevivalNow.co.uk
www.MissionsNow.co.uk

- 221 -

ByFaith Media Books

The following ByFaith Media books are available as paperback and eBooks, whilst some are also available as hardbacks.

Revivals and Spiritual Awakenings

Revival Fires and Awakenings, Thirty-Six Visitations of the Holy Spirit: A Call to Holiness, Prayer and Intercession for the Nations by Mathew Backholer. With 36 fascinating accounts of revivals in nineteen countries from six continents, plus biblical teaching on revival, prayer and intercession. Also available as a hardback.

Global Revival, Worldwide Outpourings, Forty-Three Visitations of the Holy Spirit: The Great Commission by Mathew Backholer. With forty-three revivals from more than thirty countries on six continents, the author reveals the fascinating links between pioneering missionaries and the revivals that they saw, as they sought God for the "greater things" in a spirit of holiness & worked towards the Great Commission.

Revival Fire, 150 Years of Revivals, Spiritual Awakenings and Moves of the Holy Spirit by Mathew Backholer, documents in detail, twelve revivals from ten countries on five continents. Through the use of detailed research, eye-witness accounts and interviews, *Revival Fire* presents some of the most potent revivals that the world has seen in the past one hundred and fifty years.

Revival Answers, True and False Revivals, Genuine or Counterfeit Do not be Deceived by Mathew Backholer. What is genuine revival and how can we tell the true from the spurious? Drawing from Scripture with examples across Church history, this book will sharpen your senses and take you on a journey of discovery.

Reformation to Revival, 500 Years of God's Glory by Mathew Backholer. For the past five hundred years God has been pouring out His Spirit, to reform and to revive His Church. *Reformation to Revival* traces the Divine thread of God's power from Martin Luther of 1517, through to the Charismatic Movement and into the twenty-first century, featuring sixty great revivals from twenty nations.

Understanding Revival and Addressing the Issues it Provokes by Mathew Backholer. Many who have prayed for revival have rejected it when it came because they misunderstood the workings of the Holy Spirit and only wanted God to bless the Church on their terms. Learn to intelligently cooperate with the Holy Spirit during times of revivals and Heaven-sent spiritual awakenings.

Christian Teaching and Inspirational

Tares and Weeds in Your Church: Trouble & Deception in God's House, the End Time Overcomers by R. B. Watchman. Is there a battle taking place in your house, church or ministry, leading to division? Tares and weeds are counterfeit Christians used to sabotage Kingdom work; learn how to recognise them and neutralise them in the power of the Holy Spirit.

Holy Spirit Power: Knowing the Voice, Guidance and Person of the Holy Spirit by Paul Backholer. Power for Christian living; drawing from the powerful influences of many Christian leaders, including: Rees Howells, Evan Roberts, D. L. Moody and Duncan Campbell.

Jesus Today, Daily Devotional: 100 Days with Jesus Christ by Paul Backholer. Two minutes a day to encourage and inspire; 100 days of daily Christian Bible inspiration to draw you closer to God. *Jesus Today* is a concise daily devotional defined by the teaching of Jesus and how His life can change yours.

Samuel Rees Howells: A Life of Intercession by Richard Maton is an in-depth look at the intercessions of Samuel Rees Howells alongside the faith principles that he learnt from his father, Rees Howells, and under the guidance of the Holy Spirit. With 39 black and white photos in the paperback and hardback editions.

The Baptism of Fire, Personal Revival, Renewal and the Anointing for Supernatural Living by Paul Backholer. The author unveils the life and ministry of the Holy Spirit, shows how He can transform your life and what supernatural living in Christ means. Filled with biblical references, testimonies from heroes of the faith and the experiences of everyday Christians, you will learn that the baptism of fire is real and how you can receive it!

Supernatural and Spiritual

Glimpses of Glory, Revelations in the Realms of God Beyond the Veil in the Heavenly Abode: The New Jerusalem and the Eternal Kingdom of God by Paul Backholer. In this narrative receive biblical glimpses and revelations into life in paradise, which is filled with references to Scripture to confirm its veracity. A gripping read!

Prophecy Now, Prophetic Words and Divine Revelations for You, the Church and the Nations by Michael Backholer. An enlightening end-time prophetic journal of visions, words and prophecies.

Heaven, A Journey to Paradise and the Heavenly City by Paul Backholer. Join one person's exploration of paradise, guided by an angel and a glorified man, to witness the thrilling promise of eternity, and to provide answers to many questions about Heaven. Anchored in the Word of God, discover what Heaven will be like!

Biography and Autobiography
The Holy Spirit in a Man: Spiritual Warfare, Intercession, Faith, Healings and Miracles by R. B. Watchman. One man's compelling journey of faith and intercession – a gripping true-life story. Raised in a dysfunctional family and called for a Divine purpose. Sent out by God, he left employment to claim the ground for Christ, witnessing signs and wonders, spiritual warfare and deliverance.

Samuel, Son and Successor of Rees Howells: Director of the Bible College of Wales – A Biography by Richard Maton. The author invites us on a lifelong journey with Samuel, to unveil his ministry at the College and the support he received from numerous staff, students and visitors, as the history of BCW unfolds alongside the Vision to reach Every Creature with the Gospel. With 113 black and white photos in the paperback and hardback editions!

Christian Discipleship
Discipleship For Everyday Living, Christian Growth: Following Jesus Christ and Making Disciples of All Nations by Mathew Backholer. Engaging biblical teaching with fifty easy-to-read chapters spilt into six sections, to aid believers in maturity, to help make strong disciples with solid biblical foundations who reflect the image of Jesus Christ.

Extreme Faith, On Fire Christianity: Hearing from God and Moving in His Grace, Strength & Power – Living in Victory by Mathew Backholer. Discover the powerful biblical foundations for on fire faith in Christ! God has given us powerful weapons to defeat the enemy, to take back the spiritual land in our lives and to walk in His glory through the power of the Holy Spirit.

Historical and Adventure
Britain, A Christian Country, A Nation Defined by Christianity and the Bible & the Social Changes that Challenge this Biblical Heritage by Paul Backholer. For more than 1,000 years Britain was defined by Christianity, discover this continuing legacy, how faith defined its nationhood and the challenges from the 1960s onwards.

How Christianity Made the Modern World by Paul Backholer. Christianity is the greatest reforming force that the world has ever known, yet its legacy is seldom comprehended. See how Christianity helped create the path that led to Western liberty and laid the foundations of the modern world.

Celtic Christianity & the First Christian Kings in Britain: From St. Patrick and St. Columba, to King Ethelbert and King Alfred by Paul Backholer. Celtic Christians ignited a Celtic Golden Age of faith and light which spread into Europe. Discover this striking history and what we can learn from the heroes of Celtic Christianity.

Lost Treasures of the Bible: Exploration and Pictorial Travel Adventure of Biblical Archaeology by Paul Backholer. Join a photographic quest in search of the lost treasures of the Bible. Unveil ancient mysteries as you discover the evidence for Israel's exodus from Egypt, and travel into lost civilisations in search of the Ark of the Covenant. Explore lost worlds with over 160 colour pictures and photos in the paperback edition.

The Exodus Evidence In Pictures – The Bible's Exodus: The Hunt for Ancient Israel in Egypt, the Red Sea, the Exodus Route and Mount Sinai by Paul Backholer. Brothers, Paul and Mathew Backholer search for archaeological data to validate the biblical account of Joseph, Moses and the Hebrew Exodus from ancient Egypt. With more than 100 full colour photographs and graphics!

The Ark of the Covenant – Investigating the Ten Leading Claims by Paul Backholer. The mystery of the Bible's lost Ark of the Covenant has led to many myths, theories and claims. Join two explorers as they investigate the ten major theories concerning the location of antiquities greatest relic. 80+ colour photographs.

Short-Term Missions (Christian Travel with a Purpose)
Short-Term Missions, A Christian Guide to STMs by Mathew Backholer. *For Leaders, Pastors, Churches, Students, STM Teams and Mission Organizations – Survive and Thrive!* What you need to know about planning a STM, or joining a STM team, and considering the options as part of the Great Commission.

How to Plan, Prepare and Successfully Complete Your Short-Term Mission by Mathew Backholer. *For Churches, Independent STM Teams and Mission Organizations.* The books includes: mission statistics, quotes and more than 140 real-life STM testimonies.

Budget Travel – Holiday/Vacations
Budget Travel, a Guide to Travelling on a Shoestring, Explore the World, a Discount Overseas Adventure Trip: Gap Year, Backpacking, Volunteer-Vacation and Overlander by Mathew Backholer. A practical and concise guide to travelling the world and exploring new destinations with fascinating opportunities.

www.ByFaithBooks.co.uk

- 225 -

ByFaith Media DVDs

Revivals and Spiritual Awakenings
Great Christian Revivals on 1 DVD is an inspirational and uplifting account of some of the greatest revivals in Church history. Filmed on location across Britain and drawing upon archive information, the stories of the Welsh Revival (1904-1905), the Hebridean Revival (1949-1952) and the Evangelical Revival (1739-1791) are brought to life in this moving 72-minute documentary. Using computer animation, historic photos and depictions, the events of the past are weaved into the present, to bring these Heaven-sent revivals to life.

Christian Travel (Backpacking Style Short-Term Mission)
ByFaith – World Mission on 1 DVD is a Christian reality TV show that reveals the real experience of a backpacking style short-term mission in Asia, Europe and North Africa. Two brothers, Paul and Mathew Backholer shoot through fourteen nations, in an 85-minute real-life documentary. Filmed over three years, *ByFaith – World Mission* is the very best of ByFaith TV season one.

Historical and Adventure
Israel in Egypt – The Exodus Mystery on 1 DVD. A four year quest searching for Joseph, Moses and the Hebrew slaves in Egypt. Join Paul and Mathew Backholer as they hunt through ancient relics and explore the mystery of the biblical exodus, hunt for the Red Sea and climb Mount Sinai. Discover the first reference to Israel outside of the Bible, uncover depictions of people with multicoloured coats, encounter the Egyptian records of slaves making bricks and find lost cities. 110 minutes. The very best of *ByFaith – In Search of the Exodus*.

ByFaith – Quest for the Ark of the Covenant on 1 DVD. Join two adventurers on their quest for the Ark, beginning at Mount Sinai where it was made, to Pharaoh Tutankhamun's tomb, where Egyptian treasures evoke the majesty of the Ark. The quest proceeds onto the trail of Pharaoh Shishak, who raided Jerusalem. The mission continues up the River Nile to find a lost temple, with clues to a mysterious civilization. Crossing through the Sahara Desert, the investigators enter the underground rock churches of Ethiopia, find a forgotten civilization and examine the enigma of the final resting place of the Ark itself. 100+ minutes.

www.ByFaithDVDs.co.uk

Notes

Printed in July 2023
by Rotomail Italia S.p.A., Vignate (MI) - Italy